TVEI and Secondary Educatio

TVEI and Secondary Education:

A Critical Appraisal

Edited by Denis Gleeson

Open University Press
Milton Keynes • Philadelphia

Open University Press
Open University Educational Enterprises Limited
12 Cofferidge Close
Stony Stratford
Milton Keynes MK11 1BY, England

and
242 Cherry Street
Philadelphia, PA 19106, USA

First published 1987

British Library Cataloguing in Publication Data

TVEI and secondary education: a critical
appraisal.
1. Technical and Vocational Education
Initiative
I. Gleeson, Denis
373'.01'13 T107

ISBN 0-335-15539-1
ISBN 0-335-15538-3 Pbk

Library of Congress Cataloging in Publication Data

TVEI and secondary education.
1. Vocational education — Great Britain.
2. Technical education — Great Britain.
3. Education, Secondary — Great Britain. I. Gleeson, Denis.
LC1047.G7T84 1987 373.2'46 87-2206

ISBN 0-335-15539-1
ISBN 0-335-15538-3 (pbk.)

Text design by Clarke Williams
Typeset by Burns & Smith, Derby
Printed in Great Britain by St Edmundsbury Press, Bury St Edmunds

Contents

List of Contributors

Douglas Barnes	School of Education, University of Leeds.
Brian Davies	King's College, Chelsea, London University.
John Evans	University of Southampton.
Rob Fiddy	University of East Anglia.
Denis Gleeson	University of Keele.
Janet Harland	University of London Institute of Education.
Gary McCulloch	Education Department, University of Auckland.
Val Millman	Advisory Teacher, Coventry LEA.
Murray Saunders	University of Lancaster.
Chris Shilling	School of Education, Open University.
Patricia Sikes	School of Education, Open University.
Gordon Smith	Staff Training and Development Unit, Telford College of Arts and Technology.
Ian Stronach	University of East Anglia.
Michael Taylor	School of Education, Open University.
Gaby Weiner	School of Education, Open University.

Denis Gleeson

1

General Introduction
TVEI and Secondary Education

This book examines certain fundamental issues associated with the implementation of the Technical Vocational Education Initiative (TVEI) and explores its effects on schools and colleges at the practical level. In a period otherwise characterized by cut-back and retrenchment in the education service, TVEI constitutes a novel if not paradoxical exception to the rule. There is today greater awareness of the large-scale influence of the project beyond its original pilot brief; along with TRIST and now GRIST* its imperatives for curricular and organizational change, its implications for staffing, resources, teaching relations and so forth, have reverberated throughout the educational system. Both in terms of categorical funding and delivery TVEI represents a distinct break with hitherto accepted models of curriculum development and reflects a 'new' approach to the ways in which government structures educational priorities at the local level. Following on as it does various 'crises' which beset schooling in the late 1970s, TVEI has emerged as a prototype for implementing educational policy and change. According to the Secretary of State for Education and Science, for example, the proposed City Technology Colleges (CTCs) will build upon the lessons of TVEI, both in terms of curricular planning and earmarked expenditure (DES 1986). In other respects too it is clear that TVEI extension is now closely associated with the delivery of a National Curriculum Policy.

Among much forore TVEI was hurriedly introduced into schools in 1983, following an announcement in Parliament in 1982. In a speech to the House of Commons (12.11.82) the Prime Minister expressed '...growing concern about existing arrangements for technical and vocational

* For an explanation of these and other abbreviations used in this book see the Glossary of Terms, pages 194–5.

education provision for young people...', and asked the chairman of the Manpower Services Commission, together with the Secretaries of State for Education and Science, to develop the pilot scheme. Initially fourteen LEAs were selected to take part and, by 1985, participation in TVEI had increased to include the majority of local authorities. Evidence of TVEI's major size can be cited in the £250m budget allocated to it (with a further £25m for TRIST: TVEI Related In-Service Training), in a period of falling rolls, cuts in public expenditure and schools reorganization. Perhaps, not surprisingly, the funds made available via TVEI proved irresistible to cash-starved LEAs and schools, despite the reservations expressed at the time by the teacher unions.

In essence the project may be viewed as an attempt at major innovation to stimulate curriculum development and to introduce new approaches to teaching and learning through a limited life project. Through the mechanism of categorical funding it is envisaged that the project will leave a permanent mark on secondary and further education. According to one observer 'TVEI represents one of the most significant developments in secondary education since circular 10/65, which heralded universal comprehensivisation' (Dancy 1984).

Despite its sudden arrival on the education scene TVEI has its roots in wider historical debate about the nature of schooling itself, not least regarding the ways in which schools should respond to industry's needs. In the past three decades, for example, schools have been criticized for being 'anti-industry' and for promoting academic values in the curriculum at the expense of technical and vocational skills. On this basis alone the claim that education should be made more relevant to vocational needs and aspirations of both pupils and society is compelling. Indeed, as Reeder (1981) maintains, the argument that entrepreneurial culture should find its expression in the curriculum is not new; it has its origins in nineteenth-century conceptions of schooling and is part of a 'recurring debate' (see Wiener 1981).

More recently, with rising youth unemployment, schools have been subject to a period when the very ground rules of schooling have altered. The presence of the new 'sixth former' after ROSLA, for example, promoted thoughts about changing curriculum and teaching methods and has resulted in a plethora of pre-vocational courses in the 14–18 age range (B/TEC, CPVE and so forth). At the centre of the most recent impetus for change could be seen the dramatic collapse of the youth labour market in the late 1970s. This collapse meant that for most young people schools were no longer seen as the main transition or transmission point into a job at sixteen. Change in pupil destinations has itself promoted greater awareness within educational circles of the need to initiate widespread curricular innovation and reforms. Almost simultaneously a politically inspired debate about the purposes and practices of schooling has arisen. At one level, criticism has been directed at the apparent failure of schools to ensure a proper 'fit' between the vocational needs of young people in their charge and the requirements of the economy. At another, critics argue that the current obsession with vocational education and training is flawed and obscures a more fundamental problem, namely, 'that there ain't no jobs', (Bates 1984). Either way, Dale argues (1985) the significance of TVEI relates to the prevailing crisis which it was designed to address at the time. On the one hand, the content and orientation of schooling had to be changed; on the other, the process of changing schooling itself needed to be changed. From this viewpoint TVEI is not simply a barometer of the problems facing secondary education: it is also a strategic vehicle in influencing both the temperature and climate of schooling.

Since its inception in schools in 1983 TVEI has been the object of much controversy. At one level debate has focused on the manner and mode by which the project has sought to inject greater vocational realism into the curriculum. At another, central government involvement in the running of schools and colleges, notably via MSC intervention, has drawn attention to wider changes in policy and decision making processes in education. Until the late 1970s most HMI and DES reports focused upon the broad-based nature of the curriculum, arguing for 'curricular balance' and invoking liberal humanist conceptions of education. Influenced by the Ruskin Speech (1976); FEU's *ABC* (1979) and MSC's *A New Training Initiative* (1981), the 'vocationalist' argument can be seen to have become more insistent and influential. Both government and MSC have more recently sought to change awareness about changes in the labour market via schooling. According to Youthaid (*Bulletin*, April 1984) the government views the MSC as a means of introducing market-place realities into the world of education. Vocational realism has become, in certain quarters, the order of the day. Since the so-called 'Great Education Debate' (1976–9), the MSC has been at the forefront of government training policy directly intervening in curriculum development, LEA policy and links between school/college and work. Moreover, as a major agent of the Department of Employment the MSC has bypassed conventional democratic channels and now deals direct with LEAs, schools and colleges. This model, supporters maintain, speeds up the process of change and allows innovation and resources to percolate through to the grass roots level more effectively.

This break with the previous involvement of the DES in curriculum development and a corresponding move towards centralism might be seen within educational circles as a true 'innovation', although not necessarily a welcome one. On the more positive side (if not entirely so) it is acknowledged that the involvement of MSC has brought TVEI about in rapid time compared with, for example, the Certificate of Pre-Vocational Education (CPVE), which was developed via the more established DES/LEA route. In this respect it is not simply the amount of resources allocated by central government that is important, but also the degree and means of their control; specifically, it is to the MSC that the local authorities have had to make a *contractual* commitment to deliver change. This marks a radical departure from conventional modes of curricular delivery established via relations between schools/colleges; LEAs, DES; Unions; Schools Council (now disbanded) and so forth. For the purposes of this book, what requires further analysis is the link between this model of curricular delivery and the *reality* experienced by teachers, students and others in practice.

If one attraction of TVEI is the financial and political support which it provides for a more 'realistic' student-centred approach, there are those who view TVEI as a divisive force, challenging the ethos of comprehensive education itself (Wyatt 1985; Golby 1985; Fowler 1985). The point has been made, not least by teachers themselves, that the content and experience of TVEI is not original — elements such as negotiated curriculum, vocational courses, work experience, modular curriculum and so forth, have all existed to some degree within mainstream education. What is perhaps 'new' is the speed at which centralized control of education and training has occurred, and the influence which the MSC now exerts over colleges (via YTS) and schools (via TVEI). Developments within the further education sector, such as the Unified Vocational Preparation Scheme (1976), prefigure a greater expansion of the 'new vocationalism' via the Youth Opportunities Programme (YOP), and later YTS and TVEI (1983). Yet in other respects TVEI is itself neither a universal, nor particularly as a process of innovation, a static or determined thing. The variability of TVEI nationally derives from its original and apparently 'bottom up' design in which (while broad national criteria and guidelines have been established), the detailed curricular planning and implementation has been left in local hands.

For whatever combination of reasons, once they had agreed to participate, first-round schools and colleges had to decide how best to approach the new, as yet not fully understood, undertaking. Murray Saunders (1985) has used three broad categories to indicate how schools generally responded to TVEI:

1 Adaptive Extension — A strong interpretation of TVEI: It has been used to change the whole curriculum.
2 Accommodation — TVEI adapted to fit the general shape of the existing curriculum structure.
3 Containment — TVEI absorbed by the existing school pattern.

The danger of placing individual schools at a single point somewhere along an Adaptive Extension to Containment continuum is that such a model is too static to convey the degree of past movement or future intentions. Moreover, while it may be argued that the initial approach of the individual Project schools varied from Adaptive Extension to Containment, there was, at first, a *universal* need to see how far TVEI could be 'accommodated' within the demands of the existing school organization and curriculum. These demands were themselves realized against the immediate background of falling rolls, reorganization and later industrial action. Initial attitudes were also conditioned by the early perception of the Initiative as a Technical and Vocational, theme-led project. For example, an apparent early accent on technical and craft resources led some staff in this area of the curriculum to welcome what they saw as a redress of school priorities away from 'academic' to technical subjects.

The fact that TVEI/MSC policy can be seen to bypass conventional DES/LEA channels, centralism is not necessarily felt by teachers to be the main issue. To them, the 'bypass' may be seen to indicate government intention to impose its will on schools and colleges at a time of falling rolls and industrial action. In less conspiritorial fashion there are those who argue that the project's positive commitment to mixed ability, experiential learning, equal opportunities, special needs and so forth complements rather than contradicts comprehensive principles and, if anything, strengthens democratic participation in education at the present time (Pring 1985). McCulloch's contribution in this volume maintains that the utilitarian rhetoric and objectives that accompanied the launching of the initiative have been *subverted* via their incorporation into mainstream education. Although TVEI may have been established successfully at the national level it may yet, at the local level, give way to a revival of more liberal notions of educational practice.

McCulloch's paper sets the scene of the book by looking at the historical background to TVEI development, from its inception through to its extension. According to McCulloch it is easy to interpret TVEI as just the latest in a line of attempts by employers to perpetuate traditional social and work patterns at the expense of working-class children. While it may be that TVEI emanates from particular historical ideals and attitudes identifiable as a conservative tradition, it is naïve to draw simplistic conclusions on that basis. McCulloch argues that both the character and extent of TVEI's influence remains open to question and dispute. Whether or not TVEI or other forms of technical initiative maintain a narrow vocational bias is not historically predetermined. According to McCulloch, technical and vocational education will continue to be linked inextricably with wider social and political factors, as an avenue of conflict over the nature of British Society. As such, the content and form of technical and vocational education remains contested rather than given.

From this viewpoint TVEI is seen not necessarily as a divisive force arriving out of the blue, but as a *catalyst* which may accelerate changes in schools which are already there in actual or potential form. It may be that this view of TVEI as a catalyst stretches the chemical analogy too far. A chemical catalyst promotes or accelerates a process without itself being changed and, in this sense, it could be taken out of the resulting product in its original form (Gleeson and Maunders 1985). The first part of the analogy — the agent promoting change — may be appropriate for the purposes of evaluation but the second part would direct attention away from the possible interactive nature of the catalyst itself which, in the case of TVEI, has implications for the issue of replicability. In other words, might the system revert to its original form once TVEI is taken out? (Owen 1984).

What constitutes TVEI varies widely across the country and each LEA Project differs in its institutional arrangements and model of delivery, depending on local perception, interpretation and circumstance. For Harland, in this volume, the central paradox of the TVEI phenomenon is the simultaneous emergence of two apparently or potentially conflicting features. On the one hand, it reflects strong central control of a kind which has permitted the detailed intervention of a central government agency right down to the level of the classroom. On the other hand, TVEI supports local initiatives which, in many of the pilot schemes, are highly experimental and creative. In various ways Harland's paper deals with the policy implications of this paradox with particular reference to the professional role of the teacher.

As TVEI penetrates mainstream schooling, however, variability is likely to be tempered with pragmatism, not least in relation to the imposition of curriculum and organizational change on schools and colleges. If the guiding influence of government and MSC in such development is not immediately discernible, their method of linking categorical funding with contractual delivery of curriculum is manipulative. In these circumstances LEAs can find themselves in the situation of doing the MSC's bidding, by encouraging schools and colleges to compete for a limited range of funds. The danger here is that for a number of reasons not all institutions compete for funds and resources on an equal footing, particularly in terms of falling rolls, catchment and resources. One consequence of this is the phenomenon whereby institutions feel compelled to throw themselves at innovation, without thinking through the longer-term implications.

Modularization is but one case in point. As a recent advocate of modular programmes has pointed out, if such a programme '...is not underpinned by dramatic and radical change in the mode of delivery then it is merely the same drivel packaged differently,' (Newman, *TES*, 29.11.85). Moreover, the James Report's (1972) observations on overteaching in schools confirm criticism of excessive over-direction by the teacher in circumstances where pupils have too few opportunities to learn for themselves (DES 1985). According to Lewis (1986) achieving such 'meta-goals' (learning by doing, learning how to learn and so forth) is not a straightforward activity. He argues that it is far easier to talk about the aims associated with 'co-operation not competition' in the curriculum, and quite another thing to implement this in practice. The point that is being made here is that method is no guarantee of quality. The teacher in innovative situations still has to balance the social/motivational gains against apparent academic loss. The irony is that teachers, having become more formal after the progressive era of the 1960s and 1970s (when lack of progression was blamed on falling standards), are now being asked to change track again. Willis (1984) dismisses such development as intended to bring children 'into the safe camp of conformism'; elsewhere Hargreaves (1982) restates the danger that the modern teacher may not address the *whole class* as frequently but will say 'the same thing thirty-plus times to individuals'. (Lewis 1986).

Thus, despite the rhetorical emphasis upon 'the broadening and enriching of learning opportunities', it is equally important, if not essential, to recognize the effect which TVEI has in reorganizing the environment in which such learning takes place. Sikes and Taylor's contribution to this volume focuses on the MSC's vision of implementing educational change via TVEI and the actual ways in which heads, teachers, students and administrators involved interpret received messages at school level. As one might expect perspectives and experiences vary which, again, has important implications for the replication and extension of TVEI.

This question directs attention to not only what was there before TVEI came along, but also the extent to which TVEI has brought in something different from previous curricular initiatives. Despite the refractory nature of TVEI Gorbutt maintains that the project should not be viewed in isolation, but as part of a well-defined drift towards redefining 14–18 education on more segmented lines (Gorbutt 1984). In this respect TVEI is something more than 'innovation without change'; it is linked with a broader movement to reintroduce selection into comprehensive education. This is a view endorsed by Evans and Davies whose contribution in this volume draws on case studies of four secondary schools and two colleges. It is their contention that TVEI and the many cases of *vocationalism* now found in schools may do little to lessen and, indeed, may exacerbate social and academic divisions between children inside schools and outside them. They conclude that, while TVEI may have brought about a change in the content and organization of the curriculum for the 14–16 age sector, it has left largely untouched and undebated the broader context of schooling into which this *innovation* has been introduced.

This perspective is taken up in Chapter 6 in Fiddy and Stronach's contrasting 'cases' of TVEI practice in two local areas. The experiences of 'Eastshire' and 'Westshire' are seen to have implications for the more general debate about TVEI, not least in relation to TVEI extension. A particularly telling point is the way in which *all* outcomes are taken as tokens of success at the public level. Yet, in other respects, limited time, demands from other initiatives like TRIST and GCSE, leave practitioners feeling that they seldom know enough about what they are trying to do. This, according to Shilling's paper (Chapter 7) presents very real problems in terms of ways in which teachers make sense of their professional role in relation to other teachers. Participating schools and colleges have a contractual responsibility to recruit a balanced intake of students to TVEI courses. However, Shilling maintains that in many schools it is form teachers who have the eventual job of promoting TVEI to both sexes 'across the ability range'. What this recruitment structure does not allow for is that form teachers may be affected by a number of sources of influence the effects of which do not coincide with this objective. Shilling's contribution seeks to build up a picture of the school as an 'open-ended' inter-relating totality, within which form teachers confront the demand for a balanced intake alongside a number of other, potentially conflicting factors.

The chapters which follow also lend support to the view that TVEI has, in various unintended ways, pointed up some of the more pervasive contradictions of schooling. Drawing on further case-study material of teaching and learning, work experience and gender, the contributions by Barnes, Saunders, Millman and Weiner question the degree to which TVEI practice has brought about greater vocational relevance either within or outside the school situation.

From the starting point that TVEI schools have undertaken to make their courses practical and relevant to the world which students are likely to experience, Barnes' contribution (Chapter 8) asks what progress they have made in this direction. Based on preliminary evaluation work in six schools his paper looks at four key elements of TVEI practice, associated with teaching styles, integration and what teachers say about 'negotiating' the curriculum. With reference to the latter, for example, Barnes observes that 'to make central decisions about pedagogy without involving affected teachers in the necessary rethinking is not likely to be a successful strategy'.

Similarly, with reference to work experience, Saunders (Chapter 9) points to the ways in which students' perspectives are equally overlooked. The 'bridging' between education and work that the MSC and government have stressed in recent years is an aim manifest in the compulsory inclusion in each TVEI submission of a work experience element. Drawing on survey data collected in Spring 1986 from TVEI in students from twelve LEAs, Saunders analyses their perspectives of work experience. Although many of the positive statements contained unqualified references to work experience as good or enjoyable, few contained any direct comparison with or references to school. According to Saunders, the data analysed suggests, overall, a positive yet complex picture. At present what government, employer or school considers worthwhile work experience is often at variance with what students think, a constituency largely ignored in discussions about establishing closer links between school and work.

Following on this, Millman and Weiner (Chapter 10) explore the progress which TVEI has made in its brief to promote equal opportunities between the sexes at school and work. Despite the positive effect which TVEI has had in placing equal opportunities on the agenda, the authors maintain that it has done little more than this. At present equal opportunities has all the appearances of another subject on the curriculum, while ignoring the underlying practices which characterize inequalities in the links between school and work. In making this criticism the authors offer various positive suggestions regarding the ways in which equal opportunities policies may be *engendered* more effectively in schools.

The concluding paper by Gleeson and Smith (Chapter 11) takes up the issue of 14–18 progression. An important feature of TVEI is that it represents a four-year package beginning at 14+ and progressing beyond the compulsory leaving age to 18. Moreover, a major objective is to establish curricular coherence and progression towards nationally recognized qualifications backed by coherent programmes and inter-institutional provision. Yet, according to Gleeson and Smith, such co-operation remains patchy and uneven, rendering TVEI a 14–16 school based phenomenon which has largely bypassed 16–18 provision. It is suggested that the issue of priority and status afforded to TVEI by the post-16 sector and by others in the initial planning of TVEI is an important factor in the 16–18 debate. In examining the reasons behind the neglect of the 16–18 phase, Gleeson and Smith outline some of the policy issues which need to be overcome if progression in the extension stage of the project is to take place.

As with most major curriculum development projects they have a tendency to take on a momentum of their own over and beyond their original conception. In this respect TVEI is no different. This is no bad thing and reflects the *process* of change, a starting point that contributors to this book address. Understanding curriculum innovation is, therefore, more complicated than it first appears. On the one hand, images of what constitutes the 'reality' of TVEI varies in relation to place, time and circumstance. One institution is different from another and the views of 'insiders' and 'outsiders' within each school and college influence perceptions. On the other, different conceptions of reality held by interested participants within schools and colleges (e.g. pupils, teachers, parents) and outside them (e.g. LEA, employers, careers, MSC) will affect understanding of TVEI.

Following publication of three significant White Papers: *Training for Jobs* (1984); *Better Schools* (1985) and *Working Together* (1986), it is evident that TVEI can no longer be viewed simply as a pilot scheme with a short life expectancy. With the nationwide 'replication' of TVEI announced in 1986, with a £900 m budget over ten years, TVEI is clearly being promoted as a 'success' despite there being few evaluation results. The implications of TVEI extension are that TVEI and its philosphy will become part of the national system of education and, as a consequence, MSC will have a major stake in the compulsory sector of education to complement its already large colonization of post-16 education and training via WRNAFE, YTS and ATS. Moreover, when areas of activity such as the Training Standards and Advisory Service (TSAS), and the National Council for

Vocational Qualifications (NCVQ) are considered, the enormity of its involvement becomes apparent and the fears of centralized control seem to be very real.

From this perspective TVEI contains certain unique features which have important implications for secondary education in general. At the policy level it represents a major initiative in restructuring the education and training experiences of 14–18 year olds and re-organizing the environment in which learning occurs. From conflicting evidence gleaned from research so far, TVEI is claimed to be a catalyst for change by some and divisive by others. The general view is, however, that within TVEI there is the potential for curriculum innovation, both in terms of teaching style and a better deal for many young people in schools and colleges. Perhaps the biggest constraint on implementing such change, despite the additional resources made available by TVEI, is the *time* factor. Developing cross-curricular initiatives which inter-relate such elements as profiling, modular studies, new forms of course work and assessment, are labour intensive and tend to add extra pressure on already overstretched staff.

As the papers in this book demonstrate, no neat or causal connection can be assumed to exist between the policy and the practice of TVEI. The caution here is against assuming that, for example, the MSC, LEA, employers, schools and colleges share a common viewpoint. At one level the MSC may be interested in the extent to which its innovation has brought about a turnaround in the national curriculum; at another the LEA may be more interested in managing the project and bringing about change in its schools and colleges, identifying its own influence on policy and so forth. At the school/college level practitioners may view TVEI in relation to their own particular institutions, localized problems, careers and so forth. Even if all three worked toward similar broad goals (there is some doubt about this beneath the rhetoric), perceptions vary in terms of the situations, priorities and problems experienced by different parties.

While there are no easy solutions to increasing levels of participation in post-16 provision TVEI has been positive in opening up channels of communication. Perhaps, more importantly, it has supported staff and curriculum development in the colleges, stimulated interest in cross-curricular approaches, including careers, modular studies, and accredition, and has involved FE teachers in the schools. The pressing issue is one of effectively co-ordinating all these initiatives, so that teachers, pupils and parents know exactly where they stand in relation to the content of the curriculum, qualifications, career routes, and what is on offer in the colleges. Evidence from the papers in this book suggest that there is confusion in the minds of some teachers, pupils and parents regarding how TVEI core elements (including profiling, work experience, etc.) complement GCSE, CPUE, City and Guilds, RSA, B/TEC and other courses, which affects *perceptions* of TVEI.

Inevitably the relative merits of TVEI will be judged in terms of what students and parents think, a factor sometimes overlooked in debates about the management and delivery of TVEI. Looking to the immediate future, the challenge to the project would seem to be two-fold. On the one hand establishing closer links between key elements within the programme, for example, remains a pressing concern. On the other, bringing coherence to bear in the emerging relations between modules, options and core curriculum is a major issue yet to be resolved. This has an important bearing on progression. In the circumstances so far described in this book, it would be naïve to expect TVEI to have found 'answers' to all the problems raised. Viewed more realistically the positive contribution of TVEI is in the way in which it has identified some of the limitations as well as some of the possibilities for implementing change.

Perhaps not surprisingly, research into TVEI encompasses these three different but inter-related levels. To date the emphasis of this research has focused primarily on the policy implications of TVEI, management and delivery. With a few notable exceptions little is known about the actual take up of TVEI in schools and colleges, and even less is known about how teachers and pupils make sense of the project at the practical level. What this book seeks to do is provide up-to-date information about the practical lessons that can be learnt from TVEI, and their likely effect on the curriculum, organization and management of schools at a time when the Project's extension is already underway.

While this book cannot claim to offer a comprehensive picture of all facets of TVEI development, the selection of papers has been made with school- and college-based *issues* in mind. A broad range of topics is looked at including the impact of TVEI on teacher–pupil relations, modular structures, mixed ability, work experience, profiling, progression, equal opportunities, school/college work links and other related themes associated with TVEI. It is for such reasons that this book draws on recent case studies of schools and looks closely at TVEI practice via the activities and experiences of those involved, including Heads and Principals, teachers, pupils, parents, careers personnel, LEA and MSC administrators, employers and other interested parties.

The signs are that there is widespread demand for such a book which has something to say about TVEI as it is happening now, and which can also offer some critical insight into its longer-term effects on mainstream education, particularly in terms of the emergence of a National Curriculum Policy. Consequently, the book should have wide appeal to heads, teachers, students, LEA advisers, careers and training officers, educationalists and those interested in the impact of education and training vocational initiatives on restructuring secondary curriculum at the present time.

References

Bates, I. *et al.* (1984). *Schooling for the Dole*. Macmillan.

Dale, R. (1985). The background and inception of TVEI, in Dale, R. (1985) *Education, Training and Employment*. Open University/Pergamon Press.

Dancy, J. (ed.) (1984). *TVEI Perspectives 14*, Department of Education, University of Exeter.

DES (1984). *Training for Jobs*. White Paper. HMSO.

DES (1985). *Better Schools*. White Paper. HMSO.

DES (1985). *The TVEI — Early Developments* (HMI Report).

DES (1986). *Working Together*. White Paper. HMSO.

DES (1986). *City Technology Colleges: A New Choice of School*. DES.

FEU (1979). *A Basis for Choice* (The Mansell Report). FEU.

Fowler, G. (1985). What is TVEI? *Liberal Education* **54**.

Gleeson, D. and Maunders, A. (1985). *Curricular Issues in Local TVEI Evaluation*. TVEI Evaluation Unit, University of Keele.

Golby, M. (1985). The coming crisis at 14+. *Forum* **27**(3).

Gorbutt, D. (1984). The new vocationalism: a critical note, in Dancy (1984) op. cit.

Hargreaves, D. (1982). *The Challenge for the Comprehensive School*. Routledge & Kegan Paul.

James, E. Chairman (1972). *Teacher Education and Training*. HMSO.

Lewis, I. (1986). *TVEI in Theory and Practice: A Comparative Study*. M.A. Dissertation. Department of Education, University of Keele.

MSC (1981). *A New Training Initiative*. MSC.

Newman, G. (1985). *Modules in TVEI. Times Educ. Suppl.*, 29.11.85.

Owen, J. (1984). TVEI: future control, in Dancy (1984) op. cit.

Pring, R. (1985). In defence of TVEI. *Forum,* **27**(3).

Reeder, D. (1981). A recurring debate: education and industry, in Dale, R. *et al.* (1981) op. cit.

Saunders, M. (1985). *Emerging Issues for TVEI Implementation*. University of Lancaster TVEI Evaluation Programme, 1985.

Wiener, M. (1981). *English Culture and the Decline of the Industrial Spirit, 1850–1980*. Cambridge University Press.

Willis, P. (1984). See the Conclusion in Bates, I. (1984) op. cit.

Wyatt, H. (1985) TVEI and all that. *Forum* **27**(3).

*Gary McCulloch**

2

History and Policy

The Politics of the TVEI

Policy and politics are inseparable twins, in education as in any other sphere where national and social interests are perceived. This has clearly been true of the Technical and Vocational Education Initiative (TVEI) ever since the Prime Minister, Margaret Thatcher announced on 12 November 1982 the launching of a pilot scheme in technical and vocational education for fourteen to eighteen year olds.[1] Responses to the scheme polarized on familiar political lines. Norman Tebbit, Secretary of State for Employment, saw the TVEI as providing the 'rebirth of technical education' that was essential if Britain was to compete successfully with its economic and industrial rivals.[2] On the other hand, Labour Party and many trade union leaders voiced strong suspicions on the character and implications of the TVEI. Neil Kinnock, Labour's education spokesperson and soon to be elected party leader, argued that Government policies as represented by the Youth Training Scheme and the TVEI would simply reinforce the divisions and prejudices at the root of Britain's economic decline.[3] The TVEI symbolized Conservative policy in education, training and employment, and for this reason became a scene of conflict over the character and direction of British society.

Raymond Williams argued in 1961 that historical appreciation is a prerequisite for understanding current issues and problems: 'We do not solve the critical questions by understanding the history, but still an adequate sense of the history, as opposed to the ordinary functional myths, is the basis of any useful approach.'[4] Sociologists also have an important contribution to make towards analysis of the TVEI in relation to changing social needs and attitudes. Over recent decades, historians and sociologists have been seeking a closer understanding, overcoming past rivalries to emphasize their common interests. As Asa Briggs has noted:

* The Editor gratefully acknowledges the kind permission of the *Journal of Education Policy*, 1/1 (1986) for allowing publication of this paper in this book.

'Both historians and sociologists are concerned with the same set of problems which stretch back from the present into the past.'[5] The late Philip Abrams stressed that 'historical sociology' is concerned with understanding 'the relationship of personal activity and experience on the one hand and social organization on the other as something that is continuously constructed in time'.[6]

This growing contact is clearly exemplified in the field of education, where sociology has become increasingly historical in character[7] at the same time that historians have found new interest in the relationships between education and society.[8] While the 'new' sociology of education includes historical explanations of 'what counts as knowledge', revisionist educational history is devoted to critical analysis of education as a social process. The partnership of history and sociology promises a deeper understanding of education as well as society, of the present no less than the past. For the study of an educational policy such as that embodied in the TVEI, socio-historical appraisal can help to highlight both long-term and immediate factors. The bland certainties of official policy, like the strident assertions of protest, may be explained and assessed in their wider contexts. Indeed, the social dimensions and historical context of the TVEI are most helpful in explaining not only its emergence and development, but also its essential fragility as a long-term policy.

It has been suggested by Harold Silver that in order to relate policy to 'complex processes of social interaction and many levels of attempts at influence and intervention',[9] it is important to understand the full range of opinions on a given issue. Silver seems however to neglect the key role of political dynamics in mediating between policy and opinion, explaining how issues emerge and disappear, which 'counter-pressures for innovation and established practice' are successful, why policies rise and fall. To understand why some opinions are more influential than others, and the nature of their effect on policy, it is necessary to relate them to the political context — not, it is true, at a 'traditional, elevated' level but in the many different aspects of a pluralist society. The TVEI is best understood in relation to the political climate and geography of Britain in the 1980s, as indeed is opposition to the policy. In turn, this political context is most usefully illuminated through socio-historical analysis.

History and policy

Several factors were involved in creating the conditions in which the TVEI emerged and developed. First, the direct role of governments in education generally and the curriculum in particular had grown significantly over the preceding quarter-century. The Crowther report of 1959 pointed out that education was widely regarded as 'a ''nation-building'' investment' as well as 'part of the welfare state'.[10] An area with such important economic and social ramifications was in any event a likely source of government concern, but the potential for political disputes over education was heightened by continuing problems involving the policy of 'secondary education for all' associated with the Education Act of 1944. The prevailing language of 'partnership' and consensus implied that responsibility was shared by local education authorities (LEAs), the teaching profession and the Ministry of Education. Increasingly though, as Kogan has remarked: 'From consensus between politicians and the school system itself, education became a cockpit of many of the political issues that have emerged in Britain since the war.'[11] This development encouraged successive ministers of education in the 1960s and 1970s to assert their authority under the 1944 Act 'to secure the effective execution by local authorities, under his control and direction, of the national policy for providing a varied and comprehensive educational service in every area'.[12] The 'tripartite system' of grammar, technical and modern schools was steadily undermined as difficulties of selection, assessment and rationale failed to be resolved, giving way under pressure from the Labour government of 1964–70 to a system of comprehensive schools intended to cater for all abilities and aptitudes.[13]

With regard to the curriculum, Sir David Eccles's wish that the Ministry of Education should express its views 'rather more often, more positively, and, no doubt, sometimes more controversially'[14] led him to establish in 1962 a new 'Curriculum Study Group' within the Ministry. Following protests this was replaced in 1964 by a more 'representative' body,[15] the Schools Council for the Curriculum and Examinations. The Schools Council itself represented an uneasy compromise that failed to conceal growing tensions between established educational interests and central government.[16] Friction between the erstwhile 'partners' was not lessened during the 1970s as changes in local and national political fortunes generated new conflicts and suspicions.[17]

State intervention in science and technology also increased over this period in a way that placed further demands upon the education system. The expansion of the economy and industry after 1945 required an increased supply of all types of scientists and technologists, and the schools, technical colleges and universities were expected to provide them. Lord Hailsham, appointed by the Conservative government in 1959 to become Minister for Science, tried to encourage both pure science and engineering, particularly advocating the reform of school science curricula by modernizing their content and discarding 'historical intellectual bric-a-brac'.[18] When the Labour Party came to office in 1964 the Ministry of Technology was created to work alongside the new Department of Education and Science (DES) in promoting industry and technology, only to fall from favour after the Conservatives regained power. Whereas the Ministry of Technology had aimed to maximize economic growth, recession and contraction in many sectors of the economy led to demand for devices to reduce the impact of depression. The Manpower Services Commission (MSC), created in 1973 and directly accountable to the Department of Employment, to some extent answered this need, becoming by the 1980s a powerful agency with 'a general responsibility for promoting training for employment'.[19]

The increase in direct government involvement in such areas accelerated following the launch of the 'Great Debate' in the autumn of 1976, when the Prime Minister James Callaghan stressed the need to relate education more usefully to technology and industry in a widely publicized speech at Ruskin College, Oxford.[20] DES officials began to play a more active role in the curriculum and organization of schools, a development that alarmed local authorities, teachers' associations and the Schools Council alike. This policy was maintained and even intensified after the Conservative Party under Margaret Thatcher was returned to office in 1979. The Schools Council was abolished in 1981 in favour of separate advisory bodies on examinations and curricula. All aspects of the school curriculum were subjected to critical scrutiny. Sir Keith Joseph, education secretary from 1981, reflected that: 'There is now no serious dispute that the school curriculum is a proper concern not only of the teachers, but also of parents, governing bodies, LEAs, and the government, each performing their proper role in response to the needs of the pupils and of the country as a whole.'[21] Governments of both major parties had responded to the new interest in the school curriculum which was evident in the 1960s, and this had helped to establish a 'broad presence' for national government for the purpose of educational change.[22]

The 'Great Debate' and the initiatives that followed were stimulated by a deepening sense of national decline, for which a large part of responsibility was attributed to the failures of education. *Education in Schools*, a consultative document produced by the DES in July 1977, acknowledged that recent criticisms of educational standards had been based on an underlying feeling that 'the educational system was out of touch with the fundamental need for Britain to survive economically in a highly competitive world through the efficiency of its industry and commerce'.[23] Conservative ministers took up these criticisms with vigour after 1979, against a background of economic malaise and social and industrial crisis. Education, it was urged, should be geared towards industry, commerce and technology in order to improve productivity and revive flagging national fortunes. Support for this general view could be found in many different quarters. The *Finniston Report* on the engineering profession, published in January 1980, was critical of 'the intangible influences of British attitudes towards change, industry and engineering, and the legacies of economic and social history' which had combined to produce 'an economic and cultural environment in this country frequently inimical to engendering the radical changes needed in national behaviour and priorities'.[24]

Finniston's warning that 'Unless urgent actions are taken, continued relative and possibly absolute industrial decline is inevitable with unpredictable but certainly undesirable social consequences'[25] was echoed by the Royal Society of Arts.[26] A movement in favour of 'Education for Capability' developed under the auspices of the RSA. Charles Handy, Chairman of the Education for Capability committee, spoke of the need 'to change the prevailing ethos of the whole educational system'.[27] John Tomlinson, chairman of the Schools Council and director of education for Cheshire County Council, was acutely aware that education, particularly 'the narrow emphasis on academic education', was being seen as 'a contributory factor in our industrial decline'. Critics, Tomlinson observed, were 'asking the education system to help to change the prevailing culture'.[28] The view that radical solutions were required at the educational level if 'industrial decline' was to be arrested amounted to an invitation for government intervention.

This line of thinking was further encouraged by historical analysis of the root causes of 'national decline' in Britain. Correlli Barnett has argued that since Britain's low industrial productivity has been due to negative social attitudes reproduced by education, the remedy for its problems is to be found in educational reform: 'Education for capability alone can keep Britain an advanced technological society and save her from being a Portugal, perhaps even an Egypt, of tomorrow.'[29] Martin Wiener similarly attributes Britain's relative economic decline since the late nineteenth century to the effects of 'a cultural *cordon sanitaire*' that has encircled 'the forces of economic development — technology, industry, commerce'.[30] There is indeed much truth in the view that English education has tended to encourage 'liberal' values at the expense of the 'vocational'. The revitalized public schools of the nineteenth century maintained a classical curriculum for its cultural and intellectual benefits. Science was generally admitted to the curriculum only with reluctance and even then only in a 'pure', academic, intellectual form designed to conform to the liberal ideals of the public schools.[31]

The new state grammar schools of the early twentieth century, imitating the public schools, tended to adopt a similar view of science education.[32] The Science Masters' Association (SMA) continued to insist that 'of all the claims made for the inclusion of Science in a school curriculum, the strongest undoubtedly is that which stresses the cultural value which the subject possesses'.[33] In the 1950s, as national demand for more scientists and technologists increased, the SMA sought to present science as 'part of our common cultural and humanistic heritage',[34] embarking on a curriculum initiative that had an important bearing on the Nuffield Foundation Science Teaching Project launched in 1962.[35] These initiatives were designed as much to conserve grammar school traditions in school science as to reform science curricula. Even in the new comprehensive schools, secondary science education often remained academic in character. It was acknowledged by the DES in June 1982 that 'there is wide agreement that many O-level science syllabuses are over-loaded, out of date and narrow, paying little regard to the relevance of science to industry or to adult life, and concentrating on abstract concepts from too early a stage'.[36] With economic and industrial difficulties accumulating it was perhaps natural that the liberal and academic tendencies of school science, and of the secondary school curriculum in general, should become a matter of public concern.

While public and grammar schools cultivated an intellectual, cultural approach, 'technical' and 'vocational' education seemed to have no place at the secondary level. In the nineteenth century such education was provided first in mechanics' institutes and later by institutions sponsored by the Department of Science and Art as well as several private agencies.[37] Margaret Gowing describes the growth in provision that took place from the 1870s as being 'too little and too late'.[38] Perhaps equally important, technical education became established by the turn of the century as 'a predominantly part-time education for students working in factory and office, concentrated mainly on training the technician, craftsman and office worker, and preparing students for external examinations'.[39] The higher-grade schools that developed in many urban areas in the late nineteenth century had seemed to offer an alternative approach to that of the grammar and public schools, involving 'practical' as well as 'academic' demands.[40] The *Bryce Report* on secondary education in 1895 argued that 'technical' education should be regarded as a species of secondary education that might be fostered through the spread and development of higher-grade schools.[41] Bryce insisted that secondary and technical education were mutually compatible: 'No definition of technical instruction is possible that does not bring it under the head of Secondary Education, nor can Secondary Education be so defined as absolutely to exclude from it the idea of technical instruction.'[42]

The prospect of reconciliation rapidly faded. Administrative reforms produced in 1899 a single Board of Education responsible for both elementary and secondary education. School boards and higher-grade schools were consigned to oblivion. The Education Act of 1902, and subsequent Regulations issued by the Board of Education, strengthened the dichotomy between 'secondary' and 'technical' education. Junior technical schools were accorded inferior status as compared with secondary schools, which were associated with traditional literary culture and the formation of a social elite.[43] Thus tensions between 'secondary' and 'technical' education were assimilated within the state education system of the twentieth century. It was this dichotomy that the TVEI was intended to resolve.

A major effort was made in the 1940s to reconcile secondary with technical education in the new context of 'secondary education for all'. The *Spens Report* on secondary education in 1938 described the division between technical and other forms of education confirmed in 1902 as 'unreal and unnecessary'.[44] It suggested that a number of existing junior technical schools should be promoted to secondary status and accorded 'in every respect equality of status with schools of the grammar school type'.[45] During the 1939–45 war, as it became accepted that secondary education should henceforth be available for all children over the age of eleven but that the grammar schools would not be suitable for all pupils, the notion of establishing secondary technical schools for those 'whose interests and abilities lie markedly in the field of applied science or applied art'[46] gained ground. Although the Education Act of 1944 did not specify distinctions between different types of secondary school, the existence of a 'tripartite system' of grammar, technical and modern schools was clearly spelled out by a pamphlet issued by the new Ministry of Education in 1947. Grammar schools were intended for pupils 'attracted by the abstract approach to learning.'[47]

It was envisaged that technical schools would adopt a less academic approach, 'selecting the sphere of industry or commerce as [their] particular link with the adult world'.[48] Meanwhile, modern schools would supply a broad education for 'children of widely differing ability, aptitude and social background'.[49] The *Crowther Report*, published in 1959, continued to express hope that technical schools, by cultivating a practical approach in education, might provide an 'Alternative Road' for many pupils who were not suited or attracted to traditional academic grammar-school education.[50] It was by then clear, however, that the technical schools had failed to formulate a coherent view of practical education, and that they had only a limited future as independent institutions.[51] The spread of comprehensive schools in the 1960s effectively marked the end of this attempt to encourage technical education at the secondary level. In this context, the TVEI might be interpreted as in the tradition of the *Bryce Report* of 1895, the *Spens Report* of 1938 and the *Crowther Report* of 1959. All sought to reconcile technical with secondary education by stimulating a distinct kind of 'secondary technical education'.

A further factor that helps to explain the importance attached to the TVEI was concern over the number of pupils who failed to derive any tangible benefits or qualifications from their time at school. It was hoped that comprehensive schools would encourage all pupils to reach their full potential regardless of their background, gender, aptitude or ability, but in many cases familiar problems of 'educational waste' failed to disappear.[52] The *Newsom Report* on average and below-average pupils had commented in 1963 that the country could not afford the 'wastage' that resulted from 'unrealized talent especially among boys and girls whose potential is masked by inadequate powers of speech and the limitations of home background'. It suggested that such pupils should be encouraged to stay at school for a longer period, but also that: 'The schools will need to present that education in terms more acceptable to the pupils and to their parents, by relating school more directly to adult life, and especially by taking a proper account of vocational interests.'[53] When, in spite of the spread of the comprehensives and the raising of the school-leaving age to sixteen, it became clear that such 'wastage' was still common, the idea of cultivating a more 'relevant' approach for such pupils again proved attractive. Critics of the comprehensives in the 1960s and 1970s generally stressed their alleged effects on academic 'standards' in relation to the most able pupils.[54] By the late 1970s comprehensives were also being taken to task for failing to encourage a 'practical' approach to the curriculum, particularly for pupils who were leaving school at the minimum leaving age and without qualifications.

Both forms of criticism were stimulated by Conservative policies on education. Throughout the first half of the twentieth century, academic excellence, closely associated with prevailing notions of 'liberal' education and the retention of an intellectual, social and political elite, had been a favourite Conservative theme. The grammar schools had symbolized these educational and social values. At the same time, there was a distinctive Conservative tradition favouring technical education for the purposes of national efficiency and economic productivity. The Conservative Political Centre in 1956 regarded the education and training of highly skilled people as a 'form of industrial investment' that would help the nation to compete with 'our foreign rivals'.[55] To neglect this investment was to lose the economic 'race':

> The nations that have passed us in this race are drawing further ahead, and they know what prizes are denied to the losers. They realize that lagging in this race implies lagging in the race for greater material prosperity, and they cannot understand how we dispute or disregard this simple fact. They are not surprised that our share of world trade has diminished, and they conclude that we are doubling our standard of living in a peculiarly British way.[56]

Technical education is here advocated for its economic uses rather than its educational benefits, for 'material prosperity' and a growth in trade and industry. It was a view that assumed the maintenance of a stable social and political order, and proposed educational changes designed to improve its efficiency. In this sense it was essentially a functionalist view of technical education. The same could be said of the intentions behind the Youth Training Scheme introduced in 1983. As *The Times* approvingly pointed out, it was in part a short-term 'anti-riot device keeping 16-year-olds off the unemployment record and off the streets'. No less important,

> The short-term expedient must also be used as a vehicle for a longer-term policy: equipping the work force of the 1980s and 1990s with the new array of skills required by an economy open to sharp competition from far east, far west and the Continent. A gap has long been apparent. Britain imparts to too few of its young people skills of any kind let alone new skills; we retrain too few of our adults compared with the Germans and Japanese. YTS could be a step on the path back to sustained competitiveness.[57]

A direct link was assumed between technical education on the one hand and capitalist growth, material wealth and economic competitiveness. The TVEI was highly characteristic of this Conservative tradition in technical education.

The spread of comprehensive schools helped to strengthen Conservative support for technical education at the secondary level. In 1959 Sir David Eccles as Minister of Education assured a delegation of the Association of Heads of Secondary Technical Schools that 'we equate the secondary technical school with the grammar school as being selective, which we certainly hope to defend from wholesale comprehensive schools'.[58] By 1979, only twenty years later, more than eighty per cent of state secondary schools were comprehensives. It is not surprising that many Conservatives were unhappy with this new situation, although reactions ranged from ambivalence to outright hostility. At the annual conference of the Conservative Party held in October 1978, the party's education spokesperson, Norman St. John Stevas, had to be 'the quintessence of blandness' as he 'cobbled together a garment to wear at the next election'. As the *TES* noted: 'He had to support the comprehensive schools, but also promised to keep the grammar schools: yet even in the latter respect, he had to promise to let local education authorities decide what is best for their area, which will mean letting some grammar schools go.'[59] The promotion of technical studies in the comprehensives helped signal continuing disquiet over the character and direction of the schools while also encouraging notions of 'selection'.

The accelerating pace of technological change, indeed the promise of a new 'industrial revolution' offered by advances in microelectronics, underlined the potential importance of learning new skills at the secondary-school level. This was reflected in the activities of Kenneth Baker, appointed by the Conservative government in 1981 to be minister in charge of information technology under the aegis of the Department of Industry. Baker led a government initiative to ensure that every maintained school, and selected teacher training centres, installed at least one microcomputer. Computers in the secondary school curriculum were more attractive than traditional manual or craft courses because they introduced pupils to new 'high-tech' skills and offered avenues to professional careers. As one commentator observed: 'Downing Street, bruised from battling to save dying sectors like steel and cars, has realized that some parts of industry — notably those linked to glamorous new notions like software and data flow — can kindle enthusiasm, attract large chunks of private capital and, with luck, create jobs.'[60]

Baker's activities, then, may have helped to stimulate awareness of changing needs relating to the new technology, and probably fostered greater enthusiasm among Conservatives for technological education. Even so, the microcomputer initiative did nothing in itself to rectify the problems that had been identified concerning the traditional academic curriculum, the dichotomy between 'liberal' and 'vocational' education, the needs of pupils with practical aptitudes and of the 'bottom forty per cent' in schools, the deficiencies of comprehensive schools or the growing problem of youth unemployment. The TVEI emerged in November 1982 as a response to these perceived difficulties, with the general intention of arresting 'national decline' by improving Britain's economic and industrial competitiveness.

The TVEI would not have taken the form it did, however, had it not been for a new factor associated with Thatcher's Conservative government: the 'resolute approach'. The scheme may be interpreted as a by-product of the 'Falklands Factor' of 1982. Following Argentina's seizure of the Falkland Islands in April 1982, their successful recapture not only restored the political fortunes of the government but sent its popularity to new heights. Thatcher's own reputation for strength and tenacity was greatly enhanced. This was an important advantage not only in purely electoral terms but also in addressing a range of issues, in domestic as well as in foreign policy. Thatcher was able to maintain stringent economic policies which involved a high level of unemployment and reductions in public expenditure. It was also possible to give full rein to the rhetoric of change with which the Conservatives had swept to power in 1979. Thatcher seemed indeed to offer a radical alternative to the failed policies of the past which had led to Britain's decline. As Martin Wiener has suggested: 'The general election of 1979 witnessed, in fact, an historic exchange, in which the Labour party stood for English tradition, tranquillity and ''safety first'' and the Conservatives — their leader especially — gave the calls for sweeping change.'[61]

The TVEI is an interesting example of the government's general approach. The DES and the education system were held to have failed to provide solutions for deep-rooted educational and social problems. The answer was a decisive intervention designed to oblige entrenched educational interests to change their attitudes. It was noted even before the launch of the TVEI, in relation to the MSC's New Training Initiative, that:

> The long tradition of democratic control and consultation built up over decades, has hamstrung the education interest in the face of the challenge from employment. There are, of course, many good reasons for entrusting education to democratic institutions and for engaging in careful consultation with all the interests concerned. But these count for little with brash new bodies like the MSC, in the face of a crisis of youth unemployment and strident demands for government action.[62]

So it proved also in November 1982. Thus it was the MSC rather than the DES that was chosen to administer the TVEI. Long-term trends towards government intervention in education, science and technology had combined with growing Conservative support for technical education at the secondary level to create the TVEI. None the less, the character of Thatcher's government, and the political climate of autumn 1982, had an important bearing upon the shape, direction and control of the scheme actually developed.

The TVEI

It was envisaged initially that pilot courses for about 10 000 schoolchildren would begin in ten chosen places in September 1983. The courses, which could be organized in schools, colleges and further education or existing industrial training premises, would replace the entire school curriculum for those taking part. It was to be complementary to the £1,000 million Youth Training Scheme, and would be extended widely if the pilots proved successful. LEAs were invited to submit proposals for courses for pupils in a 'wide range of ability', which would lead to a recognizable qualification. The pilot scheme was expected to continue for five years, testing ways of organizing courses and developing content and methods. The MSC was apparently prepared to spend £40 million per year by 1986. It would inspect the projects put forward by interested LEAs, select ten of them, and take part in their design and operation.[63]

The TVEI's political context gave it an emphasis on notions of nationalism, materialism, capitalism and enterprise consistent with the Conservative tradition but differing from the outlook of Bryce, Spens and Crowther. These reports had evoked what might be characterized as a 'liberal' approach to technical education. Bryce asserted a broad approach to secondary education that would embrace both 'liberal culture' and 'practical art'.[64] Spens recommended the further development of junior technical schools as 'a type of secondary school providing a liberal education based on a more realistic and scientific curriculum than that of a Grammar School'.[65] Crowther's 'Alternative Road' was marked not by 'narrow vocational interest' but by a 'broad scientific curiosity'.[66] Crowther was himself particularly concerned to ensure that:

> ... the whole of this area should be gradually transformed from being primarily designed to meet industry's needs (with some education thrown in) to being primarily designed to continue the education of a large slice of the nation's boys and girls (without destroying the usefulness to industry of the present system).[67]

The Crowther concept was seen as an alternative 'to both the merely theoretical and the rather narrowly technical'.[68] Bryce's support for higher grade schools, in common with Spens's advocacy of technical high schools and Crowther's defence of secondary technical schools, argued an important role for technical education at the secondary level not so much for utilitarian or vocational ends but rather for social mobility and personal development.

Several attempts to foster applied science and technology in schools in the 1950s and 1960s were imbued with this more liberal approach. The emphasis was generally upon finding a compromise between the academic and liberal traditions of school science and the vocational and industrial nexus of technology, craft and engineering. Dr C.G. Williams of the Institution of Mechanical Engineers suggested that the 'basic intellectual appeal' of engineering should be more widely appreciated in schools.[69] John Dancy, Master of Marlborough College in Wiltshire, argued that technology, far from being antithetical to a 'liberal education', was in fact 'an essential ingredient *within* a liberal tradition'.[70] This line of argument was difficult to reconcile with instrumental, narrow training of the kind that the TVEI seemed to imply. The consolidation of the TVEI since 1982 has involved widening its appeal to incorporate this more liberal outlook.

Once it was established, the TVEI's initiators were able to defend their policy by stressing the wider educational problems that it might help to resolve, as well as by adopting the more distinctive Thatcherite rhetoric. They could do so, moreover, in a way that suited particular audiences and interests, and so minimized hostility and resistance from those whose co-operation would be necessary for the success of the policy. The scheme was closely associated with David Young, a businessman who had become chairman of the MSC earlier in 1982. Young stressed his determination to ensure that schools should provide a broad preparation for work or more specific vocational courses, suggesting that if they failed to respond to the MSC's lead he might 'as a last resort' use the powers available under the 1973 Employment and Training Act to create technical schools run by the MSC itself.[71]

During the early development of the TVEI Young tended to concentrate on its vocational aims. He echoed Tebbit's views on the 'rebirth of technical education' and its importance from the point of view of reducing unemployment and improving national economic performance. The haste with which the scheme had been organized was explained as being due to the urgency of employment needs: 'Next summer, nearly half a million school-leavers will be coming on to the labour market, and every year that passes brings still more young people unprepared for the world of work on to the job market.'[72] Young was confident that the TVEI could help to change this situation: 'By the time they leave, our youngsters will be highly employable.'[73] This in turn would lead naturally, in Young's view, 'to Britain's industrial strength and economic prosperity'.[74] As one observer rightly noted: 'A personal adherent of the Tory economic doctrine that industrial competitiveness is the key to prosperity, he believes equally that training is the key to that competitiveness.'[75] Such views attracted many who were impatient with the traditional liberal and academic values of secondary education, anxious, like Bill Bonnen of the Confederation of British Industries' Special Programmes Unit, to 'take account of the economic and industrial realities of the society we live in'.[76] The TVEI's functionalist aspect was one of its most endearing qualities so far as organized industrial interests were concerned.

At the same time, Sir Keith Joseph as education secretary felt able to support the TVEI despite its implied criticisms of the education service and many of its traditional values. Excluded from prior discussions on the launching of the scheme, he nevertheless responded by arguing that it would help to provide a wider range and a better balance of courses in schools.[77] The comprehensive schools, he explained, were failing to draw out the full potential of many children for whom a 'technical stream' might be suitable: 'I think I'm presiding at the moment over an education system in which there really is inadequate provision for a very substantial minority. I think if what the government is seeking to achieve comes to pass, that will be less true.'[78] This kind of argument was designed to attract educators who were concerned with the apparent failure of the comprehensives to motivate the 'bottom forty per cent' in schools, although it was emphasized that the TVEI was not directed solely towards such pupils. Tebbit hoped that the TVEI would 'attract a broad spectrum of ability', but added that 'for those who do not fancy the rich academic diet, we are providing them with a rather more nourishing technical diet'.[79] Young sought to involve a 'wide range' of academic ability in the new initiative, aiming particularly for the 'fifteen to eighty-five percentiles of the ability range'.[80] The post-war secondary technical schools showed what could be done, but it was insisted that the TVEI did not mean a return to the old 'tripartite' system; it was intended not to undermine the comprehensives, but to assist them.

The new scheme also won the sympathetic interest of many who had been working within the education system to encourage more practical forms of education but had for various reasons been frustrated. Edward Semper, head of Doncaster Technical High School for Boys, attempted in the 1960s to promote national initiatives in favour of technical and technological education at the school level. He later recalled: 'I felt sure that with the onset of comprehensive education my work would die with me ... unless measures were taken to promote developments of a similar kind in all schools.'[81] The Association of Heads of Secondary Technical Schools, of which Semper was a leading figure, was renamed the Association for Technical Education in Schools in 1964. This new organization made little headway in spreading its message, and this continued failure appeared to confirm the view that 'an alternative to ''Technical'' or ''Vocational'' in the name was needed because the connotation of these words was debased'.[82] The name of the group was later changed again, this time to the Association for Technological Education in Schools. An offer by the government to sponsor a major initiative in 'technical' and 'vocational' education, which had been sought for so long, must have been attractive in spite of any reservations over the government's approach.

Semper had also helped to pave the way for a major project in technology run by the Schools Council from 1967 until 1972. The organizer of this project, Geoffrey Harrison, was hopeful that 'the craft and physics departments in a school should co-operate to evolve a true image of engineering'.[83] By 1969 his tone was more pessimistic as he had become acutely aware that 'it is difficult for any school to break out from the established conventions and traditions of secondary education'.[84] For Harrison, then, the TVEI was a welcome new development: 'Many are apprehensive about initiatives, such as this, coming from outside the education service, but in the absence of anything coming from within, what are the grounds for apprehension?.... What MSC has done is to provide the money to enable things to actually happen.'[85] Similar sentiments have been expressed by John Dancy, who in 1965–6 attempted unsuccessfully to persuade the Ministry of Technology to sponsor the development of technical project work in schools: 'After that, I personally find it hard to resent the MSC.'[86]

Sir Joseph Pope, who as professor of mechanical engineering at Nottingham University in the 1950s designed a miniature engine test-bed for the applied science laboratory at Ealing Grammar School, has also recorded his exasperation with the conservatism of the education system: 'The educational system is such a tightly-closed loop, which we've got to break.'[87] It was clearly upon such feelings that Young was relying when he explained the MSC's failure to consult interested parties before setting up the TVEI: 'Supposing we had decided to launch a debate about technical education or the lack of it. We might have had a royal commission and it might have taken five years or even ten to get off the ground. Now we have a pilot project due to start by September next year.'[88] Whatever their misgivings over the source and character of support given by the TVEI, it was difficult for sympathizers of technical education in schools to turn it down.

There were also good reasons for LEAs to involve themselves in the scheme. It provided much needed resources and revenue for curriculum development. Moreover, to ignore the initiative completely would mean the LEAs having no influence over its future direction. As Gordon Hainsworth, director of education for Gateshead, argued, the TVEI's 'announcement and approach' might be 'objectionable', but 'the best way for LEAs to make a significant contribution is to be part of the arrangements from the start and to mould them, in the interests of all youngsters, in the way that we think important'.[89] The broad criteria for LEA schemes approved by the TVEI's steering group in January 1983 probably strengthened this view. Projects for the programme were to ensure equal opportunities for both sides; provide four-year curricula designed to prepare students for particular aspects of employment and for adult life in a society liable to rapid change; and include clear and specific objectives, including the encouragement of initiative, problem-solving abilities, and other aspects of personal development. They were also to give a balance between general, technical and vocational elements of programmes varying according to students' individual needs and the stage of the course, while relating the technical and vocational elements to potential employment opportunities and including arrangements for regular assessment.[90]

There was little in this list that LEAs could reject, apart from the underlying assumption that schools were not already practising such criteria. The source of the TVEI as a policy was evident in that Conservative counties proved most sympathetic to it; the hopes of the LEAs themselves were reflected in the fact that few of the schemes submitted bore close resemblance to the notions expressed by the TVEI's initiators. Sixty-eight proposals were offered, by sixty-six LEAs. Fourteen LEAs were eventually chosen to run pilot schemes, including five metropolitan districts, seven counties, one London borough and one from Wales. At the same time it was noted that: 'While controversy revolved round the scheme's merits there was no sign in most submissions that the Authorities were busy winding the clock back to a tripartite system.'[91]

The TVEI continued to be associated closely with the outlook and ideologies of its political sponsors, although increasingly efforts were made to maintain at least the acquiescence of LEAs, schools and teachers. The Conservative manifesto for the general election of 1983 stressed the government's aim to 'make sure that children are taught and trained for the world they will grow up into', asserting also that the success of the TVEI project 'will play a vital part in raising technical training in Britain to the level of our best overseas competitors'.[92] Young himself took greater pains to explain the TVEI in terms with which educators would sympathize. He pointed out the consequences of the loss of the post-war secondary technical schools: 'In the drive towards comprehensives the technical and vocational end of education somehow got lost.' He emphasized also the need to enter for those pupils who were still leaving school without qualifications: 'It really must be recognized that young people differ in their abilities. Academic ability is given to perhaps fifteen to twenty per cent of us, but we are bright in so many different ways and our education system must learn to cater for that.'[93]

Young was aggressive in supporting the government's White Paper *Training For Jobs*, which indeed he had helped to frame, as offering 'a vision for the future taking account of changing patterns of occupations and employment and what they mean for education and training'.[94] At the same time he expressed the hope that 'before many years are out a substantial proportion of our young will have their curriculum enlarged and their studies enriched and will leave school motivated and interested and above all educated in the world in which they are going to live'.[95] The TVEI could give young people 'employable skills', but he now suggested that this was not what it was 'essentially concerned' to do: 'TVEI is about educating people, about broadening the curriculum to give them new subjects to which to relate.'[96] This new tone seemed to represent an attempt to consolidate the TVEI as a policy, to ensure its wider acceptability while keeping favour with its patrons and original sympathizers.

In August 1984 a report emanating from a proposal by Young called for further major changes in vocational education and training with the aim of competing more successfully in world markets.[97] Young's political weight was acknowledged in spectacular fashion the following month when he was elevated to a life peerage and given a Cabinet post. The newly styled Lord Young of Graffham became the head of Mrs Thatcher's Enterprise Unit at the Cabinet Office and began plans to co-ordinate the education, training and employment of fourteen to eighteen year olds.[98] Meanwhile forty-eight more LEAs began running pilot projects for the TVEI in September 1984, with a further round of projects to be launched in September 1985.[99]

Policy, politics and education

By the middle of 1985, then, the TVEI had been consolidated as an integral part of a wider policy to 'lay the foundations for a new training era'.[100] It had also broadened to take account of the views of such as Peter Brindle, TVEI co-ordinator in Bradford: 'I don't want to see a repetition of the secondary technical schools' experience — having attended one myself. We aim to broaden people's options, not funnel them towards technology. TVEI is not about producing technologists, but providing youngsters with the skills to cope with change and possibly with unemployment.'[101] It could indeed be pointed out that 'TVEI has proved to be very varied — so varied that there is no such thing as a TVEI stereotype'.[102] In another way too the TVEI had been consolidated to the extent that those LEAs still declining to take part could be depicted as doing so 'for political reasons'.[103] The implication here was that a successful policy with a wide spectrum of support was not political in character. In fact, however, the process of establishing and then maintaining the TVEI was a political one, and in so far as it had been consolidated it was a political success. Opposition to the TVEI, like the TVEI itself, was the outcome of long-term educational and social changes as well as current political problems.

Various forms of opposition to the TVEI were expressed, often provoked by the manner of its launching. Many teachers and administrators continued to resent what the *TES* called the MSC's 'imperialistic drive downwards into the secondary school'.[104] It was suggested that David Young had become 'the polished bogeyman of the education world' because he 'personified the attempted takeover of the classroom by the training world'.[105] The clear anxiety among teachers over apparent threats to their professional integrity was expressed even by those who supported more practical forms of education. For Donald Proud, head of Edge End

High School in Nelson, Lancashire, there were at least two reasons for declining involvement in the TVEI. First, it would have meant that 'we would lose our professional prerogative to think or to plan and have to hand over our accountability to a body that was not accountable to the community'. Also he continued to be sceptical of the TVEI's notion of technical and vocational education: 'Training we thought was for soldiers and circus horses ... For 14-year-olds destined to change jobs probably four times in their lives, we are happier with the idea of teaching a number of transferable skills.'[106] It was the aim of the TVEI's opponents to encourage such doubts and fears.

Criticism of a quite different order was directed at the TVEI by educators anxious to preserve at least some place for the classical and humanistic curriculum associated with the nineteenth-century public schools. The place of classics in the secondary school curriculum had declined as that of science advanced. The prospect of directly 'practical' or 'technical' subjects also being taught in secondary schools was intolerable to the more rigorous advocates of a 'liberal education'. Agitation for scientific education during the First World War was met with stern deprecations of education conducted 'in a commercial spirit'.[107] In the 1960s also, pressure to adopt school curricula to the 'practical' demands of the 'real world' was often regarded as a 'threat'.[108] Despite the fact that a Conservative government was closely involved, the TVEI renewed these fears. David Holbrook of Cambridge University argued that humanity, imagination and critical appreciation were lacking in the government's approach.[109] Maurice Holt, director of the Curriculum Development Support Unit at the College of St Mark and St John, Plymouth, also felt that the school curriculum being proposed by the government lacked a 'human dimension'.[110] The veteran politician Enoch Powell roundly condemned the 'barbarism' that education should produce economic wellbeing, insisting that it should be seen as a 'good thing' in and for itself.[111] Such protests may well have found sympathy in Conservative ranks.

The same was no doubt true of scepticism voiced by organized scientific interests. The Royal Society had long insisted that the interests of science and technology were best served by giving precedence to the teaching of general scientific principles as a foundation for various forms of specialist training. Sir Harry Pitt, chairman of the education committee of the Royal Society, criticized the TVEI on the grounds that 'it is based on the old-fashioned and outmoded view that there is a distinction to be made between science and technology'. Pitt added: 'I hope it does not go too far along the road before it is brought into line with current thinking.'[112] Academic standards as well as liberal humanism were traditional nostrums of the Conservative Party. If the government's commitment to the TVEI was undermining these other elements in the Conservative educational tradition, enthusiasm for that policy might begin to fade.

Such varied criticisms and opinions, expressed at different levels though they were, might by themselves have been limited in their effect on the TVEI. More threatening was a socialist critique of the Conservatives' policy that offered an alternative focus of political and educational activity. For over fifty years the Labour Party had represented educational attitudes antithetical to those which came to be embodied in the TVEI. As Clive Griggs has shown, the early interest of the Trades Union Congress (TUC) in technical education began to decline by the early twentieth century in favour of access to secondary education.[113] For both the TUC and the infant Labour Party, trade schools and junior technical schools seemed a poor substitute for the access to professional careers and high salaries provided by state secondary schools. By 1918 this new position had become entrenched. According to L.O. Ward: 'The Labour Party, which stood to gain from technical education, refused to accept more of it from either of the two historic parties [Liberal and Conservative], who it seemed to them had, with varying degrees of enthusiasm, justified more technical education in purely instrumental, materialistic and nationalistic terms, and never in terms of its merit as part of a general scheme of education.'[114] R.H. Tawney was especially virulent in his criticism of schemes that seemed designed to 'keep the workers' children in their place',[115] and his call for 'secondary education for all' came to occupy a central place in labour policy.

The tripartite system of the post-1944 period was soon regarded with the same suspicion as the old arrangements for the elementary, secondary and technical education.[116] For example the TUC, in a memorandum to the Crowther committee in 1957, made clear its opposition to separate technical schools on the grounds that 'it is educationally and socially undesirable that young people should be unduly segregated on the basis of their possession or otherwise of certain specific abilities, especially if such segregation is related also to different fields of future employment and consequently to different degrees of social status'.[117] Technical education was indeed, as Silver observes, 'a point of entry to debates about social class differentiation in the educational system'.[118] It was easy to interpret the TVEI as just the latest in a line of attempts by employers to perpetuate traditional social and work patterns at the expense of working-class children.

It is not surprising, then, that Labour sympathizers came to the defence of comprehensive schools, equality and the common curriculum. The TUC had generally co-operated with the schemes of the MSC, but Len Murray, general secretary of the TUC, showed little enthusiasm for the TVEI: 'It must strengthen comprehensive education, maintain the role of the public sector and ensure that vocational preparation does not mean early specialization and narrowing of study options.'[119] The Labour Party's spokesperson on further and higher education, Philip Whitehead, called on Labour-controlled LEAs to boycott the scheme. This appeal was heeded by many despite the fact that, as Whitehead himself sourly noted: 'When money is available people sometimes take it without thinking of the consequences.'[120] On the other hand, it was conceded that a more 'liberal' approach to secondary technical education such as had been current in the initiatives of the 1950s and 1960s might be compatible with the principles of comprehensive education. Such an approach would also be more in keeping with the original aims of the 'Great Debate'. The largest LEA in the country, the Inner London Education Authority, decided to ignore the TVEI but to set up a working party of its own chaired by Dr David Hargreaves to consider alternatives. Hargreaves commended the idea of more practical education and a broadening of the curriculum to recognize non-academic achievement, but argued strongly that the TVEI would tend to segregate pupils and was therefore incompatible with the principles of comprehensive education.[121]

The Plan for Training agreed by the Labour Party and TUC in August 1984, together with the party's *Charter For Pupils And Parents* the following spring, indicated the probable future direction of Labour policy in this area. As Giles Radice, Labour's education spokesperson, explained:

> Of course, we approach these questions from a quite different perspective to that of the Conservatives. From Tawney onwards, Labour has always taken a more generous, less narrowly ''vocational'' vision of education than the Tories. While we need to ensure that all pupils acquire a range of basic skills, our vision includes the creative and artistic as well as the personal and social. Hence the emphasis in our charter is on a broad and balanced curriculum.[122]

The vision here was reminiscent of the Green Paper of 1977, *Education in Schools*, which had emphasized a framework of comprehensive schools, general education and a common curriculum, rather than of *Training for Jobs*. It seemed likely that changing political fortunes at the national and local levels would have a direct bearing on the character of education policy and particularly on schemes like the TVEI.

The TVEI emanated from particular ideals, attitudes, constituencies and calculations identifiable as a conservative tradition. Opposition to the TVEI has found a natural focus in a rival source of policy, the Labour Party, with its different ideals and interests. Despite their differences, however, both the TVEI and the Labour Party now appear to be laying claim to 'liberal' views on technical education at the secondary level. In its early days the TVEI had given rise to justifiable fears that it would create 'a divided curriculum perpetuating Victorian views of knowledge and social class.'[123] By July 1985 the new chairman of the MSC, Bryan Nicholson, could express confidence that the influence of the TVEI would soon pervade the education system.[124] In the months that followed, Lord Young consolidated his place in Cabinet and it was announced that the TVEI would be extended to all maintained schools and colleges.[125] Both the character and the extent of the TVEI's influence were however still open to dispute. Technical and vocational education will surely continue to be inextricably linked with wider social and political factors as an arena of conflict over the nature of British society. It is to be hoped that whether or not the TVEI is maintained in its present form, the narrow and divisive vocationalism of its early rhetoric will continue to be undermined in favour of a broader vision more characteristic of the tradition of Bryce and Crowther.

References and Notes

1. House of Commons written answers to questions, *Hansard* (12 November 1982), cols 269–70.
2. Report, 'Tebbit starts technical education scheme', *The Times* (13 November 1982).
3. 'Kinnock hits out at roots of industry's decline', *Times Educ. Supp.* (8 July 1983).
4. Williams, R. *The Long Revolution*. London, Chatto and Windus (1961), 213.
5. Briggs, A. 'Sociology and history', in A.T. Welford, Michael Argyle, D.V. Glass, J.N. Morris (eds), *Society: Problems And Methods Of Study*, London, Routledge & Kegan Paul (1967), 94.
6. Philip Abrams, *Historical Sociology*. London, Open Books (1982), 16.
7. For accounts of this trend see e.g. P.W. Musgrave (ed.), *Sociology, History, and Education: A Reader*. London, Methuen, (1970), Introduction; P. Szreter, 'History and Sociology: Rivals or Partners in the Field of Education?', in *Bulletin of the History of Education Society*, **3** (Spring 1969), 17-24; Dennis Warwick and John Williams, 'History and the Sociology of Education', in *Br. Jnl. of Sociology of Education*, 1/3 (1980), 333–46.
8. Bernard Bailyn's *Education in the Forming of American Society: Needs and Opportunities for Study* (Chapel Hill, University of North Carolina Press, 1960) was a particularly influential work for this 'revisionist' history. The many useful analyses of this trend include Brian Simon, 'The history of education', in Paul Hirst (ed.), *Educational Theory and Its Foundation Disciplines* (London, Routledge & Kegan Paul, 1983), 62–83, and Harold Silver, *Education as History: Interpreting Nineteenth- and Twentieth-Century Education* (London, Methuen 1983), esp. Introduction.
9. Silver, *Education As History*, 11. See also Harold Silver, 'Historian in a Policy Field: A British Chef in Paris?' in *History of Education Review*, 14/1 (1985) 1–11, on the relationship between history and policy.
10. Ministry of Education, *15 to 18: A Report Of The Central Advisory Council For Education (England)* (vol. I, 1959), 55.
11. Maurice Kogan, *The Politics of Educational Change*, Manchester, Manchester University Press (1978), 51.
12. Education Act, 1944, Part 1, Clause 1.
13. Keith Fenwick, *The Comprehensive School 1944–1970: The Politics of Secondary School Reorganisation* (London, Methuen, 1976) is a useful survey and analysis of this trend.
14. House of Commons debates, *Hansard*, 21 March 1960, col. 52.
15. Sir William Alexander to Derek Morrell, 11 March 1963. (Association of

Education Committees papers, file A31(a), University of Leeds Special Collections.)

16. Tony Becher and Stuart Maclure. *The Politics of Curriculum Change* (London, Hutchinson, 1978), Ch. 3, and Barry MacDonald and Rob Walker, *Changing the Curriculum* (London, Open Books, 1976) give helpful accounts of the work of the Schools Council.
17. Such conflicts are examined by e.g. Roger Woods, 'Margaret Thatcher and Secondary Reorganisation, 1970–74', in *J. Educational Administration and History*, 13/2 (July 1981), 51–61; and Keith Fenwick, 'Changing roles in the Government of Education', in *Brit. J. Educational Studies*, 33/2 (1985), 135–47.
18. Lord Hailsham. *Science And Politics*. London, Faber (1963), 35.
19. Department of Employment. *Employment And Training: Government Proposals* (Cmnd. 5250, March 1973), 2.
20. Report, 'What the PM said.' *Times Educ. Supp.*, 22 October 1976.
21. Sir Keith Joseph. Speech at the North of England Education Conference, Sheffield, 6 January 1984. *Oxford Rev. Education*, 10/2 (1984), 142.
22. J. Myron Atkin, *The Government in the Classroom*. London, University of London Institute of Education (1980).
23. DES, *Education In Schools: A Consultative Document* (1977, Cmnd. 6869), 2.
24. Sir Montague Finniston (Chm), *Engineering Our Future: Report Of The Committee Of Inquiry Into the Engineering Profession* (Cmnd. 7794, 1980), 21.
25. *ibid.*, 4.
26. Royal Society of Arts. *The Future Of Technological Higher Education In Britain* (1982).
27. Charles Handy, in Symposium on Education for Capability, *J. Roy. Soc. Arts*, 5335 (June 1984), 431.
28. John Tomlinson, 'Education in the Eighties', in *J. Roy. Soc. Arts*, 5303 (October 1981), 731.
29. Correlli Barnett. 'Technology, Education and Industrial and Economic Strength'. *J. Roy. Soc.*, 5271 (February 1979), 127.
30. Martin J. Wiener, *English Culture And The Decline Of The Industrial Spirit, 1850–1980*. Cambridge, Cambridge University Press, (1981), ix.
31. See e.g. A.J. Meadows and W.H. Brock, 'Topics fit for gentlemen: The problem of science in the public school curriculum', in Brian Simon and Ian Bradley (eds), *The Victorian Public School: Studies In The Development Of An Educational Institution* (London, Gill and Macmillan, 1975), 95–114; and David Layton, 'Cultural contexts and science curriculum changes in England and Wales', in Philip Adey (ed.), *Innovation in Science Education* (London, Proceedings of U.S. — Japan Seminar, 1980), 105–15.
32. David Layton, *Interpreters Of Science: A History of The Association for Science Education* (London, Murray/ASE, 1984).
33. Science Masters' Association, *The Teaching Of General Science* (1936), 14.
34. SMA policy statement, *Science And Education* (November 1957), 3.
35. Gary McCulloch, Edgar Jenkins, David Layton, *Technological Revolution? The Politics Of School Science And Technology In England And Wales Since 1945* (London, Falmer Press, 1985), esp. Chs 3,5,7.
36. DES, *Science Education In Schools: A Consultative Document* (1982), 3.
37. On the mechanics' institutes see e.g. Colin Russell, *Science and Social Change in Britain and Europe, 1700–1900* (New York, St. Martin's Press, 1983), Ch.9; Ian Inkster, 'The Social Context of an Educational Movement: A Revisionist Approach to the English Mechanics' Institutes', in *Oxford Review of Education*,

2/3 (1976), 227–307; Mabel Tylecote, 'The Manchester Mechanics' Institution, 1824–50', in D.S.L. Cardwell (ed.), *Artisan to Graduate* (Manchester, Manchester U.P., 1974), 55–86.

On the DSA, see e.g. Roy MacLeod (ed.), *Days of Judgement: Science. Examinations and the Organisation of Knowledge in Late Victorian England* (Driffield, Nafferton Books, 1982), esp. Chs. 1–3; David Layton, *Science for the People: The Origins of the School Science Curriculum in England* (London, Allen and Unwin, 1973), esp. Chs. 6,7; and D.S.L. Cardwell, *The Organisation of Science in England* (London: Heinemann 2nd edn., 1972) esp. Chs. 4,5.

38. Margaret Gowing, 'Science, Technology and Education: England in 1870', in *Oxford Review Of Education*, 4/1 (1978), 9.
39. Stephen Cotgrove, *Technical Education And Social Change* (1958), 67.
40. See Gary McCulloch, 'David Forsyth and the Leeds Central Higher Grade School', in Keith Fenwick (ed.), *Yorkshire Studies In Education* (1983), 1–19, for details of a prominent higher grade school.
41. Royal Commission on Secondary Education, 1895, vol. I, 135–6.
42. *ibid.*
43. On the elitist character of English secondary education before 1940 see esp. Brian Simon, *The Politics of Educational Reform, 1920–1940* (London, Lawrence and Wishart, 1974), and Gail L. Savage, 'Social Class and Social Policy: The Civil Service and Secondary Education in England During the Interwar Period', in *Jnl. of Contemporary History*, vol. 18 (1983), 261–80.
44. Board of Education, *Report of the Consultative Committee on Secondary Education with Special Reference to Grammar Schools and Technical High Schools* (1938), 67.
45. *ibid.*, 274.
46. Board of Education, *Curriculum And Examinations In Secondary Schools* (1943), 3 (Norwood report).
47. Ministry of Education, *The New Secondary Education* (pamphlet no. 9, 1947), 23.
48. *ibid.*, 48.
49. *ibid.*, 29.
50. Ministry of Education, *15 to 18: A Report Of The Central Advisory Council for Education (England)* (1959), esp. Ch. 35, 'The Alternative Road'.
51. For further details see Gary McCulloch, 'Pioneers of an ''Alternative Road''?'. The Association of Heads of Secondary Technical Schools, 1951–64', in Ivor Goodson (ed.), *Social Histories Of The Secondary Curriculum: Subjects For Study* (London, Falmer Press, 1985), 313–42.
52. See e.g. Harold Silver (ed.), *Equal Opportunity in Education: A Reader in Social Class and Educational Opportunity* (London, Methuen, 1973), esp. Introduction, and Stephen Ball, *Beachside Comprehensive: A Case-Study in Comprehensive Schooling* (London, Falmer Press, 1981).
53. *Half Our Future: A Report Of The Central Advisory Council For Education (England)* (1963), p.3.
54. e.g. C.B. Cox, A.E. Dyson (eds.), *Fight for Education: A Black Paper* (London, Critical Quarterly Society, 1969).
55. Conservative Political Centre, *Technical Education* (November 1956), 5.
56. *ibid.*, 6.
57. *The Times*, editorial, 'Training is the Thing', 2 September 1983.
58. 'Deputation to Minister of Education', 16 March 1959 (AHSTS Council papers, c/o University of Leeds Special Collections).
59. *TES*, editorial, 'Coruscating on thin ice', 20 October 1978.

60. Richard Brooks, 'Can this man switch on Britain?', *Sunday Times*, 21 March 1982.
61. Martin Wiener, 'Conservatism, Economic Growth and English Culture', in *Parliamentary Affairs*, 34/4 (Autumn 1981), 409.
62. Stuart Maclure, 'The educational consequences of Mr. Norman Tebbit', in *Oxford Review of Education*, 8/2 (1982), 108.
63. *The Times*, report, 13 November 1982, 'Tebbit starts technical education scheme'; *TES*, report, 19 November 1982, 'Technical comeback for schools'.
64. Royal Commission on Secondary Education, 1895, vol. I. III. 40.
65. Board of Education, *Report Of The Consultative Committee On Secondary Education With Special Reference to Grammar Schools And Technical High Schools* (1938), 269.
66. Crowther report, 1959, 393.
67. Geoffrey Crowther, addendum to David Ayerst, issues paper, 'Unsolved Problems in Part 3', n.d. (1957) (Raybould papers, Museum of Education, University of Leeds).
68. 'Report of the 1st meeting of the Development Committee', 18 January 1963 (Semper papers, University of Leeds Special Collections). See also Gary McCulloch, 'Views of the Alternative Road: The Crowther Concept', in David Layton (ed.), *The Alternative Road: The Rehabilitation Of the Practical* (Leeds, University of Leeds, 1984) 57–73.
69. C.G. Williams, memorandum, 'Applied Science in Schools', 21 August 1963 (I *Mech. E.* papers, private).
70. J.C. Dancy, 'Technology in a liberal education', in *Advancement Of Science* (October 1965), 379. See also McCulloch, Jenkins, Layton, *Technological Revolution*?, esp. Chs. 8, 9.
71. *Education*, report 'Mailed fist and velvet glove from Mr. David Young', 19 November 1982.
72. David Young, 'Helping the young help themselves', *TES*, 26 November 1982.
73. *Education*, report, 'Mailed fist and velvet glove from Mr. David Young', 19 November 1982.
74. David Young, 'Equipping the young for the real world', *Times Higher Education Supplement*, 21 January 1983.
75. Donald Macintyre, 'Tebbit's ''hatchet man'' smokes the peace pipe', in *Sunday Times*, 27 February 1983.
76. Bill Bonnen, letter to *TES*, 11 March 1983.
77. *TES*, report, 'Technical comeback for schools', 19 November 1982.
78. *TES*, report, 'Good enough for your child?', 25 February 1983.
79. *The Times* 13 November 1982, report, 'Tebbit starts technical education scheme'.
80. *Education*, report, 'Mailed fist and velvet glove from Mr. David Young', 19 November 1982.
81. Edward Semper to Sir Harold Hartley, 6 May 1969 (Hartley papers, Churchill College, Cambridge, Box 328).
82. AHSTS Council meeting, 22 June 1963 (AHSTS papers; University of Leeds Special Collections).
83. Geoffrey Harrison, 'Engineering projects', in *TES*, 21 May 1965.
84. Geoffrey Harrison, 'Memorandum on Current Proposals for Advancing the Teaching of Applied Science and Technology in Schools', for Schools Science and Technology Committee, 24 May 1969 (Standing Conference on Schools' Science and Technology papers).

85. Geoffrey Harrison, 'Technology in Schools', in David Layton (ed.), *The Alternative Road: The Rehabilitation Of The Practical* (1984), 86–7.
86. John Dancy (ed.), *T.V.E.I* (Perspectives 14, School of Education, University of Exeter, 1984), Introduction, 6.
87. Sir Joseph Pope, interview with the author, 24 September 1982.
88. *The Times*, 22 November 1982, report, 'Vocational training: David Young's £7m secret'.
89. Gordon Hainsworth, 'Week by week', *Education*, 28 January 1983.
90. *TES*, report, ''More 1.e.a.s. may join the technical revolution', 4 February 1983.
91. *Education*, 11 March 1983, report, 'Mixed bag of schemes for the Young initiative'.
92. *The Conservative Manifesto 1983*, 29.
93. David Young, in *Jnl. of Royal Society for Arts*, 5335 (June 1984), 426.
94. David Young, 'Coping with Change: the New Training Initiative', in *Jnl. of Royal Society for Arts*, 5335 (June 1984), 449.
95. *Ibid*, 452.
96. *Ibid*, 457.
97. *TES*, 31 August 1984, 'Why ailing Britain needs a good VET'.
98. *TES*, 26 October 1984, 'Learning to regard service with a smile'.
99. *TES*, 3 May 1985, 'The Technical and Vocational Education Initiative'.
100. *TES*, 29 March 1985, 'MSC tries to lay the foundations for a new training era'.
101. *TES*, 3 May 1985, 'Leap in the dark'.
102. Stuart Maclure, 'Hands up for the enterprise culture?' in *TES*, 8 February 1985.
103. *TES*, 11 January 1985, '14–18 pre-vocational education'.
104. *TES*, editorial, 'Bring back the DES ...', 19 November 1982.
105. *TES*, 14 September 1984, Comment, 'The power and the pendulum'.
106. Donald Proud, 'Nothing but vinegar sponges', *TES*, 14 December 1984.
107. e.g. Frederick A. Kenyon (ed.), *Education, Scientific and Humane: A Report Of The Proceedings Of The Council for Humanistic Studies* (London, John Murray, 1917), and Victor Gollancz and David Somervell, *The School and the World*, (London, 1919).
108. e.g. Kingsley Amis et al, 'The threat of the practical', in *The Observer*, 26 February 1961.
109. David Holbrook, 'Cutting out the frills, cutting out the thrills', *TES*, 2 November 1984.
110. Maurice Holt, 'The high-rise curriculum', in *TES*, 12 October 1984.
111. Enoch Powell, 'The heresy that education must be useful', in *Guardian Weekly*, 13 January 1985.
112. *Education*, 28 February 1983, news in review, 'Young initiative condemned by leading FRS'.
113. Clive Griggs, *The Trades Union Congress And the Struggle For Education* (London, Falmer Press, 1983), esp. 117.
114. L.O. Ward, 'Technical Education and the Politicians (1870–1918)', in *Br. Jnl. of Educational Studies*, 21/1 (1973), 39.
115. R.H. Tawney, 'Keep the Workers' Children in their Place', 1918, reprinted in R.H. Tawney, *The Radical Tradition (1964), 49–54.*
116. Keith Fenwick, *The Comprehensive School, 1944–1970* (1976).
117. TUC, 'The Education of Boys and Girls between 15 and 18', memorandum to

Crowther committee, 1957 (Raybould papers, Museum of Education, University of Leeds).

118. Harold Silver, 'The liberal and the vocational', in his *Education As History* (1983), 158.
119. *Education*, report, 'Mailed fist and velvet glove from Mr. David Young', 19 November 1982.
120. *Education*, report, 'Mixed bag of schemes for the Young initiative', 11 March 1983.
121. *TES*, report 'Hargreaves in pre-voc attack on Sir Keith', 2 November 1984.
122. Giles Radice, 'Framework for radical rights', in *TES*, 17 May 1985.
123. Maurice Holt, 'The great education robbery', in *TES*, 3 December 1982.
124. *TES* 12 July 1985, report, 'MSC call for new curricula'.
125. *TES* 4 July 1986, report, 'Ten-year programme to extend TVEI'.

Janet Harland

3

The TVEI Experience

Issues of Control, Response and the Professional Role of Teachers

The Technical and Vocational Education Initiative has attracted unparalleled levels of attention and comment even though it is difficult to find people not involved directly in the scheme who have a clear understanding of what is going on. For example, many still assume that TVEI is a discrete course or, alternatively, that it represents a distinct track along the multiple pathways through our examination jungle.

The reasons for this high profile are various. For a start, as the Director of the MSC's TVEI Unit is fond of pointing out, it is the biggest single intervention ever made by central government in the school curriculum. Even before TRIST and before the announcement of plans to extend TVEI 'for all schools (sic) in Britain' (DOE/DES, 1986) there has been no attempt on a comparable scale to 'test methods of organizing and managing the education of 14–18 year olds', or any one else for that matter. Take, as a small indicator, the case of evaluation within this huge enterprise. The MSC is investing around £200 000 per annum in national evaluation; and also requiring each participating LEA to spend a minimum of £4 000 per annum on local evaluation, which amounts to a sum of well over £400 000 a year of maximum LEA participation, say 1986–7. This has produced a positive fever of evaluative activity in which the whole repertoire of methodologies, 'approaches', and 'paradigms' are being used, explored and debated; and more importantly it has galvanized the system by providing opportunities for evaluation in the field rather than in the head, resulting in the creation of new networks and much healthy cross-fertilization. Yet evaluation, and the funds put into it, is only one small part of the total initiative.

A second reason for the high level of attention relates to the impact of relatively lavish resources which seem to many like water in a desert. The *kind* of attention inspired by this bubbling well can be shaped by envy or by concern about those who remain thirsty, but at very least the resources ensure that the initiative is highly visible. A third reason, though perhaps one which is less frequently examined, is that TVEI represents a significant attempt to confront what many in the present government and elsewhere perceive to be the anti-industrial, anti-technological nature of British culture by re-ordering the value placed on particular studies at school and college, and particular occupations in adult life.

For me however the central paradox of the TVEI phenomenon is the simultaneous emergence of two apparently or potentially conflicting features: on the one hand, strong central control of a kind which has permitted the detailed intervention of a central government agency right down to the level of the classroom; and on the other a teacher response which is, in many of the pilot schemes, creative and innovative, and often indeed experimental and downright risky. This paradox is intriguing for the student of curriculum change. For so long the rhetoric of development has maintained that strong central control kills local initiative and alienates practitioners; and conversely that creativity, innovation and willingness to experiment depend upon professional autonomy and a good degree of personal security and freedom from authoritarian intervention. TVEI, then, defies this dogma. Either there are reasons why the scheme has managed to flout its precepts; or the dogma itself must be re-examined.

The aim of this chapter is to analyse this paradox. Firstly I shall explore the strategies of control and examine their wider implications for the role of central government in relation to the implementation of curriculum policy. Then I shall turn to the response to TVEI by the LEAs and their teachers, first by indicating its range and then by suggesting reasons for the apparent vigour and enthusiasm displayed by those involved in the pilot programmes. Finally I shall consider the implications of this convergence of strong control and local enterprise, both for the future of the system and the professional role of teachers within it, and also for our wider understanding of the nature of effective educational change.

Strong central control

It is one thing to aim to control the local implementation of central government policy; it is another thing to achieve it. The success of TVEI in this regard is, I suggest, the result of using 'categorical funding' and the mechanisms and relationships which have been developed within its use.

Perhaps it is useful to begin with a definition. Categorical funding is, I suggest, a strategy which can be used to facilitate a policy where the policy makers or their initiating agency, under existing conditions, have neither the *statutory right* nor the *means* to implement desired changes without the co-operation of those who have both. They do however have the *resources* and proceed to use the normal processes of contract to implement their policies. TVEI could certainly not have been implemented by the DES (though the proposal to set up City Technology Colleges may show otherwise). Despite David Young's threats, it would have been almost equally difficult for the MSC without the willing co-operation of LEAs. But that agency had not only the right and means to make direct injections of cash; it had also developed, through its earlier schemes for the young unemployed, methods of binding and then holding agencies to the implementation of the MSC's programmes by contract.

As refined and practised by MSC, policy implementation via categorical funding has several distinct stages:

1 A policy is developed.
2 Funds, generous enough to attract those who can and may deliver, are made available. (This is particularly potent, of course, when local providers have recently felt themselves starved of resources.)
3 Voluntary co-operation is invited in exchange for a share of the resources.
4 Acceptance of the resources is equated with the acceptance of policy — and also with the ability to deliver.

This describes the process by which TVEI programmes have been established and the rapid installation of the initiative is testimony to its effectiveness.

Within the mechanisms of categorical funding there seem to be certain integral themes which I shall suggest are criteria, bid, contract, monitoring, evaluation and replication.

1 *Criteria.* These specify bench-marks for those who volunteer to join the programme. They remain the explicit rules and they represent the framework within which local diversity is tolerated, even encouraged. There are often a further range of operational rules and assumptions which go beyond mere bureaucratic controls and become the 'hidden' criteria for the scheme. For example in TVEI, there is a high profile for project 'cost-effectiveness'.
2 *Bid.* The process by which the would-be provider indicates his proposals, which is followed invariably by a process of *negotiation* during which the original bid is brought as close as possible to the 'ideal' as set out by the criteria.
3 *Contract.* This represents the deal struck between the parties concerned. It forms the basis on which the licensee may proceed and the expectation is that any deviation not specifically allowed for (e.g. agreement about permitted scope for virement) should be *re-negotiated*.

4 *Monitoring.* Normal patterns of accountability would indicate that the agency providing the funds should be able to satisfy itself that the terms of the contract are being met so a flow of information as to numbers, categories, outcomes and expenditure is demanded. This of course extends to the certification of expenditure and the auditing of accounts.
5 *Evaluation.* Categorical funding requires of evaluation two somewhat contradictory characteristics: firstly a degree of independence so that special pleading and self-justification do not act as a smokescreen to ineptitude; and yet secondly, a focus on the processes of implementation rather than any form of fundamental critique concerning the underlying goals or strategies of the programme.
6 *Replication.* The funding promised is finite though it is often held out as a possibility that extensions on a similar or revised scale may materialize. Hence the stress on the experimental, pilot nature of many schemes funded in this manner and the assumption that students within the scheme form a 'research cohort'. The essential nature of categorical funding is that funds are offered as seed money, and both monitoring and evaluation (see above) are geared largely to assessing and publicizing the positive outcomes and their ripple effects through the expectant waters of the pond.

The most notable feature of this whole process is the manner in which the MSC has achieved detailed control over the operation of each LEA pilot scheme. Through a network of Regional Advisors, auditors, officials, information gatherers and evaluators, TVEI has emerged as a scheme 'known' to its sponsor to a quite extraordinary degree. There are clear echoes here of the concept of 'surveillance' as delineated by Foucault. In *Discipline and Punish* (1975) he writes of a system of control (discipline) which is based on observation and close knowledge of what is going on:

> The exercise of discipline presupposes a mechanism that coerces by means of observation; an apparatus in which the techniques that make it possible to see induce effects of power, and in which, conversely, the means of coercion make those on whom they are applied clearly visible.

This strategy is reinforced in two ways. In the first place, by shifting attention to compliance with contract, the surveillance tends to assume the flavour of neutral, technical monitoring of a freely negotiated obligation; thus avoiding at many points the implication of judging educational worth. In the second place, this discipline/control strategy must be located in the context of a discourse about desirable educational aims and choices and about appropriate pedagogical practices, to which MSC has made a very considerable contribution.

I shall return later to the effect of the new language of pre-vocational education and vocational training; but here I wish to note the extent to which TVEI 'new-speak' has successfully permeated the pilot schemes and the appropriate corners of their local authorities. The effect of this has been to create sub-agencies of MSC control among the scheme participants themselves even at moments of disenchantment. For TVEI co-ordinators and many of those involved with them tend to anticipate the response of MSC and thereby discipline themselves. Foucault again, writing of the ideal institution for the exercise of surveillance, Bentham's *Panopticon*, says:

> '... So to arrange things that the surveillance is permanent in its effects, even if it is discontinuous in its action; that the perfection of power should tend to render its actual exercise unnecessary ...' (op. cit., p. 201)

It may be argued that I am turning what should be a documentary into a melodrama. Certainly what is described here would not seem as remarkable in many other education systems. However in Britain we are experiencing a climactic change in the matter of central–local government relations and it is important to try to understand that there is more involved than changes in administrative and bureaucratic practices. With that purpose in mind, I turn now to suggest some of the reasons underlying this significant shift.

Much has been written about the relationship between central and local government in our education system. What is clear is that the relative powers of each defy final and accurate description. Most commentary consists of attempts to discern the balance between two distinct types of power — authority and influence. There is a long history of debate as to how each of these three concepts should be defined, but for the purpose of this argument I shall use authority to mean the power which is implicit in hierarchical structures where there is always at least the probability (Weber, 1947) that the superior can enforce his will upon the subordinate. Influence on the other hand is more subtle, is multi-dimensional, and consists of a capacity to affect action without a resort to, or even a right to use, sanctions. As such it depends on a range of situational and interactive factors.

Most writers on DES strategies explore both sub-categories of power, frequently asserting that the DES is short of power in the sense of authority despite its right to make certain kinds of decisions, use certain sanctions and threaten the possibility of legislation. It is generally agreed that the DES actually prefers to promote its policies by exploiting its considerable influence, thereby securing voluntary compliance without resort to crude coercion. In the degree to which this strategy succeeds, we see at work the 'politics of deference' so often remarked as a feature of our education system where subordinates make assumptions about the actual authority of their superiors which lead them to defer to DES wishes. (This paragraph draws upon a paper by Broadfoot, 1986.)

However, the argument advanced here is that the DES is attempting to supplement influence with added authority and that in this endeavour the administrative practices of the MSC, particularly as exemplified in TVEI, are proving a powerful example.

Bacharach and Lawler (1980) offer some distinctions in the concept of authority which may help to illuminate the value of categorical funding in educational policy implementation. Drawing on other theorists, they describe the bases of power, i.e. 'what parties control that enables them to manipulate the behaviour of others'. They identify four such bases: the coercive which relates to the control of punishment; the remunerative which relates to the control of material resources and rewards; the normative which relates to symbolic rewards; and the knowledge base which results from the control of information. For Bacharach and Lawler those with authority have structural access to all four of these sources of power. Those with influence have only partial and situational access to the sources of power.

As already described, the DES has for many years preferred to develop its capacity to influence the system rather than to exploit its authority, not least because of the need to operate via the LEAs who themselves have considerable authority which derives from their structural position; and so, similarly, have heads of institutions. However, as the DES seeks to maximize its authority at the expense of its 'partners', it has to look to all four of the bases of power: the coercive; the renumerative; the normative; and the knowledge base.

The coercive remains unattractive to both the professional and the general public (see for example the response to the Secretary of State's attempt to impose a teachers' pay settlement in the autumn of 1986). Hence the importance of the alternative bases. The DES has steadily increased its control over the knowledge/information base (Salter and Tapper, 1981 p. 212 and *passim*). It is also demonstrably aiming to increase its control over resources (i.e. the remunerative) by steadily escalating the importance of specific rather than block grant. (See article by Travers, *TES* 14.11.86. for exact figures which provide useful confirmation that the trend in this direction is growing and is being led by the Department of Employment via the MSC.) The advent of grant-related in-service funding is the most significant step in this direction. But to gauge the effectiveness of resource control as a strategy for exerting authority we have to see how those resources are managed and what levels of supervision and intervention are secured by the grant of those resources. In some government departments, specific grant has brought little return to central government in terms of increased authority. But the MSC has proved a fruitful pioneer. The method of bid and contract already outlined has proved highly productive. As pioneered in the 1970s with schemes such as WEP, WEEP, YOP and now YTS, as carefully developed in TVEI, and now as extended into the oversight of work-related NAFE where twenty-five percent funding has resulted in the right to a hundred percent review and co-ordination (MSC, 1985), the MSC has developed a fine-tuned system, ripe for adoption by ambitious government departments. It will be interesting to observe the implementation of the new arrangements for the approval and funding of INSET to see just how closely the same mechanisms are adopted by the DES.

The case of the remaining power source — the normative which is concerned with symbolic rewards — is not so clear-cut. The DES does have favours and rewards to hand out which are not related directly to funding but on the whole the rewards of prestige and influence in the education system are gained from other agencies — the many professional interest groups, the media, the academic world, even the LEAs. I find it more useful to see the DES as in the business of exchanging symbolic rewards. To quote Bacharach and Lawler (1980) again:

> '... organizational life is dominated by political interactions; politics in organizations involve the tactical use of power to retain or obtain real or symbolic resources'.

The exchange processes in which the DES are engaged are best understood as a three-cornered negotiation between government, LEAs and the public. The symbolic resources which government hopes to *obtain* (as opposed to those which it can bestow) are only indirectly in the gift of the education system because ultimately they come from the policy as a whole. The quid pro quo required of the LEAs in exchange for the material resources of, for example, TVEI is energetic compliance but the real prize, a symbolic resource, is public approval leading, one would suppose, to re-election. This electoral and political imperative implies a need to synchronize the product with the discourse. The product must not only be achieved but it must be seen to be achieved.

Again it is useful to observe how MSC has sought to ensure that there is an appropriate pay-off for TVEI in terms of public response, a public which in this case includes key interest groups such as employers. Clearly TVEI must succeed and therefore must be seen to succeed. Hence the need for a high profile, an active public relations endeavour, and a large network of information gatherers and disseminators. We are back to thinking about the functions of monitoring and evaluation; in part they must be about demonstrating success (or at very least a high level of activity) and they must ensure that success feeds the discourse and hence delivers the symbolic rewards. The DES has not been that adroit in attracting public acclamation for its policies. We must expect that in this too the adoption of MSC strategies will increase their access to the bases of power.

The preceding pages have sought not only to describe the manner in which strong central control is practised in the TVEI programme; it has also been my intention to demonstrate how the DES stands to gain *vis-à-vis* its 'partners' by adopting MSC strategies in the implementation of curriculum policy.

The response

I turn now to the issue of the response to TVEI on the part of LEAs but primarily of schools and teachers. This is clearly not the place to expand at length on the many and varied ways in which TVEI has been implemented. Nor is it the place to explore the inflated rhetoric with which many participants have sought to describe their activities; indeed, following the argument in the section above, we might accept that inflation is to be expected. Rather I shall suggest some of the headings under which significant innovation has occurred before turning to some comments on the quality and vigour of the response.

The most obvious innovation has to do with change and revitalization of the somewhat tired content of much practical and vocational teaching. This, I would suggest, has come about by moving it closer to the actual application in working life of the knowledge and skills acquired in classroom and workshop. Thus Home Economics has produced courses related directly to Food and Catering Industries, Tourism, Community Studies including child, family and community care, and Textiles (see the MSC's *TVEI Insight* 1986 No. 6, where one head of department is reported as saying 'TVEI is the best thing to happen to Home Economics for years'). Similary art and drama courses have been recast into such courses as Community Theatre, Television and Media Studies, Graphic and Associated Arts. Such developments go alongside the wide-scale introduction of Technology in many shapes and forms and Electronics; and the parallel development of Business Studies courses which go well beyond the old parameters of office practice and keyboarding skills. The use of information technology across many areas of the curriculum is especially notable.

The second area of change has to do with the structuring of the curriculum. It has to be said that in most schemes, at the 14–16 stage, TVEI appears as a block of grouped options available in the main to the identified TVEI cohort. Within this protected area, many schemes have found ways to reorganize the allocation of time through a series of strategies such as tasters, modules, carousels, core studies and the blocking of time. Very often the degree to which this has occurred has been determined by the importance attached within each scheme to the acquisition of conventional qualifications — where GCE/CSE results are seen as vital to gain parental and student support, the curriculum and the timetable are usually more conventional.

There is a range of practices in relation to the non-TVEI school pupil. In some schemes participation in the scheme has affected all pupils in the school, regardless of whether they are part of the TVEI cohort; in others the seventy percent general curriculum of TVEI students has been recast to make a more coherent educational experience, for example by linking

English and Mathematics teaching to the TVEI programme, or by relating programmes of personal and social education to the scheme's objectives.

The third area relates to the development of a range of new working relationships. At the institutional level there have been significant advances in co-operation between schools and between schools and colleges. In some schemes this has involved pupils following parts of their course in other institutions; in almost all it has meant the sharing of experience and in-service training among the staff of several institutions. New working relationships are also in evidence between schools on the one hand and industry and the community on the other — not invented by, but certainly fostered by, TVEI. Within institutions, too, TVEI has encouraged more co-operative methods of working among teachers, and a more open and mature relationship between teachers and students. There is emerging a set of expectations about teaching methods within TVEI courses that both result from and lead to this changed relationship. Active learning, an emphasis on experience, problem-solving, and the use of formative approaches to profiling are all part of these expectations. One common element of many TVEI programmes — the use of mini-enterprises — draws together many facets of these changing relationships, and what is more, contributes to the changes in both curriculum content and curriculum structures already described above.

This then is a brief review of the many growth points within the initiative, a number of which will have been dealt with by other contributors to this book. It is of course a very positive account and appears not to recognize that in many schemes, schools and colleges the reality is not matching the aspirations. Nor does it allow for the fact that the impact of TVEI is most marked on the 14–16 phase; at 16+ the TVEI route contains so many divergent tracks that it is seemingly more difficult to map, let alone influence. However the point of this brief catalogue was to give some indication of what a lot *is* happening, how varied is the impact, how broad are the intentions; to point to shortcomings and evasions is not to gainsay the claim that this strongly centralized initiative is eliciting a strong response. How are we to understand this response? To answer this question I would like to propose an alternative to the much cited Hawthorne effect, moving for my analogy from the production line of an electric light bulb factory all the way to grand opera, namely Beethoven's *Fidelio*. Both in the Hawthorne effect and what I choose to call the 'Fidelio effect', there is a shared metaphor of light. The Hawthorne factory workers out-performed their peers because they flourished under the spotlight of the researchers' attention. TVEI is certainly innovation under a spotlight and one often hears questions about what may happen when the spotlight is turned off and the funding is withdrawn. But in *Fidelio*, a story of imprisonment and ultimate release, the light is the light of freedom, of fresh air and sunshine, after the despair of the dungeon. For me the most memorable moment is the great chorus of the prisoners as they emerge from blackness into the free air (freier Luft) of the world above, the normal world. 'Only here, only here, is life,' they sing, 'the dungeon is a tomb!'; almost in unison they sing a great hymn of joy and returning life.

It is unduly fanciful to see those teachers leading the TVEI crusade as released prisoners? Certainly many teachers have felt personally and collectively oppressed and frustrated by shrinking resources, declining rolls, ageing buildings and a universally negative climate induced by depressed salaries and low public esteem. Many of these problems are relieved directly by involvement in TVEI. But there is yet more strength in the analogy because we are not talking here of teachers in general but of a very particular set of teachers. This set is drawn by and large from those who teach in the practical/technical/applied areas of the curriculum and it brings in also some from among guidance staff, including careers teachers. The chorus comes therefore from an identifiable group and the prisoners within it now find themselves not only in the sunlight, but singing together and what is more, holding the stage.

With this in mind, it is worth noting that teachers of practical and vocationally flavoured subjects have in many schools led rather isolated and low-status professional lives. They have often taught the more able pupils only in Years 1–3 and then often in the context of a significantly named 'circus'. They take their coffee together in the 'flat' or the preparation room attached to the workshop. They rarely aspire to achieve senior management posts and their chief line of promotion is into the advisory service where they finish up interacting mainly with their own kind. A good proportion have experience of work outside schools and curiously this too tends to distance them from teacher colleagues in other disciplines. On the whole it is true to say that they have not as a group been noted for curriculum innovation or leadership; in the matter of change they have been followers, often perceived as resisters.

(Against this, readers may quote the case of CDT where there have been highly significant developments. It would take more space than I can spare here to deal fully with that rejoinder but I would make two points: firstly there has continued to be a huge problem in recruiting the large remaining contingent of craft teachers to the new problem-solving, design-orientated approaches of CDT; and secondly, I would contend that much of the debate has been self-contained and self-addressing — the enormous potential of CDT to transform wide areas of curriculum experience is only just beginning to be realized, and that partly as a product of TVEI.)

TVEI has reversed many of these tendencies towards isolation. Teachers involved in technical and vocational education (and the associated practices of profiling, guidance and counselling, residential experience, etc.) are now manifestly in the vanguard of curriculum change. Backed by programmes of in-service training, and galvanized by the experience of holding the stage, it is TVEI teachers who earnestly discuss new structures for the curriculum and new pedagogies for the classroom. They are the practitioners of 'newspeak', the current inheritors of much innovative educational practice, now captured by MSC rhetoric and reflected back to them by TVEI practitioners and indeed TVEI pupils (see for example Appendix D in FEU/SCDC *Supporting TVEI* (1985) and various articles in the MSC's own *TVEI Insight* series, to discover how fluently pupils as well as teachers can play back the language of the initiative). Moreover, teachers for the 'central' areas of TVEI curricula have acquired an ever greater scarcity value which is likely to continue to escalate through the years of TVEI and son of TVEI. So they are ever more promoteable, to be lured only by generous scale points (or the new style allowances) and increasingly to be seen as eligible for the commanding heights in schools and LEAs.

There is another aspect to this argument about teacher response. Along with several other initiatives TVEI has offered legitimation to the more utilitarian areas of the curriculum. Despite arguments about the intrinsic values of practical studies, and the extrinsic and indeed instrumental value of 'academic' work, it cannot be denied that for teachers, parents and students, Business Studies, or Microelectronics, or Food Studies, or Technology have a meaning and significance in terms of job opportunities and career routes which is qualitatively different from that implied by History, French or Biology. It follows that on the whole those teaching in the technical and vocational areas will be more likely than others to support the government's avowedly utilitarian and instrumental policies for education because for them the price of opposition would be very expensive in terms of their professional identity.

These attempts to explain the response to TVEI are obviously only partial and much of the above is speculative thinking. However, it is the product of two years' close observation of TVEI, first hand as evaluator for one authority, second hand through knowledge gained from contact with many deeply involved in other authorities' schemes. One reservation I do however need to make. Many of the statements about the experiences of teachers of technical and vocational subjects in schools do not hold good in FE colleges where of course the staff involved with TVEI already see themselves as mainstream professionals. This is just one of many factors which may explain the less-certain progress of TVEI in that sector.

The effects and significance of the TVEI experience

Effects are of course rarely all intended effects. TVEI certainly emerges from this account as a sophisticated strategy for delivering policy both as a technical, bureaucratic structure and as an initiative calculated to secure the desired response from those who implement it and also from the ultimate audience, the electorate. But it would be wrong to suggest that all this impact and the means to secure it were fully anticipated. Effectiveness is partly a matter of persistence and consistency in working through the processes of implementation and presentation — and partly a matter of luck, that the scheme will resonate with the context. The government has been fortunate in both the performance of the MSC's TVEI Unit and also in the response from those involved in the pilot schemes. Experience however is demonstrating that categorical funding is a powerful mechanism for policy implementation, cutting as it does new routes of access to the sources of power.

In so many ways we have to acknowledge that TVEI represents a new approach to planned curriculum change. It is therefore not at all easy to relate it to some of the explanatory and theoretical models with which educationalists have sought to categorize and understand curriculum change. The model which has best stood up to the test of frequent usage is that of Havelock (1971). The strength of his taxonomy lies in the fact that it not only locates the source of change but also tells us something about the roles, and maybe even the attitudes, of those involved in the change process. The well-known distinction between the RD&D model (research, design, and development), the social interaction model and the problem-solving model give us three alternative descriptions of the role of the curriculum developer. In the first he is the expert, the authority, the creator, listening perhaps to the practitioner but making his own response and designing his preferred solution; in the second he takes a step closer to the user and the final product is developed through interaction and feedback; and in the third the developer becomes effectively a consultant, seeking to respond to problems identified at the level of practice.

These models have served well for two decades in the process of characterizing the style of particular projects. However they seem inadequate as explanatory tools in relation to TVEI. Clearly the initiative does not exemplify the RD&D approach for there is no centrally developed curriculum strategy or package. Nor can we say that the MSC is seeking to develop one through a process of social interaction. Again, although it would be true to say that some authorities and schools see TVEI as an opportunity to tackle what they had already acknowledged as 'problems', the Havelock problem-solving model implies a degree of freedom and self-determination in identifying problems and seeking solutions which is clearly not consistent with the 'contract' model delineated earlier in this chapter. It would seem that what is needed in today's curriculum landscape is an alternative taxonomy which puts particular focus on the practitioner, distinguishing the nature of the role ascribed to him and attempting to characterize the power dimensions by which that role is constrained by both central and local government. In an attempt to do this I have defined three alternative 'practitioner models': autonomy, co-operation and recruitment. These are set out in Table 1. The major difference between this and the Havelock model is that it recognizes that in each the practitioner is active and his involvement is a crucial and a

Table 1

(1)	(2)	(3)	(4)	(5)	(6)	(7)
Practitioner model	*Practitioner role*	*Havelock model of change*	*Alternative strategies*			
			A national curriculum	*Schools Council*	*TVEI*	*The DES 'national framework'*
Autonomy	Independent judgement to: (a) accept solution (b) seek solution (c) do neither	RD&D PS n/a	No	Yes	No	No
Co-operation	Partnership: co-operation on the basis of equality plus the freedom to withdraw	SI	No	Yes	No	?
Recruitment	Licensed agent: freedom within scope allowed by principal, e.g. via contract	Not covered	Yes	No	Yes	?

necessary part of successful change. What varies in this model is the degree of freedom from influence and control experienced at practitioner level.

In column (2), the role of the practitioner is described. It will be seen that within the autonomous model, the practitioner is free to make professional-type decisions to accept solutions, to seek solutions or to prefer to do neither. In column (3) I suggest that this encompasses two of Havelock's categories because when viewed from the perspective of the user, the crucial issue is not where the solution comes from but whether the decision to use it rests at the level of the practitioner. Under the co-operative model, the practitioner acquires a partner and we have a nice fit with the social-interaction model. In a genuine partnership it seems immaterial where the initial idea comes from — the essential element is the shared endeavour and the shared product, plus the voluntary involvement of both partners.

So far there would seem to be only small semantic reasons for discarding the Havelock model. It is however the new style of curriculum initiative, exemplified by TVEI, which requires that we incorporate a third model into our thinking and for want of a better word, this is labelled a 'recruitment' model. In this model, the practitioner becomes a 'licensed agent' whose freedom of action may well be not inconsiderable but always remains within the scope allowed by his principal. In the case of TVEI the 'principal' is the MSC, and the degrees of freedom are controlled by contract and the mechanisms of control and surveillance already described. With the extension of TVEI we will see the scope and style of MSC intervention penetrate a far greater number of schools and colleges; far more teachers and lecturers will therefore have experience of contractual arrangements.

In columns (4)–(7), I attempt to locate various approaches and strategies for curriculum development and/or control against these concepts of practitioner role. For example, if we consider the situation of a country where central government determines curriculum, teaching materials and assessment practices (column 4), then clearly teachers operate as licensed agents. It is worth reminding British readers that this pattern is the dominant one in much of the world even though many such centralized systems prefer the rhetoric of 'co-operation'. The Schools Council's policy (column 5) was in complete contrast to this approach. The twin principles of 'professionalism' and 'pluralism' enunciated by Caston (1970) and the Council's commitment given over two decades to teacher involvement and teacher choice, demonstrate that 'recruitment' in no way fits with its practice. Perhaps, on occasion, individual project teams might have welcomed a measure of contractual arrangements, but the very fact that there were never any substantial resource inducements to offer to participating schools meant that the Council could never, even if it had wished, move beyond the autonomous or the co-operative models. With growing experience it clearly favoured the latter.

TVEI, as has already been indicated, sets up an entirely new relationship between an innovation and those who deliver it. The MSC is clearly the principal; the LEAs and their schools are the licensed agents. At many points, the MSC acts as an enlightened principal. In other words, it recognizes that good management practices require a proper recognition of the creativity of the agent. Any initiating and controlling body which acts as if it has a monopoly of know-how and expertise is cutting itself off from the very real benefits which derive from the initiative and the commitment of those whom it has licensed to implement the programme. However it is only at the inter-personal level that the relationship appears to change its basic characteristics; at root the reality remains that of freedom within strictly defined boundaries. The Schools Council never solved this dilemma; for project teams there was always the problem that teachers could and would distort the central messages of a project in the name of professionalism. By creating a new *de facto* role for teachers the MSC would seem to have gone a long way to avoiding parallel difficulties. The key factor is clearly that of resources. One of the most important developments in educational policy making, and particularly curriculum making, in the eighties will surely be the discovery of effective strategies for linking the provision and resourcing of the system with the control of its functioning.

By way of a short digression, in column (7) I turn to the DES's notion of a national curriculum framework, developed over a decade and reiterated with considerable clarity in *Better Schools* (1985). This concept would appear to rule out the 'autonomous' model but the DES continues to underline the rhetoric of partnership. In *Better Schools* we read that 'success depends on the ready co-operation and mutual support of all the partners in education ...'. Despite a constant flow of negative ministerial comments about teachers' professional abilities and commitment, and also an increasing range of centrally authorized statements about 'broadly agreed objectives' for the curriculum and 'national criteria' for 16+ examinations, nevertheless there is still a real if grudging acceptance that teachers must be engaged with the enterprise of curriculum reform in an active and professional manner if anything much is to change. There is however a continuing ambivalence within government as to the riskiness of such a stance. Co-operation and partnership always leave room for the colleague to let you down. Perhaps the principal–agent model is less chancy? As already described, the DES is showing a growing interest in the bid and contract model and practitioners may increasingly find that they have in effect been recruited to act as agents.

But the outcome here is uncertain. Although it seems likely that a 'national curriculum framework' will remain part of our educational landscape for some time to come, no one political style is permanent and the questions about the practitioner role posed in column (7) remain fluid (though in the most recent pronouncements the word 'framework' is disappearing in favour of more precise specification of 'bench-marks'). The significance of the TVEI experience may well ultimately lie in the degree to which it influences the outcome. Put another way, will the high regard in which the DES holds TVEI mean that the question marks presently placed in column (7) will be resolved into a No and a Yes which reflect MSC strategies? Or will the traditional partnership model prevail?

To draw this wide-ranging argument to a close we have to return to the paradox that I identified in the early part of this chapter: that TVEI displays an intriguing conjunction of strong central control and local initiative. Does this lead to the conclusion that teachers respond positively to the recruitment model? Do they enjoy a role in which there is a strong framework of expectations, and in which the efforts they make are visible and recognized? If the RD&D model fails largely because practitioners resist the role of passive deliverers or alternatively use their autonomy to subvert the developer's intentions; if the problem-solving model which depends upon strenuous activity at the grassroots is too uncertain and intermittent to produce effective change; and if the social-interaction model in relying on voluntary partnership does not appear to ensure an adequate input from legitimate interests outside the immediate world of schools and colleges; then does the model developed within TVEI provide a powerful new alternative? Certainly theories about change which over-stress the importance of 'ownership', of innovation at the level of the individual practitioner, are called in question by the response to TVEI. Whether one sees the teachers involved as converts, collaborators, opportunists or traitors, clearly the sense of being part of a 'movement' has had a powerful effect. To return to *Fidelio*, singing together and holding the stage are rewarding experiences.

But I, for one, have doubts about the recruitment model. First of all it has flourished in a particular context, a context of a depressed school system, a depressed economy and a depressed area of the curriculum. I doubt whether deliberately creating dungeons in order to provide subsequent experiences of liberation is a viable strategy for policy-makers, despite many indications that the present administration is experimenting along these lines! Moreover this contract-based model has succeeded in a scheme where government (the principal partner in the contract) has secured adequate support for its initiative. The problems arise when the principal wants to pursue policies and practices which do not necessarily command the practitioners' support but to which they are recruited because the alternative of standing outside is even less attractive. In that setting, contract is replaced by conscription, and compliance rapidly becomes tokenistic. Lastly we have to enquire who is the principal? If the principal is a politician, how often will contracts be torn up and re-written as elections come and go? If the principal is a bureaucrat, is it possible that efficiency in achieving aims will become more important than selecting them? And if the principal is external to the enterprise, will the result be that the springs of genuine innovation are dried up by the hot breath of control in the name of non-educational agendas?

The challenge posed by TVEI resides in the tension between central control and local initiative. Given that more control seems inevitable and even desirable, how can we find a role for teachers which maximizes the vitality of the practitioner within a coherent national policy? In my view, the answer must lie in recapturing the role of 'principal' from the politicians by ensuring a powerful professional input at the centre in the form of a new agency for educational planning and curriculum development. TVEI has been compromised from its inception by the suspicion that its short-term political aims are more important to the government than its longer-term educational aims.

References

Bacharach, S.B. and Lawler, E.G. (1980) *Power and Politics in Organisations*. New York, Jossey-Bass.

Broadfoot, P. (1986) Power Relations and English Education: the changing role of central government. *J. Educational Policy*, **1** (1), 53–62.

Caston, G. (1970) The Schools Council in Context. *J. Curriculum Studies*, **3** (1).

DOE/DES (1986) *Working Together — Education and Training*. Cmnd 9823, HMSO.

FEU/SCDC (1985) *Supporting TVEI*.

Foucault, M. (1975) *Discipline and Punish*. Harmondsworth, Penguin (trans. A. Sheridan).

MSC (1985) *Work-related NAFE: a guidance handbook*.

MSC (1986) *TVEI Insight*, No. 8.

Salter, B. and Tapper, T. (1981) *Education, Politics and the State*. London, Grant McIntyre.

Travers, T. (1986) Destruction of the Town Halls. *Times Educ. Suppl.*, 14 November.

Weber, M. (1947) *The Theory of Social and Economic Organisations*. Cambridge, Cambridge University Press.

Patricia Sikes and Michael Taylor

4

Some Problems with Defining, Interpreting and Communicating Vocational Education

Approaching the meaning of TVEI

There are two major thrusts to current attempts to understand what TVEI is all about. One approach addresses the broad policy implications of what is in many respects a genuinely innovative programme of educational reform; the other examines varying elements of individual schemes with the aim of accumulating descriptive data on identifiable components applicable to all schemes nationally.

It would, at this time, be premature to expect either approach to offer any definitive statement on the what, why or how of TVEI, despite the considerable amount of illuminating material already in circulation. In the former approach there is a dearth of information explicating the philosophies and motives of governmental sponsors, and in the latter, a surfeit of variation between the schemes in operation. This makes it virtually impossible at present to identify any universal feature that could be exclusive to TVEI.

As with many other commentators we have paid attention to both dimensions, but we have tried to steer a course of enquiry somewhere between them, avoiding on the one hand (what for us would be) the potential sterility of a purely theoretical analysis, and on the other a confusing collection of school-based ethnographies. Instead, we have tried to bring together a preliminary and tentative analysis of the policy orientations of governmental representatives — particularly MSC personnel — and the effects of such policies upon the experiences, interpretations and perspectives of the teachers involved.

Our focus is upon how they affect the career perceptions and experiences of teachers at both objective and formal, and subjective and personal levels (see Hughes, 1937 and Sikes, 1986a). Teachers are the people who realize and implement TVEI, and whilst TVEI may affect and alter many aspects of their work situation, they, in turn, undoubtedly influence the shape and outcomes of TVEI. We feel this focus presents an important complement to the more common interest in the *content* of TVEI and the experiences of students, although we include some of their perceptions in our concluding remarks.

In the past, attempts at large-scale educational innovation have tended to be less than successful in realizing their objectives because they have encountered 'tradition', inertia and a lack of commitment on the part of those not intimately involved (see Ruddock, 1986). As will be shown, the MSC has recognized this. Despite its dispersal of generous financial resources and its ability to implement innovation more quickly than the DES (Dale *et al.*, 1986), we contend that in order to avoid (or at least, minimize) intransigence or obstructiveness, it operates a strategy of subversive persuasion based in a rhetoric of contractual reciprocity. It appears that this approach is designed to reduce appreciation of real and potential threats to professional pedagogic and administrative autonomy.

> We [the MSC] have no legal locus whatsoever to interfere with the curriculum. The fact that we fund it, nevertheless, slightly complicates that situation...The curriculum is owned by the LEA's and one of my basic problems...is to persuade the LEA's that they own the curriculum development within TVEI...Our interest in the curriculum really amounts to [whether] emerging curriculum will meet the objectives that are written into the contracts.
>
> (MSC Senior Regional Adviser addressing conference of secondary teachers, 1985.)

Our aim is to provide and discuss examples which we believe indicate the nature of the 'vocationalist' rhetoric employed by the MSC, and which is lately reflected in official and unofficial statements made by government departments and personnel. We shall also look at how this rhetoric is interpreted within schools.

Our approach to evaluation is ethnographic in the sense that we have sought to investigate the meanings that particular situations generate for those involved in them. Our intention is to provide 'critical illumination' (cf. Parlett and Hamilton, 1972) which participants may use reflectively to inform decision-making.

Our data has been collected in the course of our work as local evaluators in (between us) a total of four separate TVEI schemes. We have spent considerable time in schools, colleges and other TVEI locations (e.g. work/residential experience placements, management meetings, and education offices), observing and conversing with teachers, students, local administrators and visiting MSC personnel, and have also interviewed senior officials in government departments. Our research methods include observation, participant observation, informal and focused interview conversations (many of which were tape-recorded), questionnaires and document surveys.

Schools and vocationalism

We are particularly interested in the semantics of the discourse and practices surrounding activities in schools which are identified by participants as being to do with TVEI. The Initiative means many things to many people and particular interpretations range from broad visions of socio-economic transformation through to specific forms of relationship between two individuals.

Our use of the term 'vocationalism' is in a general, non-specific sense. It includes all aspects of institutionalized educational practices that consciously and explicitly relate learning experiences to post-school, 'adult' occupations that do not necessarily involve paid employment. In the case of TVEI, we see 'vocationalism' predominantly as an *approach* or *orientation* within schools, rather than as identifiable sets of innovative procedures that are somehow auxiliary to established forms of provision. This helps to avoid the often pejorative assumptions that 'nothing is happening' simply because little change has occurred in, for example, curriculum structures.

In a recent paper, Brian Simon (1986) refers to the argument that a more vocationally oriented curriculum was a necessary response to future technological competitiveness on an international level. He points out that this had some credence when the assumption of a return to 'full' employment was still generally acceptable. At that time the issue was one of suitably equipping the future workforce with, if not specific technical competencies, at least a so-called generic orientation to the requirements of hi-tech production processes. This belief was formally articulated in Callaghan's 'Ruskin' speech (1976) and finally became consolidated into orthodoxy with the publication of the NEDC/MSC comparative study, *Competence and Competition* (NEDO, 1984), which makes a pointed criticism of British training provision in relation to that of the USA, Germany and Japan. The orthodoxy remains in the basic formula that economic recovery depends upon increased competitiveness which, in turn, depends on increased levels of production — but, with as much emphasis on *quality* as upon quantity.

This latter point is forcefully emphasized in the government White Paper *Working Together — Education and Training* (HMSO, 1986). This document reinforces the point that a more efficient utilization of *resources* is required which, in terms of the formula, includes labour. However, a distinction that is often glossed over in the education and training 'debate' is the commonly held assumption (indeed, implication) that the attainment of efficient production and a healthy international competitiveness will mean a return to 'full' employment in the conventionally accepted sense. This is unlikely to be true, as has been recognized in documents influencing the earlier formulation of policies on education and training provision (FEU, 1982), and is endorsed by an informed spokesperson at the Department of Employment (DE);

> I think one of the aspects of unemployment of which the government [is] very well aware is the demoralising effect...OK, in a perfect world one is trying to get unemployed people into jobs. Now that is not terribly realistic, certainly in the shorter term. But what one can do is try and present...or suggest attitudes to unemployment which are slightly more constructive and optimistic...But, on present indicators...it looks as though unemployment is here to stay — at least for the foreseeable future.
>
> (Senior official, DE; interviewed October 1986)

Even so, TVEI schemes place considerable emphasis upon the development and incorporation of new forms of assessment and accreditation. These include the differentiated GCSE, a variety of established vocational qualifications (B/TEC, CGLI, etc.), CPVE, locally validated certificates, and profiles. These are intended to provide the vast majority of young people with some form of certification.

This raises the apparent paradox of accrediting a sector of young people whose current prospects for secure employment in the future remain in serious doubt. It is worth noting that the often absurd reductionism of the original 'skills-based' notion of 'competence' contained in earlier FEU documents such as *Basic Skills* (FEU, November 1982) has now shifted to a meaning that has much more to do with *attitude* and the management of social behaviour than with the attainment of specific, or even 'generic' occupational-related capabilities. This is nowhere more explicit than in *Working Together — Education and Training.*

> There must be a climate in which people can be motivated, and in which their potential and their creative capacity can be harnessed. Motivation is all important, so that attitudes change and people acquire the desire to learn, the habit of learning, and the skills that learning brings. (para.1.4)

This document's recurring emphasis upon the need for 'full-time education' to provide the motivation to acquire *'a broad competence'* (para.2.2 — original emphasis) appears to suggest that, in the absence of short- and medium-term employment prospects for young people, it has become important to legitimate *employability* as much as actually being employed.

> 'Motivation is as essential in *preparing* for work as it is at work.'
>
> (op.cit.,para.2.3 — our emphasis)

Overall, the White Paper places an accent upon more positive attitudes to 'learning skills'. In official terms these are intended to promote 'adaptability' to the demands of rapid technological change, but they may also be seen to have an *intrinsic* appeal, especially for those young people for whom the 'bridge' between schooling and work may have a very long span.

Teaching and TVEI

The message contained in the White Paper pushes the notion of vocationalism beyond the narrow confines of specific job preparation and occupational training. This enables it to fit in with the philosophies and personal aims of some teachers concerning the 'purpose' of education:

> Well, part of the job as I see it — and it's an important part — is getting them [the students] into the right frame of mind, the right attitude, that they'll need when they go to work or on a scheme or whatever. I think we should be training them to become self-disciplined. They have to learn how to behave properly, some of them.
>
> (CDT Teacher, TVEI school)

> I say to them, there are things in life that we don't want to do, and I think school is important in introducing kids to that. I make them clear up properly after a lesson. I tell them they'll have to do what they're told when they go to work. I have to, they'll have to, do things they might not agree with.
>
> (Art Teacher, non-TVEI school)

> This [TVEI] is just what we need. Academic learning isn't relevant to the vast majority of kids and that's why you get your behavioural problems. Whereas when you're doing practical work, then they're on your side.
>
> (CDT Teacher, TVEI school)

These views appear to emphasize the *protocols* of the workplace rather than the quality or type of occupation. Character building and assessment in preparation for work was a central tenet of many secondary modern schools as it was in grammar schools, albeit with different occupational destinations in mind. It is perhaps not surprising to find that the teachers quoted above (and others holding similar views) had spent periods of their careers teaching in these schools, particularly working with the 'bottom forty per cent'.

Courses, curricula and forms of assessment designed to cater for 'average' and 'below average' students tend to be aimed at inculcating 'appropriate' attitudes and types of behaviour and, as Burgess (1986) points out, this has always been the case. Yet such aims sit uneasily within the philosophy and rhetoric of comprehensive education and so 'changes have occurred in the concepts and labels that [are used] to describe educational activity' (Burgess, 1986, p.3). Some teachers see vocational education in the context of TVEI as little more than cosmetic changes in labelling:

> I think it's disgraceful. It's a return to the worst sort of grammar/secondary modern divisiveness.
>
> (Science Teacher, TVEI school)

> TVEI is about a two-tier system. There's the academic, 'normal' curriculum for the able kids, and there's the practical and vocational for the rest. I know they say it's not like that, but...
>
> (Teacher, TVEI school)

> It is divisive. It's the blue collar — white collar divide, and comprehensive education was supposed to get rid of that. It didn't but TVEI is making it obvious again.
>
> (Teacher, TVEI school)

From what we have seen, there appears to be no clear-cut understanding among teachers of what 'technical and vocational education' means in its present guise. It may, for example be interpreted, in its official presentation, as a liberating reform in the provision of secondary and further education, or as a welcome consolidation of the school's socializing role. Yet others see it as an invidious attempt to reintroduce the iniquities of occupational and even socio–cultural segregation allegedly reflected in the pre-comprehensive era of bi- (and tri-) partitism.

The role of the MSC is an important factor in these developments. It enjoys a considerable influence in nationally strategic decision-making with a wide-ranging mandate for educational reform related to employment and training, and it exercises this influence through active involvement in the organization and management of local and national educational provision. It is worth looking at some of the significant themes consistently developed by the MSC and its officials over the past three years, exploring what they are intended to mean to teachers, and comparing this with how teachers interpret and understand them.

The introductory sentence to the Aims of the TVEI states that the initiative is intended 'to explore and test ways of *organizing and managing* the education of 14–18 year old young people' (MSC, 1983 — our emphasis). The subsequent Aims and Criteria are then to provide the guiding principles upon which participating local education authorities are to construct their respective submissions (and so their schemes) in a variety of combinations.

The somewhat neglected significance of the above emphasis on organization and management raises three broad but important questions. First, what level or levels of educational management are to be addressed through TVEI; second, what aspects of the education of 14–18 year olds are to be affected by such implied management reforms; and third, what are the actual 'ways' that are being tested and explored in pursuit of the Aims of the Initiative? These questions widen the interest in the TVEI phenomenon beyond the experience and involvement of the students. Despite frequent reference to the idea of students managing their own learning processes, it is clearly stated that the environment in which this might occur must of itself be structured and managed in order to meet a range of pre-determined criteria.

This does raise a number of managerial issues ranging through the administration of projects on national and local levels, the establishment or development of work and residential experience programmes, the widespread introduction of profiling and records of achievement, and curriculum 'innovations' such as modularity. However, the level or locus of 'management' we are concerned with here is that of the *classroom* — to include both teachers and students.

To a large degree, the perceptions and experiences of these participants depend upon the extent to which they are personally involved. Our evidence suggests that those teachers most closely involved — those whose timetables include a substantial proportion of TVEI sessions, and those in posts especially created by and for TVEI — tend to regard their schemes in a positive manner, albeit sometimes inflected with a touch of instrumentalism and/or cynicism.

For many people (be they teachers, headteachers, LEA officers, local and national politicians, parents or students), TVEI means, first and foremost, an injection of money into schools. After years of scrimping, saving and making do, involved teachers have frequently found that:

> '...at last we have the wherewithal to do things properly.'
>
> (Technology Teacher, TVEI school)

For this teacher and others in a similar position, TVEI has

> ...made it possible to do all the things I've wanted to do but couldn't because the resources weren't there. It's difficult, I don't say impossible, to develop and move the curriculum forward without the financial backing. And now we've got it. At least for the moment.
>
> (Domestic Science/Childcare Teacher, TVEI school)

Financial support has therefore made it possible for some teachers to put their ideas into practice and to be involved in working with others (perhaps from other institutions) in developing and designing courses, curricula and profiling schemes. This is usually a stimulating, exciting and satisfying experience which can provide opportunities for personal *and* professional development, and is sometimes also a springboard for promotion. Although insufficient hard data yet exists, there are strong indications that TVEI has created a new career path for those teachers who either were in the right place at the right time or, in entrepreneurial spirit, took advantage of the opportunities for advancement that were potentially offered.

> I was always a bit of a computer buff in my spare time, and I could see that being Head of Drama was as far as I could get. So when TVEI came along, and there was no one else to fit the bill, I switched to IT [Information technology]. It gave me another scale point and a chance to get on — especially at my age. Ironically, I can now relate better with the kids — less of them in each class, you see.
>
> (TVEI Teacher)

The formation of smaller groups allowing improved student/teacher ratios is another financially-related benefit. This has enabled teachers enough time to build closer personal and more satisfying reciprocal relationships with students.

> They treat you differently in TVEI. They treat you more like an adult. I mean, they're always telling you to behave like an adult, but then they treat you like a kid. But they don't in TVEI. I prefer it.
>
> (Female TVEI Student)

> I don't know what it is but the TVEI teachers are different. Mrs—— is great. She talks to you just like a person. It's probably got something to do with there not being so many of us in the class, and we're all interested.
>
> (TVEI Student)

> Well, you have a much smaller group and you can get to know them that much better.
>
> (TVEI Teacher)

It is difficult to separate and weigh the various strands — smaller groups, the personalities of the teachers and students involved, the Hawthorn effect of being 'pioneers' — all of which affect and contribute to student-teacher relationships. Nevertheless, the fact that TVEI money has enhanced the conditions of work, subject status and (perceived) potential career prospects for participating teachers is, for them, a significant aspect that cannot be ignored.

However, the increased financial resourcing is also important to those teachers who do not benefit directly. They become the 'poor relations' who have to continue to cope with inadequate facilities and teach large groups. Their situation is only more pronounced for themselves, their colleagues and their students by the TVEI bounty. In some cases this is further emphasized by the way in which TVEI has challenged traditional subject hierarchies in focusing on and financing practical and applied subjects which were, and often continue to be, considered inferior to academic and theoretical subjects.

In this respect, TVEI is seen by many as a threat to liberal, arts education and some teachers fear for the continued existence of their subject area and hence for their job. The actual 'loss' of a subject from the curriculum affects directly only a minority of teachers and students at present, but organizational changes resulting from TVEI have more widespread implications. For example, in the consortia arrangements of some schemes, it has been necessary to alter the structure of the school day, sometimes involving quite radical timetable and blocking changes. These affect everyone in the school:

> I think it's a case of the tail wagging the dog. We've had to alter the timetable; alter the school day; periodically we have to provide these statistics; and then there's your comments for the profile. And for how many pupils? That's the thing — 15 in the first year, 30 in the second — isn't it? And there's the

> discipline issues. What do you do with pupils from another school who misbehave here? You need to get a policy on that one.
>
> (Teacher, TVEI school)

What this teacher says also touches on the issue of students experiencing involvement with institutions other than their own schools as part of their TVEI courses. Each school and college has its own traditions and standards concerning things like relations between students and staff and what constitutes acceptable forms of dress and deportment. Where TVEI students have entered other schools, and particularly a college of Further Education, one of their most frequent observations is how appreciative they are on being treated like an adult in being offered more respect and responsibility by the resident staff.

Many colleges do, of course, maintain a different ethos, with aims and expectations different from those of local schools, but sometimes these differences are the source of tension for both students and teachers alike especially where FE teachers find that younger students cannot always respond to teaching methods applied to older students. In schools such tension often arises from the teachers, uncertainty about their relationship with 'foreign' students, and also with the fact that these students come to them as 15-year-olds when they may well have known their own students from the age of eleven. Some teachers then experience difficulty in coping with or adapting to the different expectations that students may have.

> They come back from 'tech and they think they're all grown up. ''Oh, they let us do this, that and the other.'' They don't realize that at 'tech they don't have 11 year olds. It's not the same sort of thing, the classes are smaller for one — you don't need the same rules
>
> (Teacher, TVEI school)

> It's great, the TVEI group. The ideal size. You can really talk with the students and get to know them like people. But it's not so easy with a group of 30. I try and treat all kids with the respect I want back, but not all teachers do. There's a power thing sometimes, and with these kids going elsewhere more, they notice it.
>
> (Teacher, TVEI school)

Prior to TVEI, some schools were involved in link schemes with local colleges, but the number of students who took part in them was limited. Now, with more students venturing out from their home schools, they are able to report back to their friends about the differences and broaden the dissatisfaction with school that has always existed among some students.

We would not want to suggest that this aspect of TVEI could provoke the incursion of a 'fifth' column within the organizational and management reforms of TVEI schools. We would suggest though, that it warrants serious consideration for teachers with regard to communication processes in learning experiences and new approaches to assessment.

Teachers, like anyone else, will position themselves in relation to changes in their occupational environments according to their individual personal and professional philosophies — taking into account the degrees of advantage and disadvantage to their own and others' interests. However, the (self-) evaluative process that leads to such positioning is likely to depend considerably upon the quality and quantity of information that is known, acquired or made available with regard to the various changes occurring in particular locations. In respect to programmes like TVEI, such kinds of information will vary according to the degree of proximity to and involvement in the implementation processes as they occur within individual institutions, and at different levels of administration. Furthermore, both individual and institutional orientations towards TVEI in general can and do alter, positively and negatively, as fluctuations in the supply and quality of information occur during the period of involvement.

An illustration of this occurred during a survey one of us undertook to investigate the process of third-year option choices in one TVEI authority. All third-year students in the seven schools involved completed a questionnaire designed to discover, among other things, what they knew about TVEI generally. The responses from one school were particularly outstanding because, by comparison with the others, its students knew little or nothing about the TVEI courses available to them. The consequence of this was that the school had failed to fill its quota of placements. Further investigation revealed that almost all staff at the school had gained the impression that if students opted for TVEI courses, jobs in non-TVEI areas would be threatened. Thus, in order to preserve posts, they had undertaken very little publicity of TVEI to students and parents.

In fact, two additional (although temporary) posts had been created within the school, and once this was pointed out, the teachers expressed a willingness to offer information on TVEI as an alternative option. It was difficult to ascertain why exactly they had been misinformed. The most likely explanation that emerged was that the headteacher, in not fully appreciating the implications of the extra staffing, had been unable to provide an accurate account to the staff — including the school's TVEI co-ordinator — and had thus provoked the circulation of the negative rumours. Upon the head's retirement, the new head adopted a different policy with respect to disseminating information and effectively pre-empted further misunderstandings. This example demonstrates the effects of inefficient communications at both LEA/headteacher, and headteacher/staff levels, in this case producing a distorted appreciation of TVEI narrowly related to job security.

Poor communications are a frequent cause of dissatisfaction and complaint from teachers in general (see Kyriacou and Sutcliffe, 1976, 1979). With the recent incursion of the MSC into the chain of educational implementation, a further element of potential miscommunication is established.

Because of the MSC's dominant position in respect to funding and, less obviously, regulating TVEI programmes, it is tempting to regard it as a definitive source of information. It would be more accurate to say it is the initiator of new or modified orientations toward existing educational provision. The MSC approaches this task through various mechanisms of feedback. These include national and local evaluations, negotiations with education authority officers and, more importantly, through the appointment of Regional Advisors who, in contrast to most MSC personnel, have educational backgrounds at senior level in schools and colleges. Regional Advisers are in so-called 'partnership' with authority personnel, and they monitor the progress of schemes and offer guidance on the suitability or otherwise of TVEI submissions and particular options, forms of organization and patterns of relationships within them.

However, in spite of this, the MSC actually treads a slippery path in its involvement at the local levels of implementation. No matter how experienced its representatives may be in matters of educational reform and management, they are unlikely to have as comprehensive a grasp of local educational affairs as area administrators, senior school staff and, of course, teachers themselves. The MSC's awareness of this is one important reason why scheme specifications cannot be provided on a national basis, for what may be appropriate and viable in one school could be anathema to another, even within the same authority. Instead, the Aims and Criteria remain couched in a language of high generality allowing a diversity of local responses to be mediated, regulated and consolidated by the MSC TVEI Unit through the interpretative role of the Regional Advisers.

For this reason, Regional Advisers emerge as key figures for Scheme Co-ordinators and, to a lesser extent, headteachers, LEA officers and teachers. The Aims and Criteria are so unspecific, yet new emphases and focii emerge so rapidly that adaptations to existing scheme formats require regular referral back to MSC headquarters in order that scheme administrators may know whether they are following the right path and taking the right decisions. It is usually through the Regional Adviser that schemes clarify the acceptability of new developments whether these be courses, enhancements, off-site experiences, or appointments; and receive feedback on issues like ability spread, sex-stereotyping, equal opportunities, questions of future funding, and so on.

But the sort of straightforward, black-and-white clarification co-ordinators want is not always forthcoming. Regional Advisers have signed the Official Secrets Act and are not always at liberty to disclose what they know. Instances of this situation occurred just prior to the announcement of the National Extension of TVEI, when (some) Regional Advisers declined to answer questions from Scheme Co-ordinators on future funding, even, in one case, when accompanying the Co-ordinator to a termly meeting of his Education Committee.

A new educational idiom

It is not only misinterpretation at the practical level that Regional Advisers are faced with; they also have a delicate task of discursive diplomacy through the infiltration of a new vocabulary of the vocationalist ethos into the conventional rhetorics of educational policy-making and implementation. Their attempts to do this appear to be in a way that does not immediately threaten the identities and autonomy of established educationalists, yet provides the basis for a discourse of educational reform. When addressing a seminar programme organized by the MSC for a gathering of college principals and registrars, one Regional Adviser outlined the likely future emphases in schools' administrations:

> We...see an apparently strong wish on the part of the institutions, and a lot of teachers within them who are associated with TVEI, to begin to dismantle subject boundaries... One could observe...that many teachers see great refuge and support within their basic subject areas. Part of the process is encouraging them out of that refuge...
>
> The new teaching styles, and the broader spectrum... have quite drastically changed the teacher's role. The teacher moves from a teaching process to something quite different, which could reasonably be called 'the managing of learning'.
>
> The emphasis on curriculum development has left behind... the need for the development of assessment systems and processes. The two together have probably outstripped the necessary staff development as well.
>
> (Senior Regional Adviser addressing Joint Secretariat, Association of Principals of Colleges/Association of College Registrars & Administrators)

When speaking at a conference of teachers in a TVEI authority, the same Regional Adviser approached the issues in a slightly different way:

> ...there is an increasing emphasis on progressively transferring responsibility for learning from the teacher to the learner... I think there is an increasing emphasis towards sharing the responsibility for learning between the teacher and the learner.
>
> The really major things that's happening is that the teacher's role is changing... All that TVEI has done is to emphasize that change
>
> I think that a lot of FE structures offered information on the advantages of team teaching and a lot of schools have moved away from the notion of one teacher equals one course. But... if you are importing structures from another sector, you must not make the assumption that staff [in schools] are familiar with the assessment ethos associated with that.

To some extent, this terminological infiltration has been successful, at least insofar as the way in which some teachers have adopted the usage of language and concepts which originated in the FE sector, and had been sponsored and propagated by the MSC (see Sikes, 1986b). An example is the use of the term 'delivery'. Few teachers in the secondary sector would have considered the word appropriate to any description of their educational practice prior to its importation in connection with TVEI. Yet it now appears regularly in the plethora of documentation associated with all schemes. It is used routinely by educational administrators in planning discussions and meetings and figures predominantly in briefings from MSC personnel.

Nevertheless, the term remains nebulous for most users and it is not at all clear what it is intended to mean, either in respect to what is being delivered or how it is to be delivered, and by whom. It would seem at the present time that it has something to do with the positioning of teachers as intermediaries between some form of 'curriculum package' and the students as consumers of this package (Taylor and Sikes, 1987; Shilling, 1986). In addressing a small group of senior teachers responsible for TVEI development in one scheme, a Regional Adviser attempts to explain the process:

> TVEI is about staff attitudes to curriculum development. We have funded you to develop a product — i.e. a curriculum with also an understanding of the costs of materials and development. In an industrial context it always costs more to develop a product than to market it.

This comment seems to suggest that teachers are to see themselves as both 'deliverers' and producers of some 'product' which, however, has been designed outside of their own institutional contexts. Harland (1986) picks up this point by making the analogy with encyclopaedia salesmen whose freedom and autonomy consists in exercising their powers of persuasion to sell a product in whose content they have only a superficial input.

> A conception of the LEA and its teachers as licensed agents of the DES [and, in this case, the MSC), free to exercise initiative but within specified bounds.
>
> In considering this approach to staff development, I think we must at all times remember that it has emerged from an FE tradition of both curriculum design and pedagogy and therefore comes from the world of vocational training where it is quite normal and proper for those who practise a particular craft...to lay down what is required of the young people who are being prepared to join them.
>
> (Harland, 1986)

Even in the so-called generic skills related to the 'occupational training families' propagated by Youth Training Schemes — many of which are now serviced by FE — there is at least some putative connection with identifiable occupations. The dilemma for the MSC appears to be how curricular and pedagogic structures appropriate to the FE sector can be incorporated into the secondary sector. It remains undefined as to which 'vocational' destinations the 'delivery' systems of TVEI schools are supposed to deposit young people.

In a closely related sense, the term 'participation' becomes a neutral, though evocative, key term in communicative processes all the way down from the MSC/DES relationship through every level of implementation to the teacher–pupil relationship. For classroom teachers this involves allowing the students (previously called 'pupils') more control ('ownership') of their learning processes through various approaches such as 'experiential' learning, more general access to 'guidance' and 'counselling', wider freedom of module selection, and the 'negotiation' of content in records of achievement and profiles. But where does such participation leave the teacher? As Harland (1986) has argued, the view of the teacher's professional development appears to have been inverted in current approaches to (TVEI-related) In-Service Training:

> Apple and Teitelbaum (1986) have written recently of the trend to divest teachers of the responsibility for conception in relation to the curriculum and to restrict them to matters relating to execution [and] pointed also to the de-skilling that results from this…What the FEU model offers us I suggest is a scenario in which the arrow inevitably moves from the pre-determined curriculum towards teacher development, and never from the teacher's conception to the developing curriculum.
>
> (Harland, 1986)

In much of the discussions between TVEI and MSC personnel the notion of change is linked powerfully to curriculum development, institutional development and assessment development — all of them terms familiar to educationalists at large. What has also been emphasized is that curriculum development has diverged from and outstripped the development of *assessment* methods and procedures. That is to say, because of the predominantly academic bias of traditional in-service training, its influence on teachers has been to neglect the recognition and accreditation of pupils' *experiential* knowledge and allegedly placing a lower premium on teachers' professional skills and knowledge.

At the same time, the institutional structures that have evolved from this in the secondary sector have produced strongly insulated, examination-oriented subject specialisms which tend to exclude the majority of schoolchildren from acquiring some certificated recognition of their wider interests and achievements. By implication, this holds the danger of producing not only a supposedly ill-equiped future workforce, but, just as important, a disillusioned, alienated and aimless citizenry. (For further discussions on this and similar views, see, for example, Rees and Atkinson, 1982; Gleeson, 1983; Bates *et al.*, 1984.)

The spokesperson from the DE acknowledged that despite the Department's expressed policy of creating employment, there was another way of seeing the issue:

> If you're going to be a bit more fatalistic and say unemployment is going to be with us for a long time, there's going to be a lot of young people unemployed. We should therefore concentrate our educational efforts not on

> trying to train them or prepare them for jobs which don't exist, but instead, to actually enjoy their lives and develop interests...which will *satisfy them in lieu of a job.*
>
> (Our emphasis.) (Interview, October 1986)

This could be interpreted as meaning education or training for the vocation of leisure. Insofar as the education system might take on such a responsibility, the contribution of the teachers is obviously an important factor. For the MSC's part, it seems clear from the viewpoint of their representatives that the process of institutional development requires the importation of the now successfully established course and institutional structures from the Further Education sector. This is principally the case in relation to those courses offered by the RSA, City and Guilds of London Institute and B/TEC—which provide experimentally-based syllabii organized in modular structures that can be variously integrated, assessed and *accredited* in ways not dependent on *academic* exactitude and excellence. The task of the MSC is, in the words of their own officers, to 'strike a balance between curriculum, assessment and institutional developments' in order to ensure that 'staff development is tied to school practices'. (Quoted by an MSC Senior Adviser.)

Yet, what amounts to a strategic approach at the administrative level of implementation becomes a tactical issue at the levels of the individual institutions and the classroom, where, after all, the Aims ultimately are focused:

> The MSC's policy obligation has little if anything to do with a 'tactical' education policy. It must seek to use education to bring about changes in the world outside education....The DES, on the other hand, can only look to such strategic considerations when they are congruent with its tactical obligations....largely confined to bringing about changes good in themselves for the education system.
>
> (Dale *et al.* 1986)

The translation of strategy into tactics poses the major difficulty for the MSC. Much of the information that circulates generally about TVEI amongst practising educationalists is received with some suspicion. To many, the Initiative offers a powerful threat to the perceived professional autonomy of school personnel. Indeed, since participation in TVEI involves the acceptance of certain criteria and the contractual obligation to meet particular requirements, there is, at least in theory, a diminution of the authority of headteachers and college principals over a number of issues relating to what occurs within their institutions. Not only do heads become more directly answerable to the MSC about what happens under TVEI auspices in their school, but, more immediately, the Scheme Co-ordinator (Director) can also become a competing head-like figure to whom staff and students may look for guidance and direction (Beattie, 1986).

The way in which heads perceive and experience this potential change in their authority is likely to depend on their view of TVEI and their reasons for being involved in the first place. Many, on the whole, accept and go along with it. Others who are less happy with the situation may develop or adopt *strategies* which express their dissatisfaction or discontent. Whilst variations exist between individuals and situations, we have observed three broad types of non-cooperation. In brief, they are;

1 *Abdication* — involving the passing of responsibility for TVEI on to other senior staff and withdrawal from as much public involvement as is possible;
2 *'Working to Rule'* — strategic compromise (Sikes, Measor and Woods, 1985) whereby heads do what is required of them but in a way that reflects and makes explicit their lack of commitment. This strategy has implications for how TVEI is realized within the institution;
3 *'Filibustering'* — another variety of strategic compromise. Heads using this strategy maintain a positive public orientation to TVEI but find numerous points to question or object to and by so doing can hold up progress and development.

Although they are not widely representative, these strategies are notable because they tend to be 'obvious'. Other approaches, such as 'Delegation' or 'Heeldragging', while no less influential, are not as public. Variants of these strategies may also be used by classroom teachers thereby affecting what TVEI comes to mean within particular institutions. However, teachers' greatest influence is upon the actual experience of TVEI sessions.

The classroom is still a relatively private place. Knowledge of what happens within its walls is frequently limited to the teacher and the students, and there may be a discrepancy between what is formally described by the the teacher and what actually occurs. Although we, in the course of observing classroom activities, may sometimes witness ideal-type 'performances', we have also attempted to attune to the ways in which teachers are interpreting TVEI on a day-to-day basis. It seems to us, at times, that where changes are occurring, they are at variance with the stated aims and criteria of TVEI and the intentions of the MSC. This invariance may be attributable to deliberate 'sabotage' resulting from a particular negative interpretation of TVEI, or may be an unconscious element of a teacher's established practice resulting from a lack of information — especially where adequate in-service support is lacking. Unconscious 'sabotage' is arguably the greatest obstacle to TVEI having any real impact upon educational practices.

In order for there to be any change in the structures and processes of educational provision, teachers themselves must also change — in their practices, relations and, particularly their orientations. It seems uncertain as to whether this will be achieved within the lifetime of the Initiative or its extension. If the present shift in the deployment of TVEI resourcing away from 'resource-led' initiatives (i.e. equipment and hardware) is towards a form of 'in-service training' that concentrates on assessment development rather than a genuine staff development programme, then it seems unlikely that an authentically professional TVEI orientation will be achieved. Instead, teachers will be restricted to an operative or 'executive' level as Harland (op.cit.) has suggested.

On the unconscious level, examples of 'sabotage' have included teachers taking over students work and completing practical tasks and projects on the grounds that:

> they were having difficulty, they couldn't work out what to do, so it's better that I do it for them. At least they end up with a good piece of work.
>
> (TVEI Teacher)

Some students we have observed have been directed to certain options because they are seen as 'useful experience' for either girls or boys, despite the strong emphasis that TVEI places upon equal opportunities in relation to sex-stereotyping. Other, less academically oriented students, have been advised by teachers of the suitability of 'practical' TVEI courses because 'they will help you get a job'. We even encountered more than one teacher who regarded straightforward *dictation* as a good experiential and active learning process.

Where deliberate sabotage occurs, it is instanced by teachers successfully advising able students not to opt for TVEI courses, because it might prejudice 'A'-level subject combinations. This, of course, confounds the requirement that TVEI should be for the full ability range. On the other hand, we have documented instances where TVEI teachers — also responsible for option guidance — have attempted to induce able science students into substituting a TVEI Technology 'A'-level course for their original science option choice, thereby diminishing the saliency of their final combination for university entrance. We have also noted teachers presenting courses in a traditional didactic manner because they

> do not have much time for this experiential active learning stuff. Of course, I say I do it but nobody really expects it.
>
> (TVEI Teacher)

There are instances of residential courses being cancelled because nobody was prepared to staff them, and formative profiling sessions which consisted of a five-minute lecture from the teacher rather than the fifteen-minute dialogue described in the authority's submission. The reason given was that

> At this age its no use asking them what they think. They need telling. The theory behind it is alright and it would work with older kids, but not these.
>
> (Teacher, TVEI school)

We have also noted some cases where disruptive pupils have been placed in TVEI courses (participation should be voluntary) as an expedient means of removing them from school for a significant proportion of their timetables.

Whether such forms of 'sabotage' are conscious or otherwise, the outcomes are similar in their retrogressive effect upon the development of TVEI programmes. The implications for the MSC and, in particular, the Regional Advisers are that they are faced with the task of reassuring those who remain opposed, disaffected, or simply disinterested that TVEI offers beneficial opportunities for *all* involved in the future of educational provision.

A marketing strategy

In their paper, Dale *et al.* (1986) have pointed to the 'hybrid' quality of the MSC-sponsored TVEI, deriving from the different aims of the DES (the provision of education) and the DE (the provision of employment):

> The main relevant difference between the two departments... [is that] while education is an end in itself for the DES, for the MSC it can only be a means to achieving its (MSC's) own objectives.
>
> (Dale *et al.*, 1986)

The difficulty in establishing an acceptable rationale for TVEI thus becomes one of equating the intrinsic educational aims of schools with the extrinsic objectives of vocational curricula. The attempt at resolution is highlighted in *Working Together — Education and Training* (HMSO, 1986) where the import of the coalition between the DE and the DES is established in the introductory paragraph:

> 1.1 We live in a world of determined, educated, trained and strongly motivated competitors. The competition they offer has taken more and more of our markets — both overseas and here at home.
>
> (HMSO, 1986)

The argument that develops from this posits that 'people — with their knowledge, learning, skills, intelligence, innovation and competence' are the critical factor in gaining an internationally competitive edge. They are 'our most important asset and resource' (para.1.3). However, this resource, comprising 'their potential and their creative capacity', must be 'harnessed' by the desire to learn those things which are 'seen to lead to progress for individuals and companies' (para.1.4).

> Motivation is all important, so that *attitudes change* and people acquire the desire to learn, the habit of learning and the skills that learning brings.
>
> (Ibid.,para.1.4) (our emphasis)

Closely connected with this emphasis upon 'motivation' is the way in which the notion of 'failure' now appears to have become redundant. The implications of this were explored by a spokesperson from the Department of Employment:

> It had for long been the case that examinations like the 11+ and GCE's worked on the fundamental basis of pass or fail. If you passed your exam, on

> you went to brighter and better things. They were a passport to progress. If you failed, then you were a failure and that was that. The damage this must have done to youngsters' self-esteem was inestimable and it produced.... alright, a sense of alienation. At one time this was offset by a more fluid job market, so that some fulfilment could be found, even if only a pay-packet at the end of a week. It would be much better if young people were helped and encouraged to value themselves in ways that do not entirely depend upon academic and intellectual ability.
>
> (Interview, October 1986)

We do not have the room here to explore the number of ways in which such a statement may be interpreted. However, we do not underestimate the extent to which educationalists, particularly teachers, will appreciate the sentiment contained here and be motivated to take on and make TVEI their own. MSC Regional Advisers are frequently heard talking about the importance of teachers and their LEAs assuming 'ownership' of their schemes. Ownership in this sense meaning commitment — professional, philosophical and financial — in relation to the TVEI Aims and Criteria. Yet, as we have tried to indicate, this form of commitment is not always apparent in the way in which teachers present and represent TVEI to the students in their schools.

Furthermore, the various interpretations of what TVEI means to teaching staff is paralleled by those held by the students themselves regarding their involvement in TVEI schemes. However, we have not attempted an evaluation of students' experiences of TVEI in relation to the previously established curriculum. This is because no comparison is possible between their involvement in newly modified course structures and those they might otherwise have chosen to follow but didn't. Rather than attempting to compare 'experience' with 'experience', we have found a more fruitful approach to be comparing 'experience' with *expectation*. Almost all students we spoke with interpreted TVEI as a means to improve or promote post-school career opportunities for satisfying employment of some kind. Their expectations thus revolved around more 'mature' relationships with teachers and other adults, the acquisition of work-related competences and information, and the chance to accumulate some direct experience of a desired occupation. These views were sometimes expressed as an antipathy toward the perceived infantalizing atmosphere of everyday school routines where TVEI options offered a legitimate means of withdrawing:

> This course is brilliant. It's good preparation for drama school.
>
> (16+ student, Entertainments Industry Course)

> I think it gives you a good basis for getting a job. I don't mean you're bound to get a job because you've done it, but it helps, and since there's so much unemployment here anyway, you've nothing to lose.
>
> (16+ student, Entertainments Industry Course)

> It offers more opportunities and the equipment is much better than in the

> ordinary lessons....I'm going to university but I still thought this was the better course.
>
> (4th-year student, Electronics/Control Technology Course)

> I'm going to work in electronics and this course has been very good. Good equipment and good visits [to local industries]. What we saw there we could do back here. The only thing that worries me is that all this hardware stands idle for a lot of the time. Other departments, like Physics, could use some of this stuff.
>
> (5th-year student, Electronic Engineering Course)

There exists some contradiction between the generally accepted view that employment prospects will be improved for young people through a 'vocational' emphasis in education, and the less publicized admittance among government-sponsored agencies that unemployment levels are expected to remain proportionately high. It does not seem to us that either teachers or students are generally aware of this paradox. The tone of *Working Together — Education and Training* offers a clear indication that, in the event of continued high unemployment, the task of schools is to prolong the interest and involvement of (many) young people in *preparatory*, work-related programmes that sustain high levels of motivation through practical and self-regulated participation. In our view, the extension of TVEI beyond its original experimental status, serves to further consolidate this process. It is as a contribution to this aspect of the debate that this chapter is addressed.

References

Apple, M. and Teitelbaum, K. (1986). Are teachers losing control of their skills and curriculum? *J. Curriculum Studies*, **18**, (2).

Bates, I., Clarke, J., Cohen, P., Finn, D., Moore, R. and Willis, P. (1984). *Schooling for the Dole: The New Vocationalism*. London, Macmillan.

Burgess, R.G. (1986). Whatever happened to the Newsom Course? Paper given at the Education and Training: 14–18 Conference, St. Hilda's College, Oxford, 15–17 September 1986.

Dale, I.R. *et al.* (1986). TVEI: A Policy Hybrid. Paper presented to BERA Annual Conference, Bristol, September.

FEU (1982a). *Basic Skills*. Further Education Unit, November.

FEU (1982b). *Skills for Living*. Further Education Unit, December.

Fiddy, R. and Stronach, I. (eds) (1986). *TVEI Working Papers 2*. CARE, University of East Anglia.

Gleeson, D. (ed) (1983). *Youth Training and the Search for Work*. London, Routledge & Kegal Paul.

Harland, J. (1986). The New Inset: A Transformation Scene, in Fiddy and Stronach (1986).

DES (1986). *Working Together — Education and Training*. HMSO, Cmnd. 9823.

Hughes, E.C. (1937). Institutional Office and the Person, in *Amer. J. Sociology* **43**, November.

Institute of Manpower Studies (1982). *Foundation Training Issues: A Report for the MSC*. IMS, University of Sussex.

Kyriacou, C. and Sutcliffe, J. (1986). A Note on Teacher Stress and Locus of Control. *J. Occupational Psychology* **52**, 227–8.

Kyriacou, C. and Sutcliffe, J. (1979). Teacher Stress and Satisfaction. *Educational Research* **21** (2), 89–96.

McCabe, C. (ed) (1986). *The Organisation of the Early Years of the Technical and Vocational Education Initiative*. Avon, Multilingual Matters.

Manpower Services Commission (1983). *TVEI Manual*, MSC.

National Economic Development Council (1984). *Competence and Competition*, NEDO.

Parlett, M. and Hamilton, D. (1972). *Evaluation as Illumination: A New Approach to Innovatory Programmes*. Centre for Research in the Educational Sciences, University of Edinburgh Occasional Paper No. 9.

Rees, T.L. and Atkinson, P. (1982). *Youth Unemployment and State Intervention*. London, Routledge & Kegan Paul.

Ruddock, J. (1986). Understanding Curriculum Change. Inaugural Professional Lecture, University of Sheffield, 19 February 1986.

Shilling, C. (1986). The Schools Vocational Programme: 'Factories and Industry, a Deficit Programme for the Commodification of Youth'. Unpublished paper.

Sikes, P.J. (1986a). *The Mid-Career Teacher: Adaptation and Motivation in a Contracting Secondary School System*. Unpublished PhD Thesis, University of Leeds.

Sikes, P.J. (1986b). Headteachers and the Organisation and Management of TVEI Schemes, in McCabe, C. (1986).

Simon, B. (1986). Education and the Social Order: the contemporary scene. Paper given at BERA Annual Conference, Bristol, September.

Taylor, M.O. and Sikes, P.J. (1987). *The Two Faces of TVEI*, forthcoming.

John Evans and Brian Davies

5

The Social Context of Educational Opportunities in New Vocational Educational Initiatives

In July 1986, prompted by 'the encouraging progress made with the pilot TVEI projects' the Conservative Government announced its decision to extend this initiative from a pilot to a national scheme beginning in Autumn 1987. It was quickly pointed out however that the level of funding for this phase of TVEI was considerably lower than had been provided for the pilot project; that '£90 million a year to cover all schools and colleges is less than twice the amount currently being spent under the pilot programmes on only 39 000 pupils in 500 establishments, (*TES* 4 July 1986, p.1). This critical retort to *Working Together* properly raises questions not only about the overall cost of achieving innovation in the 14–18 curriculum on the grand scale envisaged but also the specific prices of meeting some of the more laudable, particular aims contained in the document. *Working Together* clearly carries forward the Government's intentions to alter the 14–18 curriculum in every state secondary school England and Wales. It also repeats some of the commitments and criteria explicit in the pilot TVEI requirements. In the pilot schemes, for example, local authorities were held contractually responsible for, among other things, attracting to TVEI pupils representing 'the full ability range', and achieving 'equal opportunities for young people of both sexes' (*TVEI Operating Manual* 1983).

In a similar vein *Working Together* (DES, Department of Employment 1986) along with the supporting literature (MSC 1986) submitted to LEAs, carry a vision of educational practice in which children from across the ability range receive a broad, balanced and 'relevant' curriculum, one in which they 'progress to the limit of their creativity and potential'. The Paper conveys an imagery which seems as persuasively liberal (see Holt and Reid 1986) as it is socially and academically all-embracing. Moreover, the very title of the White Paper also carries with it a conception of the system at work in co-operative and collaborative endeavour, of schools working together with colleges and industry in the vocational and educational interest of every adolescent child.

At this point in time, we can only begin to speculate on what might be achieved in our whole school system with this meagre proposed level of funding. The data provided below may well give something of a coarse glimpse of a future inhabited by lowly funded TVEI types as might be found within the difficult conditions of educational practice already routinely experienced by many teachers in our beleaguered state secondary system. These conditions are hardly conducive either to collaborative activity between schools, or the realization of 'equal opportunities'. Our attention centres on the activities of one 'TVEI' consortium consisting of four secondary schools and two colleges which, in 1983 had failed in its bid to become 'the' LEA scheme put forward for MSC funding (see Evans and Davies 1986a). Nevertheless, its members had worked on in the hope that there would be a second coming, another round of MSC handouts in which they would be financially favoured. In the meantime, 'the consortium' had received a small amount of money from the LEA to purchase additional resources and, in the first year of its life, for supply 'cover' for teachers from the four schools to meet and develop what we call New Vocational Educational Initiatives (NVEI). Although the schools and teachers involved in NVEI were in no way contractually tied to the MSC, they had attempted to adhere to the principles, criteria and characteristics of TVEI when effecting change in their upper-school curriculum and they continued to use the term 'TVEI' to describe their work.

In this discussion we want to focus attention on the processes of selection and differentiation in NVEI and the mechanisms by which social and academic hierarchies and division are achieved and sustained. We draw attention to the difficulties which these schools faced when trying to effect NVEI for pupils from 'across the ability range' involving curriculum and pedagogical change in the direction of what teachers thought to be more interesting and vocationally useful and relevant forms of educational practice. At the heart of our argument is the contention that TVEI and the many cases of NVEI now found in schools may do little to lessen and, indeed may even exacerbate social and academic divisions between children inside schools and outside them (see also Holt and Reid 1986). The achievement of 'equal opportunities' in the 14–18 curriculum may have a lot less to do with the abilities of teachers as innovators, or for that matter the amounts of money expended on educational change, than the social *context* of educational practice in which teachers and pupils are compelled to work. This context is constituted by a range of factors of long standing such as the expectations of parents and pupils, the biographies and identities of pupils already established in the lower-school curriculum and the awesome power of the examination system, all given fresh meaning and edge by the conditions created by falling school rolls which government policy has translated into greater legal, practical and ideological prominence for 'parental choice'.

Maindene and *Rainford* are both large co-educational schools on the outskirts of a city. Both are set within working-class communities and have largely working-class intakes skewed towards the middle to lower end of the ability spectrum. Both are plagued by falling rolls though the problem is especially acute at Rainford. Here the rolls are predicted by the LEA to fall all through the period up to 1993 and while the characteristics of the population in its catchment area are such that this school should attract most of the local children 'about 30% of them do not seem to go to it' (Mar Molinero 1986). *Cranfield* and *Barton* by contrast are large, single-sex schools set more within the city in what is mainly a middle-class area. They enjoy intakes socially and academically more mixed than those of Rainford and Maindene. The numbers on roll in these schools are about '20% larger than the size of the secondary school age population in the area' (Mar Molinero 1986, p.25). Their 'good reputation' attracts children from other catchment areas and while neither school is particularly plagued by falling rolls, both are concerned with their public image and eager to protect the quality of their intakes. In effect, although the four schools had joined to work towards the development of NVEI, they were unavoidably in the position of competing with each other for a limited supply of pupil talents, their intake upon which would depend their levels of human and physical resource. This situation inevitably created tensions between schools and some curtailment of the consortium's collaborative zeal (see Evans and Davies 1986 a and b).

Differentiation and selection in NVEI

In each of the schools NVEI had meant the revision of some old and the inclusion of perhaps one or two new options within the upper-school curriculum. But in each of the schools these options tended to be disproportionately filled by the average and less able pupils though the emphasis varied slightly from school to school. Indeed in this respect, it seems that a much greater injection of official money alone into the system would not alter this pattern. As the recent HMI report on first-generation sponsored TVEI schemes also found (Bolton 1985, p.15) 'pupils of average and low ability were represented in all projects, but few of very high ability or very low ability appeared to have joined'. It does not go on to explain how or why this outcome is achieved so regularly.

At Maindene and Rainford, both schools seriously concerned with their pupil intake, NVEI options were intentionally offered largely for the average and less-able pupils. At Rainford NVEI was seen as something which could fit fairly comfortably into the existing pattern of curriculum provision and it seemed ideally suited for the school's disaffected and uninterested majority of middle ability children. As the NVEI co-ordinator stated:

> We'd just revised the curriculum for the less able and given them what we thought was a fairly good deal.... The more able we felt were able to cope, to cater for themselves in that they were much better motivated because they had much more success. But the middle lot, we were thinking, good grief, you know, lots of courses offered to them are just not relevant to what they want, they are not particularly well motivated, they are not interested in what they are doing and we are looking for others things in many cases for them to do...

This middle-ability range presented the school with its main problems of pupil control and motivation which the more experientially based curriculum of NVEI was seen as a means of better managing. Indeed the Business Craft course (referred to in the next section) was held as something of an exemplar of good practice, in just this respect.

> We thought that problem solving and the whole business about being involved in the conceptual idea of a project, the sort of working out where they were going to go, the design of the object, the marketing of the object and that whole land of .... would be just what they wanted.
>
> (NVEI co-ordinator, Rainford)

As we see however, the school's success in achieving this goal of better controlling its disaffected children through the pedagogy of NVEI was extremely short lived.

At Maindene, the NVEI principle of providing access to all pupils was rationalized and interpreted as the responsibility of the consortium rather than any individual school.

> Now that it (providing access to all pupils) is the responsibility of the consortium... it doesn't mean that every single school in the consortium must put in the full ability range...
>
> (NVEI co-ordinator, Maindene)

This is somewhat ironic, for Maindene, despite its relative lack of able children, stood nearest to having mixed-ability options thrust upon it by falling rolls. They had achieved:

> a huge impact on our staffing, on our option system and what we can offer, irrespective of TVEI... we had a banded system of options up until I think last September — was the first time we departed from it. We've now got as you

> can see, an all through option system, then in the fifth year is the banded option...
>
> (NVEI co-ordinator, Maindene)

In this context then, a mixed-ability option system was purely an accident of falling rolls, which meant that '*in theory* any child can choose any subject now which he couldn't before when it was in two bands...' (NVEI co-ordinator, Maindene).

In practice however, a number of factors combined to ensure that this mix rarely happened:

> You see we have a very complicated option system as you can see, that is the top two lines of that timetable and it works out, not intentionally — but it works out that those children who want to take things like German or Integrated Science, you know this 11+ double entry 'O'-level, cannot by practical nature of things do a TVEI course where you need two modules of PVE [Personal and Vocational Education] because the options boxes will not allow you in the time you're allowed in a week.
>
> (NVEI co-ordinator, Maindene)

and

> It's quite a complicated system but it does sort them out in a fairly logical way... self sorting if you like. It takes a lot of time but...
>
> (NVEI co-ordinator, Maindene)

Elsewhere we have argued that these statements hint at not only the mechanisms by which pupils are differentiated in the upper-school curriculum, but also the rationales which accompany, support and legitimize this process. Both mechanism and rhetorics were featured in the perspectives of teachers at Maindene, Barton, Rainford and Cranfield. In each of these schools, the sorting process was neither direct nor 'intentional'. It was not achieved by teachers simply telling pupils which block or option he or she should choose, nor was it something which the teachers particularly desired. More subtly, the option/selection system worked by providing a framework of limited opportunity in which children were expected to recognize for themselves the limits of their own ability, and secondly to choose curricula appropriate to their 'status' and expected post-school occupational routes. Failing this, the school seemed to act only in an *advisory* capacity, very often appealing to the help of parents and with special reference to the biographies of the children themselves, to ensure that any mis-recognition of talents did not take place (Evans and Davies 1986a).

> You see here we've got this advisory section here, we tell the kids look, you first have two choices. Your first choice... we advise these sets to make the first choice in this band, etc... and PVE is open to all these sets but notice we miss out (sets) 1 and 1A which are our top two sets. So they opt for a first choice in these bands and then for the second choice they can opt across the bands...
>
> (NVEI co-ordinator, Maindene)

and

> We say to the parents and to the kids, it's no good going for German or for IS if in the years 2 and 3 you've had no experience of these. There's no point. Why deny someone else who's had experience a place when you'll foul it up and want to leave after a few weeks. They do opt within their abilities and capabilities...
>
> (NVEI co-ordinator, Maindene)

At Maindene, as indeed in all of these schools, the system of selection built up on pupil/curriculum hierarchies already established in the lower-school curriculum. Neither Maindene nor Rainford could afford to indulge in forms of curriculum reorganization which would or could place at risk the identification of their already scarce supply of 'superior' pupil talent.

A similar picture is evident at both single-sex schools. At Barton, while in theory all pupils had access to vocational options, in practice pupils were 'selected from across the ability range with the exception of the top 20% who are *guided* into a highly academic curriculum' (NVEI co-ordinator, Barton) while those at the lower end of the ability range had only 'a limited selection from the vocational options since some courses will be beyond their capabilities...' (ibid.) The NVEI options here, again as in all the other schools, were essentially for the middle-range pupils, some of whom were also difficult pupils. As at Maindene and Rainford the NVEI options were intended to be more interesting to the average pupil and help lessen pupil management and control problems. As the NVEI co-ordinator at Barton stated:

> The extreme low were ... this is an awful thing to say perhaps, but the extreme low were too slow to create a problem because they could always be picked up easily. Problems I believe in school exist in the lower middle to middle middle .... The upper middle were quick enough to realize that they weren't taking GCEs they were taking CSEs and that the GCEs would be in front of them in the job queue and then they became disaffected and that tended to affect some of the GCE candidates...

The 'guidance' system here involved tutors making assessments both of a pupil's social and academic credentials — an assessment which was then passed on to a senior teacher, the Curriculum Co-ordinator, for further screening. Again, the organization of the option system firstly set limits to the choices available to pupils, the less able, for example, being 'directed' into a Basic Studies course, which in taking up two option blocks effectively limited their opportunities to take up other vocational 'subjects' while, as the NVEI co-ordinator put it; 'We steer away the top 25%... the real high fliers in the hope that they might go on to further professional training or to University... .' But there was no simple intention or hope that vocational education could achieve some sort of blanket control. Here, those pupils who were of average ability *and* behaviourly difficult were carefully screened out of those options which demanded that they travel to neighbouring schools. The school's concern to protect its public image, to confine its behavioural problem to the boundaries of the school, had thus given rise to a peculiar form of the Catch 22 of educational practice — if you can't do the practices required to learn in 'conventional' academic curriculum and you don't 'behave' then you don't get access to those alternative curricula in which you might learn and so *want* to 'behave'. Protecting school 'brand image' in the newly marketized fight for entrants had set limits to the opportunities of using vocational options for the purpose of social control (Evans and Davies 1986a).

At Cranfield (the girls' school) both Head and Deputy were concerned to introduce a more comprehensive curriculum to their girls. Here the 'control' motivation did not feature in the perspectives of teachers. These teachers, as indeed all those above, were very conscious of academic (ability) divisions, but they also saw the examination system along with the expectations of their 'client' parents, as imposing severe constraints on any ambitions which they might have to challenge curriculum status hierarchies. As the Cranfield NVEI co-ordinator put it: 'Parents won't let their children opt for anything without an examination, that hasn't an 'O' level attached to it...' Moreover the curriculum, co-ordinator felt that it was their duty to help girls achieve all that was possible within the conventional subject hierarchies...

> We can't gamble with these girls, we wouldn't want to put a real high flier into these [vocational] options ... if they are going on to University.

Again, the concept of *self selection* is invoked to explain how the problem of differentiation and assessment works.

> They were all offered to take option X and we've got two bands. Those in TVEI came from both so it's right in the middle I'd say... none of them very low and none of them really high fliers...
>
> It's just the way it happens... because the high fliers want to get their 'O' levels don't they, they can't afford to drop out...

It is our view (see Evans and Davies 1986a) that the language used by all of these teachers when describing their option systems (including concepts such as 'self selection', 'guidance' 'advice', the denial of 'intentionality') functioned to resolve not only a contradiction between the 'principles' of NVEI and their within-school organizational practices, but also a tension in their own thinking and ideals about how educational practice ought to be. Each of these teachers would have liked to have seen more movement between the practical and academic options and a weakening of the boundaries between high- and low-ability pupils and subjects. But they were also, as managers, realistic enough to know that attracting a good clientele was an essential first priority. Moreover, gaining legitimation by meeting the expectations of parents meant making the most in 'conventional terms' of what available 'talent' their school had acquired. There was nothing conspiratorial or dishonest in their actions. By the age of thirteen/fourteen, differences between children had already been produced within and by the lower-school curriculum. Thus the task which senior management saw as quite legitimate was that of ensuring that children could themselves recognize their ability, build on it and channel it into appropriate curricular routes. The interest of the school and teachers was firstly and foremostly to improve the lot of pupils *within* existing structures of curricular organization and practice.

The overall pattern to emerge in this NVEI consortium is of senior teachers building on and sustaining conventional academic and curriculum hierarchies. But these hierarchies are not only sustained by the expectations and actions of senior teachers. The pupils themselves also play a part in the differentiating process as they too determine to find a curriculum which is best suited to their career interests and vocational needs. Inside classrooms, as we see, the interests of senior teachers and pupils can interact not just to temper the intentions and ambitions of innovatory teachers, but to severely constrain and even deny them. In the next section therefore, to highlight this process, and for the sake of space and time, we concentrate on two of the four schools involved in the consortium, *Cranfield* and *Rainford*. We draw attention to only the actions and perspectives of four teachers within these schools — to *Food Studies* taught by Mrs Bates and *Business Craft* team taught by Miss Smiles and Mr Trough at Rainford; and *Science in the Home* taught by Mrs Paterson at Cranfield. These teachers' opportunities to effect NVEI for pupils across the ability range were already circumscribed by the decisions of senior management as high 'ability' children were channeled away from NVEI into high-status subjects. Management 'felt' the pressures of falling rolls and the 'need' to sustain or attract a 'better' middle-class intake.

Understandably examination success was taken extremely seriously and these senior teachers pointed to the local communities or the relative success of other schools as the sources of the pressure for results. However, although the pressures for examination results were similarly felt by senior management in each of these schools (all were concerned to sustain their numbers, protect or improve the 'quality' of their intake), the constraint of falling rolls and parental expectations was experienced in a qualitatively different way by teachers within their classrooms. In this context at Rainford, teachers had to contend not with the educational 'codes' of those children which the senior management within the school *would like to have* attracted in far greater numbers, but of those (often the less able and the disaffected) who stood more immediately before them. At both schools the expectations of middle- and working-class parents, mediated by their children's actions, could further set limits to a teacher's preferred way of working and the delicate process of curriculum innovation.

Teaching for a change in NVEI

The Business Craft course began at Rainford in September, 1984 and was constructed and staffed by two teachers Miss Smile and Mr Trough, the first a Design and Art, the second a CDT teacher. It has attracted twenty-four pupils, the majority of whom were boys. These pupils were not, as the NVEI co-ordinator put it:

> particularly well motivated kids ... well certainly not but they were the ones who opted to do the course ... potentially we could have selected 30 but as it turned out twenty-four 'self selected' (see Evans and Davies 1986a) and that was it. It was really good for a pilot group. I mean one to twelve is a bit sort of favourable as a staff/pupil ratio but it's worked out superbly really ...

As we have noted the course was looked upon (and talked about at interview) with a great deal of enthusiasm and it received strong support from senior management. To the NVEI co-ordinator, Business Craft not only expressed the spirit and content of vocational education, it met the needs of those pupils who provided the school with its most pressing managerial and educational concerns. The 'very favourable pupil/teacher ratio' consequently seemed an acceptable, if slightly worrying, small price to pay for the educational satisfaction of previously uninterested pupils and better order within the school system.

However, Miss Smile's and Mr Trough's motivations for involvement in NVEI did not have any straightforward origins either in some vocational educational ideal or the concerns of their senior management for the achievement of greater order and control over disaffected children. Indeed the thought of dealing with some of the pupils with whom they had been presented had filled them initially with considerable trepidation. For Miss Smile, NVEI represented firstly, an opportunity to resurrect an ambition — 'to run a business' — which she had failed to realize before entry to the teaching profession and secondly to teach a curriculum which she had been unable to express through the content of her Design and Art teaching. She had, as she stressed, 'always wanted to run my own business doing the production, design and management bit'. The Business Craft Course 'allowed me to do this'. Mr Trough also found this idea of taking pupils through 'the whole process of production, design and management, hugely attractive. Although he was already teaching a practical subject, he felt that neither he nor Miss Smile had 'really given thought to the vocational elements in what we did'.

Both teachers saw NVEI as an opportunity to make their curriculum, combining elements/skills from Design and Art and CDT, more relevant and related to what they saw as the future work opportunities of their pupils. Their aim, indeed, was to provide a course which was both vocationally orientated and occupationally useful. They visualized a future for their pupils of limited employment opportunities and thus saw themselves providing not only the knowledge and skills to help them 'better understand the world of industry' (Mr Trough) but also the 'confidence' and 'initiative' to start up on their own when faced with unemployment. Consequently their objective in the classroom was not to create the conditions of factory life for them, with its oppressive hierarchies, depersonalization and divisions of labours, but rather the environment of a 'small family craft business', with more personal social relations and flexibility of labour and skill. Indeed, any move in the pedagogical content in the direction of something approximating 'factory life' was, in these teachers' view, a change also strongly resisted by the pupils.

> If we tried to link it more clearly with industry it wouldn't work ... we wouldn't get away with it ... it's more like a small family craft business not a large factory. (Mr Trough)

Together these teachers had intended to establish a course which had at its heart the ideal of producing the 'creative, confident and industrious individual'. Theirs was the *romantic individualism* to which Cohen (1984, p.108) has referred — it was a commitment to self help and self employment. The small enterprise was seen as a major source of job creation for young people in the foreseeable future. It was a vision, a 'romance', however, which seemed not to be shared by the pupils themselves.

However, there was other attractions too, associated with an involvement in NVEI. Both teachers saw in the Business Craft course an opportunity to shake themselves free of the examination system and the structure and organization which it imposed on their curriculum and teaching. To them NVEI offered a 'freedom to do anything that you like to put forward', and they had created a curriculum in which 'you're never quite sure what's going to happen next'. In fact the syllabus of the Business Craft course was little more than a half page statement of aims and intent — to use Bernstein's (1971) terms, the curriculum and pedagogy featured weak classification and framing. They talked of 'ad libbing' the curriculum. Content (within broad parameters) could be negotiated (between staff and pupils) as could the timing and pacing of the lesson:

> Last week for example (we were just back after the hols) nobody felt like doing anything ... so we didn't; we talked about what we might do and had done in the holidays, we casually worked on bits and pieces...
>
> (Mr Trough)

For these teachers, NVEI was the means of achieving greater professional autonomy and responsibility. To them the MSC was neither task master nor ogre. Indeed, its 'initiative' had weakened at least some of the frames on their professional work, and had created a space for development and the realization of the latent content of their skills and ambitions and professional identities.

But the motivations of these teachers were not the same as those which underpinned the *Food Studies* course or the teaching of Mrs Bates, the Head of the Home Economics Department at the same school, Rainford. This teacher also expressed firm opposition to the view that school should be in business of producing factory fodder, of only preparing pupils for the world of work. Like other teachers at Rainford she resisted what she saw as the MSC's endeavour to vocationalize the curriculum:

> There was a very anti-feeling amongst teachers, against being made to do that kind of thing really. Well it's sort of manipulating the curriculum isn't it ... from the top. Well you know, there's this big lump of money for something called TVEI and that will change everything to how you want it to go. So there was a suspicion that we were being led to produce whatever is wanted at the end of the day, and that's not really what education is about.

Yet this teacher had eagerly embraced the opportunities presented in the TVEI bid — opportunities as she saw them, to disestablish boundaries between community and industry and between subjects within the curriculum. As she put it:

> I'm not a very subject-orientated person. I think subjects are educationally confining. I mean, my subject (Home Economics) can relate to anything and I'd much rather it did. I mean, what I teach in here (HE) is fine but the ramifications of that ... and to some extent this being able to integrate the curriculum, to my mind is positive. I don't like these boxes we live in ...
>
> What we do in schools is a nonsense anyway, because not only do we live in our own little subject areas but we live in our own primary, secondary, further, sectors. We ought to be thinking more of what went before and what is coming after ... from the point of view of the system ...

For Mrs Bates, TVEI was a means to the sort of 'pedagogic liberation' described by Jamieson (1985, p.37). It was a step towards challenging the organization of schooling and of teaching and learning within it. Indeed, Jamieson goes on to argue that radical teachers (of this sort) 'often join with industrialists in claiming that "real world" problems do not fall neatly into academic subject divisions' (p.37) and he notes that in the area of assessment they can 'embrace many of the changes which are supported by industry. Pupil profiling is a good example' (ibid.). This was already a view taken by Mrs Bates:

> You've got some employers saying you don't tell us much about the whole child either. There is this argument you can't go against really. Exams don't tell you much about the person and if you don't get exams you go out at the end of the fifth year with nothing really....

NVEI had presented this teacher with an opportunity to shift her curriculum and teaching 'in the right direction', away from the home centredness of Home Economics and towards a curriculum which was underpinned by a more comprehensive range of aims and intensions. It was intended to develop in pupils 'life', 'leisure', 'social' and 'work' skills, which would be of use to them *irrespective* of their future occupational destinies. The vocational utility of the course, however, was not in any way underplayed, but this feature was simply one (and not the most important one) among others expressed through the course. But the course did offer pupils a way into a career:

> If they feel inclined to go into the work skills area then they have got a link with the tech. college. So that they can see what it's like. They can try catering, hotel work, or related industries ...

Again, however, like Miss Smiles and Mr Trough, this teacher celebrated the freedom from examinations which NVEI had given her, and she preferred instead to develop her own system of profiling. The course contained no highly organized or elaborate syllabus / defining in detail, content or pedagogy. As Mrs Bates remarked:

> Even now we've got a very rough idea ... we don't know what we are doing ... we are just looking at it as a taster that's all ...

Emphasis was placed on the possibilities for a negotiated curriculum, for spontaneity and creativity. There was again a weakening in both the classification and framing of the education process, a shift which Mrs Bates hoped would allow greater sensitivity to the developing needs and interests of her pupils.

Cranfield (the all-girls school)

At Cranfield, the Science in the Home (SH) course was one of two new NVEI options and had been introduced to the curriculum by Mrs Peterson (Head of Home Economics) in 1984. For this teacher NVEI was an opportunity to get out of the rut into which six years of Home Economics teaching at Cranfield had placed her. It was an opportunity 'to do something different' and to rethink the bases of her teaching and curriculum. Again, however, this teacher's motivations for involvement in NVEI were complex and differed markedly with those of the teachers at Rainford — a difference which expressed not only this teacher's idiosyncratic values and orientations, but the values, the dominant code, of the school system within which she operated. Indeed, it is in the contrast between these two schools and these teachers that we can see how NVEI is 'shaped' not just by the interpretations and intentions of individual teachers, but as Dale puts it *within* 'explicit conditions based largely on the existing history, ideology, structure and location of the school' (1986, p.44).

For Mrs Peterson, the TVEI bid was an opportunity not just to create an entirely new curriculum but to effect a significant shift in the content of Home Economics teaching away from its Humanities base in the direction of something more 'scientific'. This teacher was keenly aware of the hierarchy of subjects at Cranfield, a structure (of opportunities and opinions among colleagues and pupils) which placed her subject, like other practical and physical subjects, low in the status heap. Her goal, through, NVEI, was not essentially to challenge this hierarchy (distasteful though she found it) but to elevate the status of Home Economics teaching by injecting into it a component (Science) which she felt or hoped would give it greater *academic* respectability. To this end, in stark contrast to the teachers at Rainford, Mrs Peterson was desperately keen to provide an examination ('O' level) certificate at the end of the course and had quickly entered into negotiation with an Examination Board to effect this. The Board has assured her that an examination would be available for her children by the end of the course in 1986. In this way (offering science and an examination certificate) it was anticipated that the course would attract pupils from across the ability range, even those 'able' pupils who might not usually have taken a Home Economics option.

To achieve the backing of the Examining Board, the course devised contained a sophisticated syllabus outlining week by week its structure and content. In sharp contrast with the courses at Rainford, the syllabus implied very strong classification and framing. Indeed the content of the course contained rather less of a vocational component than was evident in the Food Studies option at Rainford. In many respects it remained quite 'home-centred', and set out 'to give insight into the link between science and everyday substances, make them (pupils) more aware of their surroundings and the part that science plays in life...' (syllabus). Neither did the course provide any link with the tech. college. Its vocational relevance lay not first or foremost with the transmission of work-related skills, but in the provision of an academic credential, an examination certificate, that most marketable commodity expected and desired by the school's middle-class and able clientele.

The social limits of educational change

Our conversations with children in each of these new options revealed that they derived an enormous amount of satisfaction from their lessons and that they very frequently rated the 'subject' and the teacher as among the 'best' they had encountered in their secondary school careers. In the space available here we could not do justice to these teachers' work or fully describe the skill with which they operated in the classroom. Yet one year after the inception of these options, Business Craft at Rainford, Science in the Home at Cranfield, lay 'dead' in the curriculum unable to attract the numbers which would make them viable concerns. Brief recourse to the pupils' perspectives gives some clues as to the origins of this outcome.

The Business Craft course had attracted nineteen boys and five girls, over the selection of whom, as indicated above, the teachers had had little control. Our conversations with some of these children revealed that most had 'chosen' the option either because there was little else they could do which was not 'academic' or 'high powered', or because they saw the option as being 'like woodwork', or providing 'practical work' — that is, it seemed to have on offer at least some of those components/elements or skills which they associated with their future careers. At least half of the boys interviewed wanted to be 'mechanics', others 'bricklayers' or 'welders'. However, at the time of interview (towards the end of their first year of the course) these pupils seemed to be in the business of extracting as best they could from the course those skills which would be of use to them in their future working lives. All had come to see only the most tenuous of connections between what they were doing in the Business Craft course and the skills which they felt would be required of them if they realized their preferred job aspirations. None of the pupils articulated any semblance of the ambition to 'run their own business' which had been expressed by the teachers and which had underpinned both the content and teaching of the Business Craft course. The course was not in any sense seen in this holistic fashion, as a package preparing them for a future as independent entrepreneurs. Indeed, Mr Trough had commented that the pupils thought they were simply making things for other teachers.

Our observation and interview data suggests that the pupils simply pressed on in routine fashion de-contextualizing and re-contextualizing (Bernstein 1977) the Business Craft curriculum to suit their own anticipated needs, and occupational interests. Thus although the course seemed to offer these pupils an immensely satisfying *context* of learning which they both highly desired and appreciated not least because of 'the freedom you get', 'you're always working together', 'it's the way we can talk', the *content* in their view had been unrealistically aligned to their future prospects and job opportunities. By the end of the year, the course was attracting little interest among pupils. This, along with what was seen by Mr Trough and Miss Smiles as the failure of senior management to publicize the option adequately (they also thought the course would be largely 'self-sustaining', that is, that it would recruit largely by word of mouth/recommendation), had ensured its demise, much to the despair of the teachers concerned and not a little to the surprise of senior staff.

The destiny of the Science in the Home course at Cranfield had also similarly rested upon its capacity to meet the expectations of both parents and pupils to provide a vocationally useful 'academic qualification'. The course in the first year had functioned largely as the teacher had intended and had attracted eighteen pupils from across the ability range. However, mid-way through the course it was learnt that the Examining Board (perhaps now overtaken or over-burdened by GCSE developments) would not deliver the required examination. This left Mrs Peterson deeply frustrated and very angry, in a position of having to drop the valued science component and to revert to the Home Economics syllabus and examination.

In 1984, eighteen pupils had opted for this course and at the time of observation, the class had been divided into an 'O' level and a CSE group of six and twelve pupils respectively. Most of the 'O' level group had it seems chosen the option *because* of its science component. It promised a way into a subject which they had found difficult *and* it provided them with an academic qualification which would be useful whatever their future careers. Most of the pupils interviewed in the CSE group, however, seemed to have chosen the option because they were 'forced to' by the organization of the option system. As one girl stated, 'we couldn't do anything else and do the secretarial course'. Most thoroughly enjoyed Mrs Peterson's teaching but found the science component immensely difficult (a view endorsed by Mrs Peterson) and had been glad to see it dropped. They favoured the move back to Home Economics and most would have preferred to have done this course which they saw as being 'more practical' and useful in making them 'a better wife' or 'a better cook'. Others however, felt that a CSE would give them a chance to go on to the tech. college, to do hotel management or 'secretarial work'.

The absence of an exam and the reversion to Home Economics status, had ensured that the option could not attract pupils from 'across the ability range'. Only one pupil had subsequently opted for the course which was dropped, resigning Mrs Peterson to finding space for her aspirations for science-based Home Economics through developments in the GCSE syllabus. It was also pointed out by Mrs Peterson that her endeavours to establish a mixed-sex group in the Science in the Home course by attracting boys from Barton, the neighbouring single-sex school, had been thwarted at the inception of TVEI by the then Headteacher who, in this teacher's view had been

> very worried both about boys being in the school and the effect they would have on girls, and the lack of facilities (toilets) to provide for them.

Although, as Mrs Peterson went on to stress, the present Headteacher offered a much more enlightened attitude towards TVEI, she also felt that senior management at Barton (also with a new Headteacher) were now even more orientated towards producing examination success in high-status curriculum areas, than was previously the case.

Among three options which we have looked at, then, only the Food Studies course at Rainford 'lived on' in the curriculum. We want to suggest that it did so not because the pupils shared Mrs Bates' liberal philosophy but because it met their demands both for skills which were perceived to be occupationally related and provided a route to a career through the links with the tech. college. These were achieved within a classroom working context which was reported to be both satisfactory and sensitive to their educational needs and abilities.

The course began in 1984 with some sixteen pupils who were, in the teachers perspective, of 'average to low' ability. At the beginning, the course attracted more boys than girls. The pupils clearly felt that they could derive from the course skills which would be occupationally useful. Some of the boys wanted to be chefs, one or two already had brothers or fathers 'working on the boats'. Others saw themselves taking up a trade in the hotel or catering industry. Only one of the (seven) boys interviewed had no clear conception of what he would do on leaving school. He saw the course offering the skills 'to help his wife so she doesn't have to do all the cooking' or 'if you stay single'. In the perspective of these boys the curriculum of Food Studies was viewed quite instrumentally. It was a content for boys leading towards men's work. They were equally eager to differentiate the content of this new option from the Home Economics courses which they saw as essentially for girls and as having 'more to do with the home' and the kitchen. Mrs Bates acknowledged that the boys saw the course in much more instrumental terms than herself:

> They do see it as a route to a job ... because there *is* this link with the Tech., and if the Tech. knows them and finds them ... well ... unless they blot their copy book they don't have to go through the process of selection at 16, but they are offered a place on the course there. So that in a sense is a career choice, isn't it? So that's why we've got the large number of boys in particular who are interested ... .

On the girls' part, two of those interviewed also saw the course as a way into a job. They had, for example, mothers or sisters already working in 'hospital catering'. Others seemed to be hedging their bets about their future careers. 'Learning about cooking' would be useful to them whether they ended up working in the home or elsewhere. These pupils, like Mrs Bates, were realistically considering that their career might be confined to the home and the task of servicing and caring for husbands or family (see Millman 1985). As Mrs Bates put it:

> For these girls ... this (the F.S. Course) will always be useful ... you know they'll always have to look after somebody and there's a lot of them *do* have to look after homes and children ... There's very much of this on this estate. Their actual horizons are very limited ...

The vocational utility of this course had by 1985 begun to attract pupils from across the ability range. But as the above comments suggest, although the option was now achieving an ability mix it had done little to challenge pupils gender expectation or career aspirations (see Wallace 1986, Millman 1985). The growing interest in the subject was not shared equally by boys and girls and not untypically (cf. Millman 1985) the option had become increasingly popular as a choice for the boys:

> It's quite funny really. I mean in this subject there is sex stereotyping ... but then in this sort of area I suppose boys do see relevant opportunities with the boats and that ...
> (Mrs Bates)

Ironically it cannot be over-stressed that Mrs Bates was acutely aware of the problem of sexism in the school curriculum and had fought hard to confront pupil stereotypes and expectations both by ensuring that Home Economics was compulsory for all pupils in the lower-school curriculum and by directly confronting pupil expectations and remaining sensitive to interaction patterns in her own lessons. However, there was in her view only so much she alone could do. Her view that the 'skills' of the option were not gender specific might be seen to be justified by the 1985 Food Studies intake, where the sixteen (the maximum she could take) pupils divided evenly between boys and girls. They were however all drawn from the school's 'top-ability range'. In contrast, her 1984 Home Economics course drew sixteen girls and four boys, mostly from the low-ability range. The 'success' of Food Studies has created its own tensions for Mrs Bates who would strongly prefer to retain a profile type assessment, whereas its clientele are now well within the conventionally examinable range. As a piece of NVEI it has certainly served to sieve out the least able and employable from those who see it either as a job route or at worst, useful life preparation. Somewhat typically, in response to Mrs Bates' request to her new intake to write down the reason for their choice of Food Studies, one of the boys says:

> I chose Food Studies because it has a good preparation for tech. college and there is a lot of jobs for chefs. If I choose to follow another job it would help in life if I live alone, or just feel hungry. I gives me the peace of mind to know I can look after myself without starving. (Martin)

Discussion

TVEI and the many cases of NVEI which undoubtedly exist have brought about a change in the content and in some cases the organization of the curriculum for the 14–18 age sector but it has left largely untouched and undebated the broader *context* of schooling into which this innovation is introduced. Like Raffe (1985) we have argued (Evans and Davies 1986a, 1986b) that the context of educational practice is to a large extent constituted by the structure of selection and differientation within the educational system and by its relation to differentiation within the labour market and within society as a whole. This structure is sustained not only by the selective grouping and curriculum practices and policies of teachers, but also by the choices, movements and decisions of parents outside them. Although TVEI may sometimes seem like a generous, even liberal (and liberating) intrusion into the state secondary, other Government policies over recent years have often seemed bent on damaging if not slowly dismantling on already fragile Comprehensive system (see Simon 1985, Davis 1986). The 1980 Education Act for example, issued parents the right to send their children to a school other than their local one, provided that the chosen school had enough space capacity to take the child.

By extending the scope of parental choice and, largely through the publication of an examination league table, exacerbating the conditions of competition between schools, 'popular' schools have tended to become middle-class enclaves often at the expense of working-class schools which are forced to struggle for their resources, even their future survival. The schools in this study functioned in areas in which there were significant amounts of transfer from 'working-class' to middle-class areas and schools (Mar Molinero 1986). In these conditions, as spare capacity appears in middle-class schools a process of creaming develops which further widens the social and academic differences that exist between schools. Unsurprisingly, falling rolls have a more serious effect on those schools that are situated in working-class areas. Framed thus by the principles of parental choice joined the exigency of falling rolls, teachers like those in the schools described above are confronted by the often increasing vagaries and inequalities of their pupil intakes and the capacities of their parents to offer compensatory support in the form of money or care to allay the effects of Government underfunding.

It is into this context, these conditions of schooling, of intensified competition and limited resources that NVEI (and TVEI) are introduced. As we have stressed, we should not then be surprised to find teachers, particularly those at the sharp end of parental demands and expectations, rather unwilling to risk innovations which might either impair the efficient identification of their scarce pupil talent, or hamper the progress of 'able' children into conventional, publicly acceptable high-status curriculum areas (Evans and Davies 1986a and 1986b). Senior management were acutely aware that academic standards are the prime motivation of many parents when choosing a school and there is ample evidence to suggest that doing well in exams bears some connection with social background. Consequently transfer between these schools ensured the persistence of differences in academic results. This in turn makes schools in working-class areas even less attractive to academically minded parents and children.

The 'code' of the school and its teachers and the kind of pressures that the parents exert (directly or indirectly through the supply of pupils and parents evenings, etc.) on the attitudes of senior teachers, are of some considerable importance. But it is the pupils, as conveyors of parental codes who directly confront classroom teachers and provide a frame in which 'new' curriculum and teaching have to be negotiated not determined. Pupils are representatives of the local society, of their families and of their social class and its habitus and interests. They carry to the school and the individual teacher their communities' expectations, their prejudices, class expectations and aspirations. Teachers, as the above analyses has suggested may be more or less sensitive to these aspirations, for example, to working-class codes.

Like Dale (1985) we would want to argue that understanding other sponsored (unsponsored and now meagrely sponsored) schemes will mean examining how and how far their 'origins, aims and structure and ideologies affect and are reflected by the existing patterns of educational practice in the local authorities and school involved in the scheme' (p. 30).

As we have argued elsewhere, 'It is this 'accommodation' which may be the means by which schools reproduce their local societies, their socio-economic divisions, by fitting pupils to curriculum slots which suit their imagined vocational destinations and their economic futures'. (Evans and Davies 1986a). In the schools described here, NVEI teachers had gladly acclaimed TVEI and the opportunities it gave them to realize latent aspirations or indeed in their view pursue more worthy educational goals. But despite some of its best endeavours and the creation of a learning context which could at least on the surface look very different to that usually found in academic classrooms, they were ultimately forced by the actions of pupils and their consumption or otherwise of new options, to engage in socially and economically *re-productive* activities.

TVEI (and NVEI) does focus attention on curriculum provision for the 14–18 age range, and it may also have begun to raise questions about who, in terms of ability and gender, get what subject diet, where, when and how. But meeting the criteria of TVEI in ensuring that boys and girls, whatever their measured or peceived abilities, get access to the full range of curriculum, vocational or non-vocational, will also mean considering how the supply of pupils is arrived at and then examining how their identities are variously channelled, constructed and constrained in the earlier years of schooling. It is quite unlikely that the attitudes and expectations of children post thirteen can be 'influenced' if they have not first been examined earlier *and* in relation to our own attitudes and practices as teachers or policy makers of one sort or another.

Most of us have been brought up through an educational system which many would accept has functioned primarily and efficiently, to lift and to separate the undifferentiated 'chaff' from the gradeable 'wheat' and to dampen and disperse the seeds of despair. So often in our Secondary practice, being 'academic' has meant 'intellectually bright', being 'practical' has meant 'intellectually less able'. Within these conditions of thought and their associated practices, TVEI or NVEI are likely to do little to challenge existing curriculum hierarchies or extant conceptions of ability and educability. More damagingly still it may viciously compound or at least further promote a divided curriculum structure post-14 (see Holt and Reid 1986). It may also help us to avoid the more difficult and challenging business of considering what kind of *educational* practice, in form and content, is capable of reaching and teaching not some but *all* our children.

References and bibliography

Bates, I. *et al.* (ed.) (1984). *Schooling for the Dole?* London, Macmillan.

Bernstein, B. (1971). On the classification and framing of educational knowledge, in MFD Young (ed.) 1971. *Knowledge and Control*. London, Collier Macmillan, pp. 47–69.

Bernstein, B. (1977). Aspects of the relations between education and production. In *Class, Codes and Control*, vol. 3 (2nd edn), London, Routledge & Kegan Paul.

Bolton, E. (1985). TVEI; very good and very bad, in *The Times Educational Supplement*, 15.11.85, p.15.

Clarke, J. and Willis, P. (1984). Introduction, in Bates et al. (ed.) 1984. *Op. cit.*

Cohen, P. (1984). Against the new vocationalism, in Bates I. et al. (1984) pp.104–170.

Dale, R. (1985). The background and inception of the Technical and Vocational Education Initiative, in Dale, R. (ed.) 1985. *Education, Training and Employment*. Oxford, Pergamon, pp.41–57.

Dale, R. (1986). Examining the gift horse's teeth: an analysis of TVEI, in Barton, L. and Walker, S. (eds). *Youth, Unemployment and Schooling*. Milton Keynes, Open University Press, pp.29–46.

Davies, B. (1986). Halting progress: comments on recent British educational policy and practice. *Journal of Educational Policy*, 1, 4, 349–59.

DES/Dept. of Employment (1986). *Working Together, Education and Training*. London, Her Majesty' Stationery Office.

Evans, J. and Davies, B. (1986a). Fixing the mix in vocational initiatives. Paper presented to the International Sociology of Education Conference, Westhill, Birmingham, January 1986.

Evans, J. and Davies, B. (1986b). The rise and fall of vocational education. Paper presented to the conference Education and Training, 14–18. St Hilda's College, Oxford, September 1986.

Holt, M. and Reid, W.A. (1986). Instrumentalism and education: 14–18 rhetoric and the 11–16 curriculum. Paper presented to the conference Education and Training, 14–18. St Hilda's College Oxford, September, 1986.

Jamieson, I. (1985). Corporate hegemony and pedagogic liberation: the schools–industry movement in England and Wales, in Dale, R. (ed.) *Education Training and Employment*. Oxford, Pergamon, pp.23–41.

Manpower Services Commission (1983). *TVEI, Technical and Vocational Education Initiative, Operating Manual*. Manpower Services Commission.

Manpower Services Commission (1986). Extension of the Technical and Vocational Education Initiative (TVEI). Proposals for programmes to start in 1987 — Guidance for Educational Authorities. The Manpower Services Commission.

Mar Molinero, C. (1986). Statistical Information and School Reorganisations. Department of Accounting and Management Science, University of Southampton.

Millman, V. (1985). The New Vocationalism in Secondary Schools: its influence on girls, in Whyte, J. *et al.* (eds). *Girl Friendly Schooling*. London, Methuen, pp.45–71.

Pickard, J. (1985). The Technical and Vocational Education Initiative, in *The Times Educational Supplement*, 3.5.85, p. 23.

Pring, R. (1985). In defence of TVEI, in *Forum* 1985, pp.14–17.

Raffe, D. (1985). The content and context of educational reform, in Raggat, P. and Werner, G.F. (eds). *Curriculum and Assessment*. Oxford, Pergamon, pp.67–75.

Simon, B. (1985). *Does Education Matter?* London, Lawrence & Wishart.

Wallace, C. (1986). From girls and boys to women and men: the social reproduction of gender roles in the transition from school to (un)employment, in Walker, S. and Barton, L. (eds). *Youth, Unemployment and Schooling*. Milton Keynes, The Open University Press, pp.92–118.

Wallace, R.G. (1984). From concept to reality, in *TVEI Insight* No. 1, September 1984, pp.3–5.

Rob Fiddy and Ian Stronach

6

Fables and Futures

Cases in the Management of Innovation

It is the lot of programme evaluators to forever tell the story of the Three Little Pigs and sort stick from brick, flimsy from substance. It is also their lot to see the audience drift away in disbelief and disgust at tales of straw and wolves, in search of another fairy-tale. By the time the story unfolds to that solid house, on whose foundations we may build futures — even educational futures — no one is listening. The evaluator delivers a last report to an empty room.

For this reason we have decided to cheat in this chapter. If we are to be formative in the future, we must be summative now. We must gather what data we have (recognizing that straw and sticks, as well as bricks, are our materials too), assemble what issues we find, and present them now as an anticipation of TVEI. We must try to be the historians of the future.(1) What will be the status of such an account? It will not be case study, nor history; it may not even be true (although we use real data). But it will represent important possibilities within TVEI — representing them because people may want to use them to make TVEI more than it is now, or to go beyond our present understanding of the programme. If our account creates that kind of effect, then it will be educational, as a way of learning and as a forum for debate, rather than true. (Those who object that we cannot be educated by that which is not true must return to the Three Little Pigs, and consider the educational potential of analogy.)

Our intention in this chapter, then, is to invent two contrasting 'cases' of TVEI practice. The cases represent tendencies in TVEI. The data which inform these accounts are real, but are not always drawn from the same LEA. Our cases of Eastshire and Westshire are inventions, not anonymizations. The data on which this account is based derive from the local evaluation of three TVEI projects, from workshops and informal discussions within the TVEI network and from the authors' editorship of the *TVEI Working Papers* series.(2) The data reveal different styles of management of innovation, and different assumptions about values and outcomes. We adopt this approach so that we can anticipate the claims that politicians and administrators are already making, or are going to make about TVEI and its extension. (This is not so unconventional a step in the TVEI debate. The five-year pilot was declared a 'success' in its first year, and judgement on it has consistently run ahead of evidence since 1984.) These claims concern a wide variety of areas — from pedagogy to the politics of education and the management of innovation. A critical foreshadowing of the issues they raise is vital: TVEI and its offshoots — CPVE and the proposed City Technology Colleges — are attempting to shift radically the definition and practice of secondary education in the UK. Beyond that, it is also becoming clear that while we still may have to guess some of the features of the new 'educational settlement'(3), we no longer have to guess at its delivery system. In short, we cannot wait until the roof is finished before we begin to inspect the foundations.

TVEI in Westshire LEA

'Conceived in haste and born of Caesarian section', was how an LEA officer described the advent of TVEI in his county. At the time of its birth — following a short gestation period of December 1983 through to September 1984 — much alarm was expressed about the speed of events, a speed unknown in previous educational innovations with which this county had been involved. On top of this concern was the unknown effect of 'the new masters', the Manpower Services Commission. Some looked to FE to provide what hints they could based on their previous experience of the Commission through YOP and YTS. But the current situation was somewhat different. From a fiscal point of view, categorical funding had emerged from the murk of central government, and new buzz words such as 'delivery' and 'targets' were in vogue. Industrial action by the teachers had not helped to smooth the path of the innovation, nor did it do anything to relieve the anxiety of teachers who feared that the whole profession might soon be working for the D of E or the MSC. In fact TVEI entered the world of Westshire LEA, as it did for all Round Two TVEI LEAs, at a time when teachers as a whole were probably more politically aware than ever before.

There is a tendency in heavily funded innovations that take-up will be based on a desire for extra resources rather than a perceived need for change. Back in the early days of TVEI tales were told of the bait — around £400,000 per annum — being the prime motive behind Westshire's involvement. The speed of events resulted in, as one headteacher put it, 'concertina planning'. LEA officers and headteachers of Westshire jointly decided that TVEI would best be conducted under a consortium approach and, moreover, that the consortium of five schools should be placed in a geographically confined area. Various reasons were given, including political expediency, and the fact that unemployment was high. Many teachers thought, however, that the selection of venue was as much to do with it having been identified as 'an area of educational deprivation'.

An LEA official even introduced a notion of financial quarantine:

> It really needed to be a compact area of schools. Fairly isolated from all the other schools. That would actually be very suitable for the introduction of all that extra money. And I suppose that there was an element of saying, 'Well, it's all or none of you, you know.'

The decision to submit a proposal to the MSC was made in early November 1983 and the proposal deadline was a mere five weeks later. The official continued:

> That's quite a lot going on in just over a month. Now, how can you actually consult with everybody else in that period? It's actually very difficult as you can see, I mean, that's the way it had to be handled...the prevailing economic view is that competition produces the most efficient system in anything. And the problem with the public sector is that there really isn't competition, is there? So do you have to actually, um, design a system that creates competition for LEAs based upon an economic theory that they will become more efficient and effective if you stimulate competition between them? Based on an economic theory? And do you actually put the money through MSC on purpose to stimulate the DES? Do you actually create rival firms as it were within the public sector to get them to get their fingers out? I mean, that's how I understand it. You can be seen to create rival firms within the school as well because the LEAs will be adopting the same process down into their schools. And if you're not careful Heads will be doing the same thing to Heads of Department which will be fatal. Some......,um, it's been very difficult to know when creative tension stops and unbearable breakdown tension comes.

Thus Westshire, pressured by the speed and novelty of the development, settled for a consortium model. The major principle behind the location of the project was needs-based (rather than the ability-based criteria of Eastshire); it rested on a compensatory notion. Consultation was limited.

The LEA also retained a scepticism about the planning context of TVEI at a national level. This was reflected in their concern for the metaphors of TVEI. Indeed, throughout TVEI, Westshire officials continued to re-define the metaphors of the enterprise:

> I am actually very interested in the MSC's obsession with the word 'delivery'....'delivery' really, I think, stems from its root 'to rescue', to save people from something. And yet I suspect that they really tend to use it meaning 'a successful outcome'....and you actually only deliver a baby at birth if in fact the mother and the baby can't do it for themselves....you really only talk about the delivery when nurses are there and otherwise it seems to be a natural birth. I suppose that's their deduction, that we need to be

> helped. To speed up. It doesn't happen quickly enough. But you're going to do a lot of damage with forceps....!

The County Co-ordinator of Westshire was appointed as a specialist in computer studies, an expertise with the 'new technologies' being seen as crucial to progress within the project. He also had to liaise between the MSC, the LEA and the headteachers of the five consortium schools, some of whom felt they'd had TVEI thrust upon them. Nearly one year into the project, evaluation field notes record a chance meeting with the co-ordinator:

> 'I'm on a tightrope,' says Tom Jones, the Westshire TVEI Co-ordinator. 'The MSC have a long pole and are pushing from one side, the LEA have another and push from the other side....when I go into meetings I think, "Now, who am I batting for today?" '

The Co-ordinator felt himself located in a 'Bermuda Triangle' between MSC, LEA and the schools. Little wonder that he seemed to employ a resource-led approach to the schools. The field note continued:

> It is the role of the Co-ordinator to be pig in the middle, relationships are everything. Tom is neither fish nor fowl, not really accepted by the LEA hierarchy — not really seen as legitimate by the staff but seen as very kickable by Heads. Is this his true role — scapegoat for both sides? No wonder he always arrives bearing gifts — 'Ah, Tom, I want to talk to you....' 'O.K. but first let me give you this dictaphone/keyboard/tricky little plastic gizmo'.

The headteacher of one of the consortium schools gave his impression of the TVEI Co-ordinator.

> He's not been a curriculum change agent himself. He's not, I think, influenced change in management styles in any way whatsoever. Erm, I think I thought that his particular skills in curriculum innovation, the High Tech. area, could have been used more. But I think that the way the job seems to have been directed from MSC's point of view precluded that from happening. Maybe the job required more of the managerial type skill than curriculum expertise and administrative skills.

Thus TVEI in Westshire was seen as an uncertain thing. In a pattern familiar to this style of innovation in the UK(4), the LEA alternated between public expressions of solidarity and private concern, while the project Co-ordinator groped for a role and the schools kept much of their autonomy. In an equally familiar way, LEA claims moved straight from the stage of administrative 'teething problems' to the stage of 'consolidation', leaving their audience feeling that the development stage had been missed out.

The initial development strategy of TVEI in Westshire was called 'black box' by some of those involved in its management. Each level of the hierarchy passed down a prescription to the next — again a typical pattern and almost an inevitable one in cases of 'concertina planning'. The TVEI parcel came to rest with the school Directors and they began to feature as the real change agents in the project.

At first the aspirations of the school Directors carried them outside the walls of their particular educational institutions. It began to look as if they had gained the space to define their role for themselves and were doing so according to their own particular chosen career route. Those of the TVEI Directors who saw their future in school, perhaps the next stage being a deputy headship, tended to focus their energies on developing TVEI within one particular institution in the consortium. Those who saw their future as advisers, on the other hand, began to direct their energies at a consortium level. Neither the LEA, nor the school heads played a very active role in this second stage of project development. This was a period referred to by one of those headteachers as 'the time of the five barons', each with their own fief in their schools. The TVEI Co-ordinator was allowed to go his own way and the TVEI Directors in various schools began to make their own plans according to their own aspirations.

Toward the end of the first year one of the heads began to feel that the project was getting out of hand, in terms of the consortium arrangements in particular. Encouraged by an evaluation exercise in his school he decided to put pressure on the other headteachers with a view to revitalizing their Management Group, a team consisting of the heads of all the consortium schools, the TVEI Co-ordinator and the Deputy Chief Education Officer. The Group had been in existence since the beginning of the project, but had not met on a regular basis up until this time. The group began to meet monthly and one of their first acts was to 'pull in the reins' of the TVEI school Directors.

The Management Group felt that the organizational arrangements for the consortium were in danger of breaking down. Schools were not 'pairing' as had been planned. Equipment was not being shared as had been hoped. Moreover, more radical proposals such as the introduction of a modular approach to the curriculum were being aired by the TVEI school Directors. The Management Group tried to redress its balance by taking over the decision-making role for the consortium. Up to this point decisions had been undertaken largely by TVEI school Directors and the TVEI County Co-ordinator. From this point on, TVEI school Directors were to have an almost exclusively in-school role and the County Co-ordinator was to become a 'liaison person'. This suited those TVEI school Directors who saw their future as deputy heads, but those who felt that their future lay outside the school were less than enthusiastic. Some strongly felt that their talents and enthusiasm had been curtailed, particularly when they considered that the most stressful period of the project might be coming to an end. The headteacher of St Luke's High School looked back at that time:

> The Management Group had ceased to function or it didn't start functioning until late. I mean really, if we're honest, didn't start functioning did it, until the County LEA came back into it? Up to that point, er, I think it was an

> unmanageable group...it was a non-group. There were too many forces pulling in conflict for anything creative to come out of that conflict. One puts so much time and energy getting the actual, um, grant from MSC, there wasn't time and energy of people to, um, put the sort of consortium issue to the forefront because you've got to come back into your own school.

By 'pulling in the reins' the Project Management Group forced the school Directors to look to their own institutions. There was some bitterness expressed by individuals in terms of the Management Group having re-defined their roles for them, just when some of them felt that they were beginning to 'get somewhere'.

The school Director of St Mark's began applying for jobs in other counties, 'But they won't let me go,' he said, 'Who would do what I do here?' Over at St Jude's another evaluation field-note captured a different attitude from the school Director:

> ....the Directors carry on as before, they continue to ignore the restraints, according to John. But they have no list of priorities — no meetings arranged. The Directors are left to themselves. The Advisors are due in St. Jude's. John says the Head is extremely worried — he wants a 'snow job'. John says he wants the Advisors to 'see the reality....they will be disappointed.' John seems happy to jog along waiting to be told what to do — not apparently worried by the lack of direction for the project — maybe he never saw it as his problem.

Westshire's consortium project was in danger of becoming a resource-led initiative in five neighbouring, but not always neighbourly, schools. The apparent lack of communication and subsequent disorganization evident within TVEI in Westshire, particularly within the first eighteen months of the project, tended to divert attention away from what was actually happening in the classroom. That distraction included the evaluation. The formative intent of the evaluation produced a follow-my-leader stage in the study, wherein the management preoccupations of the project became the sole focus.

But what of the classrooms? Were the tensions reflected here? At this stage the data on Westshire grew more surprising. Early on, there had been a congruence between the data gathered at different levels of the project. There seemed to be a general agreement that all was not well, and only the usual disagreements about whose responsibility that was. Pupils and teachers were unimpressed. A girl at St. Mark's remarked:

> ....this is only a trial this TVEI thing. I mean, they said to us we were guinea pigs! Testing it out...one of the teachers in school in TVEI said, 'We're all guinea pigs in this.' I said, 'Yeah, well I don't see why our education has to suffer. We're getting messed around up here.' And he sort of said, 'Well, you know, we're, sort of, being trialed on as well. We're guinea pigs as well.' I put it back to him that he already had a job. He was paid and everything. He didn't have a lot to say to that.

Her comments were echoed by a member of staff:

> This first year should be seen as a trial period — we should have the freedom to experiment, but there are kids involved. We can turn round and say, 'O.K., we've got it wrong — start again,' but the kids are the ones who really suffer.

The 'freedom to experiment' was a recurring notion among TVEI staff. At that stage the speed of events and the lack of consortium support was pressuring them to take 'blind' risks at a level that they were unused to. They wanted to take the opportunity to 'experiment', but were concerned about possible negative side effects on their pupils.

Westshire's TVEI development had been characterized by a rough sequence of stages. Insider descriptions looked something like this:

1 *Concertina planning* — tight schedules, poor consultation and inexperience in large-scale curriculum development lead to *ad hoc* structures and off-the-shelf solutions.
2 *Filling the black boxes* — school Directors and teachers are left to make sense of the initial proposal; project lacks power — high levels of anxiety in the project, low levels of priority in the project schools in the LEA.
3 *The bid for a 'school within a project' formula* — school Directors try to build a project dimension as opposed to a school dimension (consortium activities, modular development, etc.) but the attempt founders; LEA opts for 'consolidation'.
4 *Piecemeal development* — project retreats to a 'project within a school' formula, each Director concentrating on in-school development; more support from heads — LEA dimension recedes.

These stages were regarded as pathological by those most closely involved with the project (school Directors), but as a sensible accommodation to other priorities by Heads. The formula seemed to point to minimal change,(5) and to minimal impact on the pupils and classroom teachers.

Ironically, as the project went on, the lack of support and the management dilemmas did seem to be creating space for experimentation within the curriculum. The school Director of St Mark's produced a revealing comment early on in the initiative:

> ...there were a lot of children who were underachieving...there had to be different ways of looking at education within our school. As a form teacher I had seen a lot of students go out of school without the academic qualifications they could have gained...We perpetuate a system. TVEI was a chance to stand still and analyse what we were doing...

The evaluator asked him about the apparent paradox contained in the notion of the speed of TVEI actually producing the opportunity to 'stand still and analyse what we were doing'. He went on to explain that it was the lack of direction, the lack of plan in the consortium arrangements which had almost forced him to look at practice within his own institution. This had helped him to recognize gaps and to begin to facilitate changes. The energy that was consequently redirected back into the school did not go unnoticed by members of staff. One commented later:

> It's the most exciting two years I've had in teaching, probably ever. Things have gone on very fast...What I'm trying to say is TVEI initiated a whole series of options and changes for me. And once it had started I was able to pick up these options and develop them....We are in a period of critical change and I'm talking about fundamental change, not top surface change. And it's happening very quickly and it is part of a teacher's job to recognize those changes and cope with them. Manage them. And if that means that you have to scrap and rethink and work from bottom up, then that's what it involves... people know something is wrong. They are part of a structure. They can't see how to get an overview of that, to say 'how do I shape it?' One of the key things to recommend TVEI is that it will give you the opportunity to say, you don't have to do what you were doing before. You can do other things, well bloody well go ahead and do it. Um, well, there we go.'

Pupils were aware of a change as well:

Girl 1:	In normal subjects you just get pampered don't you? In TVEI, in the practical bits especially, you're allowed to get on with it. You're responsible. It's much better. You're given more responsibility.
Int:	How does this freedom that you get in TVEI make you feel in other lessons?
Boy 2:	Sometimes it makes other lessons easy. Easy but boring.
Int:	So you find TVEI hard work? (General agreement)
Boy 2:	Sometimes if you say to teachers, like, we do this differently in TVEI. Or if you say this isn't as good as TVEI, they get annoyed. Some teachers say they're not quite sure about TVEI. Some of them are not aware of what goes on in TVEI
Int:	Do you find that odd?
Boy 2:	Yes
Boy 3:	Like our physics teacher, she thinks it's a really bad idea.
Int:	Do you feel different from your friends who're not doing TVEI because of that?
Boy 3:	Not different, it's just a lot better. You still get into trouble and that sort of thing, but a teacher in TVEI, when they tell you off, what they'll do is stop you working. Like if you're doing a practical they'll stop you doing it. But in other lessons where you're just have instructions to follow and things like that, if you mess around then they send you down the administrative corridor. And kids just treat that as a laugh.
Boy 1:	They just expect you to do it properly in TVEI and you sort of do it properly.
Int:	So the reverse of that is that you keep on telling kids off they're going to mess around?
Boy 3:	If they treat you right you work right. We get stopped doing practicals as a punishment. We get stopped doing work. If you mess around in other lessons then you get sent down the administration

> corridor and you're made to work. The punishment in other lessons is to do work. The punishment in TVEI is not to do work.

'Well,' wrote the evaluator in a private memo, 'this is a change, this is novel. This is a paradox, even. The County Co-Ordinator is virtually invisible, the consortium structure is shaky to say the least, a good proportion of the school Directors feel that they have generally been misled and abused — particularly this school Director — and yet here are glowing reports from elements of both staff and pupils.' What seemed most significant in these 'glowing reports' was the shared notion that TVEI was visible. Staff, even non-TVEI staff, were aware of a difference in approach and, most importantly, a measure of opportunity within the initiative. The project seemed to have gained space, not only to allow teachers and pupils to experiment, but also to enable them to be creative within the curriculum of the school. The project did seem to be beginning to afford participants a creative opportunity, and the opportunity seemed to have emerged from the evident chaos that the mode of adoption of the project in Westshire had spawned.

TVEI in Westshire had always felt different from TVEI in the other LEAs to which the evaluation had access. At first the difference was pathological — everyone agreed that Westshire's TVEI was 'doing badly' — lack of plan, lack of direction, poor communication, general bad feeling. Then the data began to suggest that TVEI in Westshire had somehow prospered. There seemed more distinct evidence of creativity at a school and classroom level than in Eastshire; across the curriculum initiatives began to appear in practice before they appeared on paper (unlike Eastshire). Actual rather than rhetorical instances of negotiated pedagogy and curricula were discovered. 'With TVEI you feel that you are learning it together,' said one teacher. Resistance came not from the teachers and pupils, but from the inspecting Advisor: 'Do you think it's right to encourage children to go up and speak to strangers in the street?' Pupils and class teachers were more certain of the difference than management figures. It began to seem to the evaluation that TVEI in Westshire had prospered despite its manifest failures in management. Chaos had produced holes in the fabric of project management. Creativity out of chaos?

TVEI in Eastshire LEA

Imagine. It is 1995 and the CEO of Eastshire is speaking at a conference of Headteachers:

> ... and if you ask me what TVEI gave birth to, I will tell you. It gave birth to itself. At the time, we counted babies and claimed multiple births up and down the County — student-centred learning, profiling, negotiation, active pedagogies, hi-tech this and hi-tech that ... But it turned out that we mistook

> birth for adoption. When we came to take stock, we found that our novelties were largely imported from previous initiatives. Pedagogies courtesy of the FEU, hi-tech courses from the exam boards (although we gave as good as we got here), profiles from the Profiling Network of the early 1980s or from CGLI ... No, we did not give birth to very much that was really new if you consider the millions of pounds that we collectively invested. But we certainly fed and spread these initiatives. That was new. And that is what I mean by claiming that TVEI gave birth to itself. TVEI created a way of managing curriculum change. It linked the whimsical innovation of the '60s and '70s to the categorical change of the late '80s. And if I can labour my metaphor for a last time, it made us realize — and I mean all of us in this education business — teachers, administrators, co-ordinators and advisors — that we were not the mothers of invention but the midwives of change. That was the lesson of TVEI, and it changed the face of education and training in our secondary schools. It linked top and bottom, centre and periphery — not directly, not manipulatively — but in partnership. It linked teacher and student, Head and staff, LEA and schools. By 1990 Bid, Negotiate, and Contract had become the ABC of educational management at all levels and in almost all situations. For once it worked, and not before time ... we were in the business of curriculum change at last.

The evaluation had heard the Watershed theory before. There was even the unusual feeling of having contributed to it. At first Eastshire had been unwilling to concede the point that curricular invention had not been very significant. Now, Eastshire's 2-line retrospective of TVEI and TVEI extension read:

> TVEI re-invented the wheel in curriculum change
> but invented the steering wheel of management change

It was a good argument, and the evaluator felt that there was some truth in it. But it left him uneasy. Perhaps the triumph of process over product had been too complete. The evaluation imagined the old Schools Council as the engine of educational innovation. Had we swopped the engine for a steering wheel? The evaluator recalled a hot day in July 1986 when he had first heard the watershed theory.

It had been a pleasure and a challenge to interview the Eastshire officials who ran TVEI. They were skilful, articulate and decisive. When one official referred to appointing a 'chap', the other instantly added, 'or a lady'. And when one of them mentioned over-hasty resourcing at the beginning of the project, the other immediately pointed to the necessary morale booster in the first few months — 'it was the only evidence of TVEI being in the school. Because it's no good having additional staffing when you don't actually see it. It doesn't come through the door in a box.' The answers came easily and quickly. They supported each other like jugglers taking turns with the clubs.

Int: How do you know that negotiation, or pupil-centred this and that, actually works?

Official 1:	Where are the outcomes in education anyway?
Official 2:	The outcomes, the outcomes. I suppose one would have to say the outcomes are in the pupils that are about to leave the 14–16 stage. The words that keep cropping up from people are 'self-confidence', greater awareness of their own ability and what they want to do with that ability. They are able to see much more — the linkages between the various subjects in the school, much more inquiry, much less prepared to accept things without questioning, greater analytical ability ...
Int:	If they've gained all of these things then why is there a problem recruiting to Years 3 and 4?
Official 2:	One of the problems is that local employers see the youngsters as far more attractive because of these various abilities and are preferring them to non-TVEI.

'Are they managing the project as well as this interview?,' the evaluator wondered. The answer seemed to be 'yes'. A coherent and original picture emerged from the interview. Before all else, TVEI was seen as a management tool. For the first time (the phrase recurs) they had a managerial purchase on the curriculum and could demonstrate to the government that education could deliver the goods — 'our last, our golden opportunity, our golden chance to show them what resources are needed to get the changes that we are talking about'.

An evaluation statement about the management model was negotiated with Eastshire at the time. The LEA made three claims and articulated a model for future curriculum management:

1. TVEI is seen as a success in Eastshire. A most important aspect of that success is that TVEI has helped to pioneer a new pattern of curriculum management at LEA level (other LEA initiatives are also involved). Potentially, that new model is a watershed in educational development.
2. The old patterns of development were haphazard (e.g. Schools Council), uncoordinated (within LEAs), and voluntary (the Head or teacher's enthusiasm). They also depended on a Big Bang theory of change. Every few years, a national report would trigger projects. The educational engine was one-cylinder and it fired every 5/6 years. LEAs administered rather than managed.
3. The new pattern offers — above all — coherence and continuous development. It makes change an intrinsic possibility within a system of management, rather than an external imposition. It is based on a series of partnerships (DES–LEA; MSC–LEA; LEA–school). These partnerships are made through negotiated contracts. The funding partner offers support for policy development within guidelines. A system of bidding offers incentives to LEAs, and within LEAs to schools. That system is also a rational principle for the distribution of scarce resources. As a management tool it offers — at all levels — both control and devolution. For the LEA, it gives a steering mechanism for directing curriculum policy. Previously, LEAs were more preoccupied with PTRs and contact hours — units of administration and economy rather than units of productivity. For the school, department or

> teacher, it offers a say in policy and participation in development, accompanied with practical support from Curriculum Centres.
>
> Thus TVEI is a new delivery system. It has delivered more employable, better motivated students with relevant technical and vocational skills. The model is MDDMER — manage, devolve, develop, monitor, evaluate, replicate. We should use the process of TVEI development in our LEA strategies for educational management in the future.

They were going in that direction anyway — in management and in curricular terms. They had good relationships with the TVEI Unit and saw a coming together at every level — national partnership (MSC/DES), national/local liaison, and LEA/school partnerships. The negotiated contract coupled the systems. A rational model for policy and curriculum development was emerging at last — 'not centralism but partnership'.

How did the model emerge? In Eastshire, winners got TVEI—a long list of twenty invited bids from individual schools, a short list of eight and six selected. They were schools that were already active in innovation — CGLI 365, work experience schemes, CDT courses, a record of innovation, and so on. Unlike Westshire, the principle behind selection was competitive rather than compensatory, and the extension phase maintained something of that competitive institutional bidding. The secret garden had become a market garden. Eastshire also resisted the integration of the Consortium model. The TVEI schemes were deliberately spread across the County, to aid dissemination. Unlike Westshire, a dissemination model was implicit in the original TVEI design, both in the spread of schemes, and in the twinning of TVEI and non-TVEI schools. The data also showed much less of the confusion and strife that had attended TVEI in Westshire. At school level TVEI found a readier constituency, with more powerful internal support (school Directors were senior teachers in Eastshire, rather than scale 4 as in Westshire):

> There was a group of us, really, who happened to believe in something and TVEI came along and happened to match what we believed in...

Thus Eastshire was efficiently managed. Project morale was relatively good. The management structure and development rationale was clear; the extension plans logical. Communication from LEA to project schools was effective. To a much greater extent than in Westshire, the project spoke the language of TVEI without irony. It had been a lot less fun. The evaluator reflected, to do research into Eastshire's TVEI. No one played with metaphors. While Eastshire's Co-ordinator described his role as 'facilitating the management of change', the Westshire Co-ordinator explained:

> 'You need a metaphor to get you through the week, like a lilo on the water.'

But Eastshire was dry land. The LEA's teachers had reported on TVEI fairly positively. They thought TVEI had been fairly successful. Its main benefits had been pedagogical. Pupil-centred, more practical, more problem-solving. Perhaps smaller groups had been the most important factor in this success. As a result the pupils had shown greater confidence and had taken more responsibility for their own learning.

In many ways, then, Eastshire differed from Westshire. And in one other respect: The zeal with which claims for project success were made ebbed as the evaluator worked his way down through the levels.

The higher the status, the greater the claim. Nothing remarkable in that, but it contrasted greatly with Westshire. Indeed, in Eastshire, teachers had begun to find TVEI indistinguishable from other initiatives like TRIST or GCSE. The other major contrast was the low levels of positive reaction from pupils. They found the project unremarkable, although they recognized its main features.

Boy 1: Not what I thought it would be.....
Int: Are you disappointed?
Boy 1: No, not really, It don't bother me.
Int: But didn't you know before you signed up that that'd be what it was like....?
Boy 2: Nah. We didn't know what we was doing for anything.
Int: Is there anything different about it?
Boy 1: About what?
Int: About TVEI. I mean, OK, the groups are smaller. Right? That's one thing. But is there anything else?
Boy 2: Teachers can teach more when there's a small group. I think. So I'm glad we're all in small groups. I think.
Girl 1: It's just like normal options, but you're just taking the course. Nothing special about it.
Boy 1: Except residential experience......

Their reactions stand in considerable contrast with those of Westshire LEA — and of course we have to recognize that the contrast may be a reflection of how different schools are in the two TVEI projects. Competition winners versus compensation victims. But, however we explain it, we can clearly see pupil enthusiasm in Westshire, a sense of difference and novelty, and much less of an effect in Eastshire. So, well-organized, efficient and concerned. Yet it seemed that justice did not have its reward. If chaos led to creativity, did efficiency lead to ineffectiveness?

How was this disconnection to be explained? The following table and 'Issues' section point to some of the differences between Eastshire and Westshire, and begin to develop an explanation and a more general interpretation of TVEI as an educational initiative.

Table 1 TVEI implementation in two LEAs

Eastshire	*Westshire*
Project schools volunteer	Project schools may be conscripted
Project typically technological/bureaucratic	Project critical/creative
Enhances existing good practice	Enables new practice — invokes 'brand new' options
Director support	Directors de-skilled
Co-ordinator has high profile in project structure/LEA hierarchy	Co-ordinator may be less visible/role may be ill-defined
Innovations for school — 'off the shelf'	Innovations for school created in-house
Project typified by intended and accommodated enclaves or 'pockets'	Project typified by unintended enclaves or 'bubbles' and subsequent 'ripple effects'
Central LEA involvement	Peripheral LEA involvement
Strong structure — high level of support	Loose structure — low degree of support
Stable project organization	Unstable project organization
Consistent 'top-down' delivery system	Inconsistent 'top-down' delivery system
Clear project–schools relationship	Contentious project–schools relationship
Over-claiming student outcomes/project delivery	Under-claiming student outcomes/project delivery
Weak student image of TVEI	Strong student image of TVEI
Predictable project progression	Project proceeds via 'creative spaces'
Project model has potential for dissemination	Project model has potential for development
Potential for replication high	Potential for replication low

Issues

Issue 1

Eastshire introduced a mini-categorical funding scheme within the LEA. Educational policy implementation was 'contracted' down the line from

LEA to classroom. This negotiated coupling — apparently flexible and consensual — linked national and LEA policies to classroom practice. The system was deemed successful by the LEA and by the MSC Regional Advisor. It became standard practice in the management of educational change in the Authority.

Westshire introduced a more devolved scheme, with a weaker 'co-ordinated' model of TVEI management. Privately, it was deemed a failure. There was a 'management gap'. The model (or absence of a model) led to high levels of anxiety, and the experience of TVEI at middle-management levels became surreal:

> 'I feel like a hamster in a wheel.'

The model was seen as a standard pathology of Westshire's pattern of educational management.

The evaluation assumed the virtue of the Eastshire model in planning its formative strategy. To return to the analogy with which this account began, Eastshire was the brick house, and Westshire the straw hut. The evaluator tried to help Westshire develop a more effective model of innovation management — meetings, discussions, analyses and options. But the evaluation shared a misunderstanding with the project. It linked efficient management to innovative achievement in the classroom. It assumed the rationality of the system. Had the evaluation succeeded in helping Westshire to become more effective in these terms, it might well have foreclosed on the possibilities of real development. Formative evaluators beware!

Questions

In any formative strategy, what assumptions are project and evaluation tacitly sharing? How will the evaluation critique these assumptions? On what grounds will the evaluation predict success?

Issue 2

Worse still, there were signs that Westshire's traumatic management problems were productive in development terms. The failure to create effective co-ordination, liaison, resource-sharing and consortium-based development had made key actors in the project sufficiently introverted ('sod the consortium') for creative development to take place. By making these administrative roles untenable it had inadvertently created room for development:

> You need mental space round it. And the fact that you've got an hour, you've been teaching, and you've got one hour, and you're going back teaching (...) it gets deferred because you never actually have that big space.

Westshire now had 'big space', and was roundly condemned for it by MSC — the 'management gap'.

Where does that take us? Planning for high anxiety, role confusion, irrational decision-making, and ineffective co-ordination, is an implausible recipe for success. Yet if success is measured in terms of creativity and originality — of development rather than importation — then Westshire's chaos seemed more productive than Eastshire's efficiency.

The evaluation was on the point of burying this finding (midnight, full moon) when it came across a similar conclusion in US literature on the management of innovation. D.L. Clark cites an evaluation of the Pilot State Dissemination Program. That project was surprisingly successful while fulfilling all the criteria for failure. 'Beneficial handicaps' included 'uncertain conceptual foundations, weak technology [in the social sense], unclear preferences, ambiguous authority relationships, inexperienced and/or changing program participants'. (Clark *et al.* 1980:4). Essentially, Clark argues that proposals for change are always rational, but institutions always aren't — we must differentiate between the 'logic-in-use' in educational organizations and the 'reconstructed logic supporting rational planning systems'. Goals, they conclude, are fantasies, rationality an illusion. His reasons are summed up as follows:

1. In most educational organizations most of the time, goal-based planning models are orderly facades that inhibit the management function of planning.
2. Their use is especially suspect in periods of planning for change, because during this period the organization is experiencing maximum uncertainty.
3. Their use is most damaging in planning for interorganizational arrangements for school improvement since, under these conditions, several organizations are being brought together into a macro-level organized anarchy.

Returning to the data, the evaluation found that the more creative moments in the projects tended to have something of an anarchic rather than a planned quality. The rational model of planning, so zealously pursued by the project — and by the formative evaluation strategy — began to look vulnerable. Creative moments in the project tended to have the following characteristics:

Individual: those engaged in creative work had a high personal investment in a particular situation, and relatively low administrative duties.

Critical: creative moments were attended by high levels of stress and uncertainty, often following (though not immediately) the failure of more conventional initiatives; 'exasperation' appeared to be a valuable emotion for education development.

Experimental: an element of experimental play, of trial and error, was present.

Focused: the development was highly specific and unconnected with developments elsewhere in the project.
Voluntaristic: initiatives tended to be personal digressions rather than mainstream policy; there was little connection with the prompts of management or remit.
Informed: individuals had either high levels of expertise in the area, or access to considerable support.

There were signs that the current MSC/DES wisdom in innovation (consensual, negotiated, collaborative, facilitative) was ineffectual or stifling. Indeed, the evaluation began to feel that it had hold of a paradox: the more efficiently an innovation is conducted in terms of its original remit, the more prone it will become to mildly adaptive strategies, off-the-shelf solutions, and limited change. Good management and creativity stand in a contradictory relationship.

The literature on educational innovation also looked vulnerable. Dalin (1974) deals with innovation in terms of the 'barriers' to change. In his account, innovation is a political construct (promoted, resisted, subverted, disseminated). Similarly, House (1979) sees innovation as 'the deliberate, systematic attempt to change the schools through introducing new ideas and techniques'. Both accounts are typical in that they address one possible meaning of innovation, but not another. Innovation may mean (SOED):

1 to change into something new;
2 to bring in or introduce novelties.

The second meaning is familiar to education. Innovation is portrayed as a stranger — to be introduced, to be brought into a situation. But the creative act within an innovation that defines its 'newness' is neglected, dismissed as unproblematic. Newness may be imported, but it also may be created. So the question, 'Under what conditions can educational creativity be engendered?' is both important and quite separate from the question, 'How can improvements in practice be introduced into educational institutions?' The literature seemed less interested in the first question. As the school Director said:

> I was so fed up, that I thought 'sod it, go for it, there are kids here who can get into this, there are staff here who can handle it.' So I took some hardware round and said, 'Here you are, this is how to set it up, get on with it.' Couple of weeks later I find these amazing digitized posters round the school in the name of TVEI...

Innovation theory is reticent about these creative moments. Richard Pring has argued about TVEI: Because there was no ready-made formula, teachers were being forced back to deep and significant questions about educational purposes, aims and values. (*TES*, 7.11.86). On one level, of course, the notion is absurd. We know from Eastshire and Westshire that the absence of ready-made solutions and short time-scales led to *ad hoc*, hastily adapted, off-the-shelf and superficial innovation — it would be silly to deny that that was the norm. But it might be argued, however, that it was where improvisation — in the administrative sense — was weakest, where project structures were the least efficient, that 'anarchic' possibilities began to appear, and where teachers began to respond imaginatively rather than just pragmatically.

The evaluator began to wonder: are straw houses better than brick ones when it comes to project design?

Questions

What creative potential has TVEI mobilized and realized? Is innovation being defined in developmental terms (creative/original) or in dissemination terms (new for the teacher/school/project/LEA)? What balance of these two forms should be struck? How can curriculum creativity be prompted?

Issue 3

The experiences of Eastshire and Westshire also have implications for the more general debate about TVEI. The philosophers have argued over vocationalism (skills v. disciplines, common-core v. vocational, ends v. means). So too have the social theorists (comprehensive v. differentiated schooling). Curriculum theorists have sought to tease out the curriculum and professional models implicit in TVEI rationales. But both critics and apologists of TVEI assume at least a loose coupling between the rhetoric of the innovation and its various practices. The evidence of Eastshire and Westshire suggests that this may be unwise. So loose or contradictory is the coupling, so extensive the accommodation to institutional norms, or so eccentric the creative moments, that there may be little reason to assume that the philosophies or models embedded in the rhetoric act potently on educational practice. Are our commentaries fantasies about fantasies? At the very least, we need to know a lot more about the mediations between policy and practice in categorically funded initiatives.

Eastshire and Westshire illustrate something of the dilemma. In Eastshire's case the rhetoric is believed. Purposeful and efficient attempts are made to implement it. The effect is rather small (good steering, but no engine, we might conclude). In Westshire, there are areas of considerable change but they are unpredictable in nature (no steering, but good engine). Neither case suggests the kind of 'tight coupling' assumptions that have to be made for the debates of the philosophers and theorists to be grounded in empirical realities. Neither case encourages us to try to understand TVEI at a distance.

It also follows that there is no compelling reason to take categorical funding too seriously — at least as current practice, as opposed to future possibility. As a steering mechanism, it is extremely loose and prone to all sorts of legitimate and illegitimate redefinition. It is prudent, of course, to note its centralist intentions: but it is no more likely to be effective than other models of centre–periphery change.

As things stand it seems prudent to conclude that categorical funding, as expressed by TVEI, represents a fantasy of control that appeals equally (but oppositely) to national policy-makers and radical theorists, both of whom acknowledge the 'strong' but not the 'weak' argument. Thus Harland (1986) offers a convincing account of linkages between the logics of categorical funding and a training model of curriculum and staff development. Categorical funding, she concludes, devalues local autonomy — 'freedom within tight rules'. But such an account finds a mixed reception in the data. MSC's tight monitoring, for example, seems arbitrary rather than sinister. There is detailed concern about TVEI and non-TVEI boundaries, a deep anxiety about who uses the TVEI rooms and equipment, but only a vague concern for and knowledge of broader and more central issues, and a contradictory policy towards project integrity as opposed to the need to disseminate the innovation. The restraint could be regarded, in the same project, as a 'skeletal script' or as an invitation for teacher emancipation: 'Teachers initiate, own and self-evaluate their particular contribution to the Project.' (Vincent 1986: 1,4)

Questions

What are the steering mechanisms and developmental moments of TVEI? What kinds of connection or disconnection link TVEI rhetoric to TVEI development? Do these connections represent centralizing or decentralizing effects?

Issue 4

If it is hard to know what TVEI is, how can we judge its claims? Eastshire was a 'southern TVEI', and sought to be judged in terms of occupational skills and destinations. Claims were high: employability up, problem-solving and initiative recognized in the marketplace. The achievement was a better product. Yet the evidence was highly problematic. In making these claims the project made no attempt to sort 'Hawthorne' effects from programme effects. There was no recognition that these sorts of outcomes were echoed in most transition projects (of whatever kind) in the last ten years. Nor was there any attempt to be precise about the kinds of 'transfer' involved (was 'problem-solving' a transferable skill — across subjects, in the workplace?) or indeed to establish if the new pedagogy (negotiated, problem-solving, active, and project-based) actually delivered the intellectual goods. As a pilot, an avowed experiment, TVEI in Eastshire was happy to cook the books. Where claims were challenged, or did become untenable, the grounds for success were simply shifted. The danger was that all outcomes were taken to be tokens of success:

Staying-on rate goes up? — Revolutionized attitudes to education.
TVEI students leave at 16? — Cohort so attractive to employers that they all get jobs.
TVEI students flock to YTS? — Attitudes to training transformed.
On the dole? — Young people better skilled and motivated for the upturn.

Questions

On what grounds are success claims in TVEI being made? How are local economic and transition realities influencing these grounds? What grounds for failure are projects willing to recognize?

Issue 5

A further aspect of TVEI outcomes for both Eastshire and Westshire was an all-pervading sense of reinvention. Limited time, demands from other initiatives like TRIST and GCSE, left participants feeling that they seldom knew enough about what they were trying to do. Innovations like profiling and Work Experience have accumulated a considerable range of practice and an extensive literature. But it seemed to be only in the hi-tech areas that the projects were in touch with the latest developments. The norm was for individuals to depend on local networks, chance encounters, and the occasional conference and workshop. The constraints of time and task made that inevitable. Few people knew what other TVEI projects did; fewer still were familiar with the numerous developments in the transition and prevocational fields since 1977. The decentralization of curriculum development led to a systemic loss of memory that applied as much to evaluations as to developments. For example, a researcher into gender issues pointed out that the TVEI debate about Equal Opportunities was unnecessarily deficient:

> I was disappointed to see that gender was viewed [in TVEI Working Papers No.1] as a new and unexplored area. Perhaps it truly is for some of the TVEI evaluators but haven't they heard of libraries?(6)

Eastshire had set out to create through TVEI 'a model for curriculum development'. They had ended up with a dissemination model instead. In so doing, they had overcome what was always taken to be the great weakness of the Schools Council model of curriculum development. But at what cost? In terms of innovation, the education system had learned how to trade, but forgotten how to produce.

Questions

What degree of reinvention has characterized TVEI developments?

Does TVEI represent an adequate vehicle for CD? What are its costs and benefits?

Issue 6

What to make of it all? That was the evaluation's last question to TVEI. The evaluation came to feel that TVEI was an educational initiative trying to redress an economic problem. Better and more relevantly trained and skilled pupils, a brighter economic future, an end to decline. But the patterns of the innovation seemed to enact the problem, reflect its structure rather than address its solution.

As with the economy, so with education. A long period of restraint — some would say depression — was followed by the sudden demands of TVEI. In the interim, specialist curriculum firms had gone to the wall (the Schools Council, LEA Curriculum Centres). For each project, therefore, the boom led to the sucking in of imports as managers scrambled — on inadequate time, and with key deficiencies in CD skills — to meet demand and produce a marketable product, such as a profile, a new course, suitable software, etc. Off-the-shelf innovation was the immediate consequence along with a lot of unavoidably mediocre domestic production. Also the welter of other changes (Records of Achievement, GCSE, TRIST, GRIST, etc.) made it likely that few of the early improvisations would deepen into original and creative development. TVEI became, therefore, a dissemination project for the innovations of the past, or a multiple process of reinvention. Some innovation processes must have been repeated hundreds of times up and down the country. Profiling, for example, must be the only new territory in education or history where pioneers have so outnumbered settlers. (It was interesting to see how the rhetoric of the process curriculum was used to justify these duplications — repetition and duplication became the necessary steps to 'ownership' of the innovation, in terms of the new pedagogical metaphysics.) Where creative developments did take place, it was quite usual for them to pass unnoticed, as in Westshire.

Far from being the major innovation and redirection of education in the twentieth century, the TVEI pilot programme is more likely to be remembered as a minor bump in the resources chart, sufficient to admit hi-tech into certain classes in a few schools. But TVEI is being, and will continue to be, replicated across the vast majority of LEAs in the country. Lessons 'learned' from the first three years of the pilot — in spite of the inability of the various evaluation systems to report adequately during this time — are being reproduced on a grand scale. TVEI is a success — because it has been so declared.

Also it seems inconceivable that TVEI — whether in Eastshire or Westshire guise — could ever have lead to the careful and technically sophisticated developments of MACOS, or HCP, or even SCIP. Indeed, their reinvention would have been beyond its scope, despite vastly greater resources. Is this the consequence of the de-industrialization of educational innovation and evaluation? Are the TVEI projects the equivalent of the new small business enterprise culture? And if they are, is that good enough?

Issue 7

Finally, what had the evaluation learned? It has learned to mistrust the power of analogy. The three pigs were deceptive: it was hard to sort 'brick' projects from 'straw' ones. Evaluation seldom offered the neat choice between options that the analogy implied (or that decision makers demanded). On the other hand, at least the wolf had been revealed, because it had turned out that what threatened both innovation and the evaluation's attempts to understand it, was the wolf of rationality.

But rationality was to be mistrusted rather than rejected. The economic metaphor with which the evaluation had ended would no doubt fall to more compelling parallels. Meanwhile, its provisionality might help the evaluation and others to go beyond it, to find a more educative purchase on the implications of TVEI.

Notes

1. Or, to put it another way, we must 'feedforward' as well as 'feedback'. See I.A. Richards, 'The Secret of Feedforward', *Saturday Review*, 3.2.86. Richards sees feedforward as those anticipations that we all make based on a 'selective reception of what has been relevant in similar activity in our past' (p.15). We are indebted to David Hopkins for the reference.
2. TVEI Working Papers 1 and 2, Spring and Autumn 1986. R. Fiddy and I. Stronach (eds), CARE, UEA, Norwich (for the MSC).
3. The term 'educational settlement' is often used to describe the educational policies of the Thatcher administration, especially in so far as they threaten to upset the 1944 settlement. See CCCS (1981) *Unpopular Education*. Hutchinson, London, p. 229.
4. The European Community 'Transition to Adult Working Life' projects (1978–82) in the UK were similar in many ways to the TVEI projects. They were externally funded, based on bids against EC guidelines, run by the LEAs, and often managed as consortia. See Varlaam C. (ed.) (1984). 'Rethinking Transition: Educational Innovation and the Transition to Adult Life'. Falmer, Sussex.
5. On this point, MSC, external evaluation, and project personnel all seemed to agree. Similar patterns of minimal change had occured in the EC programme.
6. Letter from Gaby Weiner to Ian Stronach 21.11.86, quoted with permission.

References

Clark, D.L. (1980). In consideration of goal-free planning: the failure of traditional planning systems in education, in Clark, D.L. *et al.* (eds) *New Perspectives on Planning in Educational Organizations*. Far West Laboratory, San Francisco.

Dalin, P. (1974). Innovation in Education — a systematic view. OECD mimeo, p. 8.

Harland, J. (1986). The New INSET: A Transformation Scene, in *TVEI Working Papers 2*. CARE, UEA (for MSC).

House, E. (1979). Technology versus Craft: A Ten Year Perspective on Innovation. *J. Curriculum Studies*, 11 January, 1–15.

Vincent, G. (ed.) 1986) *Inside Buckinghamshire TVEI*. Buckinghamshire LEA.

*Chris Shilling**

7

Implementing the Contract

Front-Line Teachers in the TVEI Classroom

Introduction

There is a growing body of literature concerned with the historical background, organization and sociological implications of the Technical and Vocational Education Initiative (e.g. Dale 1985, 1986; McCulloch 1986; Pyart 1985). Through the national and local evaluation of schemes, a mass of data is also being collected concerning issues such as teacher and student experiences and perceptions of the Initiative, the detailed content of regional programmes, and the post-school destinations of those leaving TVEI.

Rather than dealing comprehensively with any of these questions, this paper has a more limited aim. My focus is on those features of TVEI within schools which may influence the attitudes and actions of form teachers in recruiting students to the Initiative. This involves looking at those aspects of the school organization of TVEI which may hinder the full dissemination of information about the Initiative, create antagonism toward it as a new curriculum development, or, alternatively, predispose teachers favourably towards TVEI as a 'relevant' development which could ease those problems they may face in the classroom. Any of these factors might affect the advice given by form teachers to their students when considering TVEI as an option choice.(1)

The Manpower Services Commission (MSC) requires that TVEI

*The Editor gratefully acknowledges the kind permission of the *British Journal of Sociology of Education* for allowing publication of this paper in this book.

programmes 'should cater for young people *across the ability range* and offer *equal opportunities* to boys and girls' (MSC 1984). As a condition of acceptance, participating schools must undertake to promote this goal and, through requiring such details as the numbers of girls and boys on the course, the MSC monitors progress in achieving a 'balanced intake' to TVEI. Such a demand may impinge on teachers involved in the school option choice process. This may be especially so for those form teachers who are supervising students involved in choosing the subjects they will study in the last two years of their compulsory education.(2)

It is under the auspices of form teachers (or their equivalent) that students make their academic options. While the influence that form teachers' advice may have cannot be determined precisely — it may vary in relation to the sex/race/social class of the student and form teacher, whether horizontal or vertical pastoral grouping exists, etc. — it could be vital as *the* causal factor in a student's option choices (Bhaskar 1979;106). Such influence could, therefore, be essential for recruiting a 'balanced intake' to TVEI programmes.(3)

In the Autumn term of the 1985/86 academic year, I interviewed the form teachers of the previous year's third year at Borough School. Their students had made their option choices and had recently begun their fourth year of study. I had decided to use structured interviews as I wanted to establish their views on particular aspects of their role. How they saw their role as form teachers, the information they received concerning TVEI, their opinions about TVEI, its suitability for their students, and their own subject specialisms were all relevant to my study. My aim was to discover if there were any factors which might lead form teachers to mediate or oppose the requirement of a 'balanced intake' to TVEI. As a 'case study' it is difficult to generalize the results of this paper or speculate as to how representative they may be. Their applicability may be limited to those TVEI schools with a similar organization to that of Borough School.

The organization of option choices

At Borough, the 1985 option choice process started some four weeks before the end of the spring term. Students attended 'options talks' given by teachers whose subjects were on offer in the fourth and fifth years. 'Advice sessions' were set aside where form teachers discussed and explained options with their group (experience had shown that few students absorbed much information from the 'options talks'), and answered specific questions concerning the relevance of particular subjects for individual students.

The school was keen to involve parents in this process. They had the opportunity to attend an 'information evening', where the option choice procedure was explained, and a 'parents' evening' where potential subject choices and academic progress were discussed with their child's form teacher.(4) Finally, students submitted their provisional option choices, before being sorted into exam/non-exam groups and, in some cases, redirected into what senior teachers considered 'more suitable' subjects shortly after Easter (cf. Woods 1979, ch.2; Ball 1981, ch.5).

It requires only a very brief account of the organization of option choices to see that a number of factors may contribute to producing students' final decisions. In addition to the effects of peer group interaction, students may be subject to a number of pressures, from the school and family, to take or reject certain subjects.(5) However, central to Borough's organization is the form teacher. She/he is in the best position to gather information on students and is a figure who represents a 'bridge' from school to the family, through the performance of activities such as attendence at 'parents' evenings' and summarizing, in termly reports which are sent home, the general performance of students at school. In what follows, I shall be focusing on the influence of this figure in relation to the recruitment of a 'balanced intake' to TVEI.

The role of the form teacher

The importance of the form teacher to the school is reflected in the writings of those concerned with pastoral care. This literature can be seen collectively as representing a 'model role' of the form teacher. The centrality of form teachers in relation to the academic and pastoral spheres of school life has been emphasized by a number of people (e.g. Hamblin 1974; Marland 1974; Blackburn 1975; Hamblin 1981; Rees 1985). The constituent elements of what is viewed as the form teacher's role are often catalogued and generally include a 'first-level' responsibility for pastoral, academic and even sometimes career matters. During the options process, the form teacher's role is seen as extending to the provision of an 'impartial relationship' through which students may come to make their subject choices:

> The model that I would propose for the tutor is that of 'enabler'. It implies a tutor–pupil relationship which leaves the pupil free to make his choices but provides a relationship...through which he can come to those choices. (Blackburn, p.215)

In talking to the form teachers of Borough's previous third year, it was clear that they viewed their role in terms similar to this 'model'. They may not have had the time to do all they would have liked, but all eight (see Figure 1) mentioned their participation in pastoral, academic and career matters with their students.(6) The following comments were typical:

> Well, we (form teachers) have to look out for any problems the kids might have, personal or academic. At options, and later on in the fourth and fifth

> years, jobs and college courses are prominent in their minds so we give them what advice we can on careers and sometimes tell them to go and see the careers teacher for further advice.
>
> To be honest, I just don't get enough time with all the other demands of this place to do all that I should. But I'd say I spend a lot of time on discipline and general welfare problems. Often you've got to keep on at them — some don't make any effort at all academically. From about the third year, there's an emphasis on what they want to do later and it's important to get them to think and talk about jobs they may want to do.
>
> ...I meet their school problems, with work and problems they may have with others, and their personal troubles. There are some seriously deprived kids in this school. You also need to be a jobs and college courses expert — a right 'Jack of all trades'.

After commenting on their general role, I asked these form teachers what specific advice they gave to students when considering option decisions. Despite variations in the content of their answers, all said they asked students to bear a number of factors in mind when making their final decisions. For example:

> Well, whether they like the subject, if they are any good at it, if it's relevant to what they want to do after school. I also make sure I go over any new subjects, to make sure they know what they are opting for.
>
> They should be competent at those subjects they have already taken, although this is just not realistic with all of them. I also ask them to think about what they'll need after school.
>
> ...talk to their parents, or whoever is at home, about their choices, and to others who are already on them in the fourth year. I also tell them to think if they're good at the subject, enjoy it, and if it's going to be useful to them.

The matter of 'ability' and whether a subject will be useful for students' post-school intentions were factors mentioned by all eight form teachers. Enjoying the subjects was something seven form teachers asked their groups to consider. Consulting with parents was included in the comments of four of them, as was the need for the form teacher to explain what was involved in any new subject on offer to students.

Through presenting such advice to their groups, these form teachers can be seen as creating a 'tutor-pupil relationship... through which (students) can come to (their) choices' (Blackburn 1975). Furthermore, Borough's form teachers were all keen to stress that final decisions were the responsibility of individual students, attitudes congruent with the other aspect of the 'enabler role' proposed by Blackburn.

Now, that form teachers mention their concern with pastoral, academic and career matters, and seem to hold views which approximate to an 'enabler role' during option choices, does not confirm the reality of the 'model' constructed by the pastoral writers. The group I interviewed may well have been unrepresentative of most form teachers, and even they were conscious of not having enough time in which to fulfil their general role. Trying to 'fit a quart into a pint pot' was how one form teacher summed up all that she tried to do. Despite these qualifications to the 'model role', it remains a useful 'yardstick' with which to compare the effects recruiting a 'balanced intake' had on these form teachers.

The 'Irreducible Demands' of TVEI

The demand made by the MSC for a 'balanced intake' to TVEI courses requires form teachers, alongside other members of staff, to become effective 'policy bearers' (Blackburn 1975;6). By implication, form teachers should encourage students from both sexes across the ability range to consider opting for TVEI. This would alter substantially the role of the form teacher as an 'enabler' at option time. Furthermore, being subject to pressure from form teachers, certain students may not opt for the Initiative in an entirely voluntary manner. This reveals something of a contradiction in MSC guidelines. While requiring a 'balanced intake' to courses, the MSC also stipulates that participation in TVEI should be 'voluntary' (MSC 1984). It is not difficult to see how these two conditions could become contradictory if in one year the course was undersubscribed.

Diagrammatically, the requirement for a 'balanced intake' can be seen as altering the 'enabler role' of form teachers. Figure 1 illustrates how the requirement for a 'balanced intake' to TVEI may affect the advice form

Figure 1
(a) *The 'Enabler' Model*

(b) *TVEI's Intake Requirement*

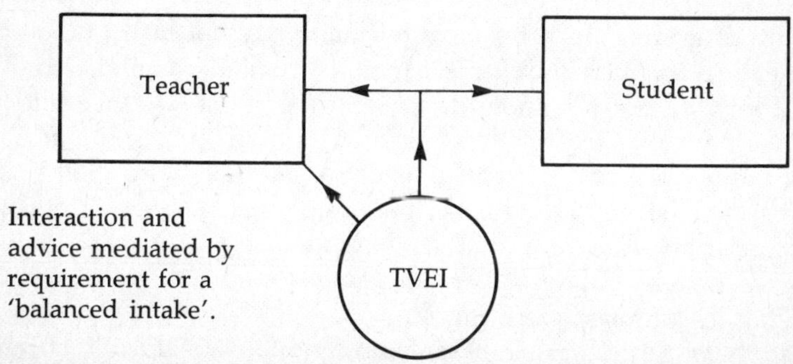

teachers give to their students. In suggesting this I am not ignoring other factors which may have a similar effect, such as the form teacher's subject specialism. However, recruiting a 'balanced intake' to a particular subject is a marked departure from the existing practices form teachers are required to engage in. Furthermore, it is an externally imposed requirement which is relevant to *all* form teachers in a uniform manner. Here, form teachers do not play a role in *creating* policy, they are merely cast in the position of *implementing* policy for others.

The TVEI influenced 'model' proposes significant changes to the 'enabler role' of the form teacher. However, it neglects a vital factor which could introduce a large disjuncture between practice and theory, 'what is' and 'what ought to be'. The TVEI influenced 'model' fails to account for the fact that form teachers are not just passive individuals willing to take on board external requirements without question. As those I spoke to at Borough made clear, they had their own views concerning the advice they gave to students at options time which may not be compatible with recruiting a 'balanced intake' to TVEI. In addition to asking students to consider a number of factors when making their option choices, the 'student-centred', 'enabler' approach articulated by Borough's form teachers, may direct individuals toward or away from certain subjects depending on how suitable they may be seen for those in their group. For example, a form teacher may view TVEI as a course for only the 'most able' in her form:

> I encourage the most able to take the course, those who are most reliable and would get most from the course. (Ms Jay)

As all those form teachers I spoke to expressed their advice in terms congruent to an 'enabler role', it is not surprising that there was no uniform sense in which they could be said to have promoted TVEI:

> ...in advising on options I try to give as much information as possible for all subjects, to create real educational choice for those in my group. I didn't push TVEI. Most boys in my group didn't want a science-based course, while the girls saw it as a boys' course. I let them get on with their choices after I'd given them details about TVEI — it didn't change any minds, so that was that. (Mr Peebles)

There are other reasons why form teachers may not take on board the aim of meeting the MSC's requirement for a 'balanced intake' to TVEI. Form teachers are not just individuals with a general advisory role, they are also usually subject specialists. As such, they may be influenced by a number of other factors pertinent to teachers generally, and their position within the school structure. For example, it may not be in the interests of a form teacher who is also a non-TVEI language specialist to promote the Initiative to students. Success in encouraging students to opt for TVEI may lead to a fall in language recruitment.

Form teachers are active, not passive, individuals who have a number of views and interests which may impinge upon the advice they give to students and affect detrimentally the achievement of a 'balanced intake' to TVEI. In itself, the identification of these factors, or sources of influence, is not enough to determine individually form teachers' views of TVEI or the advice they will give to students about it. However, they do suggest the outlines towards building up a picture of a number of interrelating factors whose influence may be asymmetrically weighted in relation to each form teacher.

The existence of various sources of influence impinging on form teachers assumes particular significance when it is realized that schools bear close similarity to what Dorothy Smith has characterized as a 'front-line organization' (1965;381):

> In a front line organization the locus of responsibility for organizational performance and policy-making at the center is peculiar in being divorced from the locus of organizational initiative in units at the periphery.
>
> (1965;394-5)

Features of front-line organizations include the peripheral units performing their tasks independently of other like units, and the existence of obstacles to the direct supervision of the activities of such units (p.388). If peripheral units are seen as teachers operating in classrooms, the relevance of Smith's work becomes obvious. The success or failure of much educational policy is dependent on the classroom teacher, working in an environment far removed from the policy making centres of local education authorities or government. At the same time, teachers are usually autonomous agents within the classroom. For the most part they work independently of their colleagues without formal supervision. The organization of teachers into groups via 'the department', is sharply contrasted with their entry into the classroom as individuals. Similar features apply to form teachers in their role as advisors. With regard to the objective of a 'balanced intake' to TVEI, it is up to form teachers, not central policy makers, whether or not they use their influence towards achieving this goal.

The degree of autonomy form teachers have in advising students within the front-line units of the classroom has important consequences for the attainment of a 'balanced intake' to TVEI. To the extent that sources of influence impinge upon form teachers' perceptions of TVEI, their autonomy allows them to translate these views into concrete action via the advice they give to students about the Initiative. An important set of questions relevant to this, then, are which sources of influence are encountered by teachers? How do they interact, and what are their points of intersection within the school? Furthermore, just where are form teachers located within this system?

Three sources of influence will be identified as relevant to form teachers and the achievement of a 'balanced intake' to TVEI. These are 'divisiveness', 'dissemination' and 'ideology'. Divisiveness concerns the potential rifts which may be caused within schools by a curriculum development which concentrates resources around certain subjects. Dissemination is concerned with the effectiveness with which information about TVEI in general, and the objective of a 'balanced intake' in particular, is communicated to teachers. Ideology concerns the rationality with which the Government and MSC have imbued TVEI. This presents the Initiative as a substantial response to the problems of youth unemployment. Throughout this discussion I will include three additional factors which impinge upon teachers. These are, the recurring themes associated with the school as a front-line organization, the deskilling of teachers (by which I am referring to a reduction in the ability of form teachers to carry out their role as they view it, see pp.121–3), and the politics of TVEI within the Borough curriculum.

My aim is to build a view of the school as an interrelating totality within which form teachers can be located as individual agents actively confronting the sources of influence they encounter in their multi-level and complex manifestations.

Form teachers, sources of influence, and the 'Irreducible Demands' of TVEI

Eight form teachers were responsible for guiding the 1984/85 third year through their option choices at Borough School. They are listed in Table 1 according to their subject specialisms, whether they were involved in teaching TVEI groups, and whether they were in charge of an 'alpha' or 'mixed ability' form group.(7)

Table 1

Form teacher	*Form group*	*Subject*	*Teachers TVEI?*
Mr Peebles	alpha	Maths	Yes
Mr Brown	mixed ability	Craft	No
Mr Osgood	mixed ability	English	No
Mr Simpson	mixed ability	P.E.	Yes
Ms Blackwell	alpha	Humanities	No
Ms Jennings	mixed ability	Home Economics	No
Ms Jay	mixed ability	Maths	Yes
Ms Lawson	mixed ability	French	No

1 The 'Dissemination of TVEI'

In a school which requires a particular composition of students on a curriculum innovation, the effective dissemination of information concerning the course is extremely important. The communication of such goals is a precondition for teachers to become 'policy bearers' (Blackburn

1975). However, the evidence is that this has not occurred at Borough. During the introduction of TVEI, an afternoon's in-service training was devoted to the implications of TVEI for Borough. This was the first, and so far the only time teachers were brought together and given the formal opportunity to ask questions about the course. Not surprisingly, this was regarded as inadequate by the one form teacher who referred to it:

> There was no consultation as to whether we wanted TVEI in the first place. Then, all we got was a totally inadequate afternoon which was meant to be staff training.

That no other teacher mentioned the afternoon as a source of information perhaps confirms this view. It is notable that unlike previous curriculum developments (such as many Schools Council projects), classroom teachers were not involved in the formation of TVEI or in the decision to have it in their school.

This lack of consultation can be seen as an aspect of the contemporary deskilling of teachers (see Lawn and Ozga 1981; Apple 1985). Teaching has been identified as undergoing a process akin to 'proletarianization' whereby the capacity of teachers to initiate and execute their work has been diminished. This is reflected in the introduction of curriculum developments which bypass teachers in their conception and formation, and adoption within schools. While the deskilling of teachers' work has been seen as starting long before the introduction of TVEI, the formation of the Initiative at the level of government and its often hasty adoption within schools by Headteachers, can be seen as part of the same process.

At Borough, an indication that the adoption and initial implementation of TVEI had bypassed many teachers was provided by those form teachers who were dissatisfied with their knowledge of the course at Borough and those who felt unable to offer adequate advice about the Initiative to their students (see pp.128–9). Furthermore, of direct relevance to the 'irreducible requirements' of TVEI, three form teachers were completely unaware of the 'balanced intake' objective. Being free to form their own judgements about the Initiative, no guarantee existed that form teachers would promote TVEI to both sexes across the ability range. These are the opposite conditions to those suggested by Smith for realizing centrally formulated goals in front-line organizations. Here, form teachers would be left 'ideally' with the 'minimum leeway for judgement' (Smith 1965; 393).

The second source of information to which form teachers were exposed came indirectly, through escorting their groups to a TVEI 'exhibition'. Established by the school TVEI co-ordinator, the exhibition illustrated what was done on TVEI and the career opportunities it offered. Form teachers who attended were impressed by the interest this stimulated in some of their students:

> It seemed an excellent package. You couldn't help but want to take the course having seen the exhibition. (Ms Jay)

Valuable though this may have been for many students, it was a source of information aimed only indirectly at teachers. They were not the 'target group' for the exhibition. In two cases it was the co-ordinator who showed third-year groups around, leaving their form teachers free to get on with other things.

A third source of information, directed toward form teachers, was literature about TVEI. This was distributed regularly by the school co-ordinator and clearly informed one form teacher not involved in teaching TVEI:

> Stuff gets thrown into my hands all the time. Fortunately, I can't help but know what TVEI's about. (Ms Lawson)

Two other form teachers mentioned that they had received 'some information through the pigeonholes'. However, none of the other five received literature apart from 'right at the beginning of the course' (Mr Brown). It was only several days later that I realized Ms Lawson was the only form teacher based in the same building as the school TVEI co-ordinator. The others were based in separate buildings. It appeared that an erratic internal mail system may have been responsible for this communication failure. To 'test' this, I forwarded two notes to myself care of another member of staff in a different building. Seven weeks later I was still waiting for one of them!(8) The erratic nature of the dissemination of knowledge about TVEI meant that only three form teachers, two of whom taught TVEI, were satisfied with their knowledge of the course at Borough. Moreover, it is doubtful whether this would be rectified merely through an improvement in the internal mail system. Much of the literature distributed in this way was concerned with TVEI at a national level, not the specific features of the Borough programme.

The indirect effects of 'separating' form teachers from detailed knowledge of the Initiative, was that they were largely removed from being able 'officially' to advise students about TVEI. Four of those I spoke to felt distanced from the job of guidance with regard to TVEI and were unable to offer what they considered to be adequate advice. As far as TVEI was concerned, many of Borough's form teachers were unable to carry out the role they perceived themselves to have. Typical were the following remarks:

> I had nothing to do with the options concerning TVEI. He (the school co-ordinator) came into my form, said a few brief words and showed them around the exhibition.

> We were in the dark about it. Nothing was sent to form teachers about TVEI. I had one kid who asked me about it and I had to say, 'Look, I'm sorry Richard, but I don't know.' To be honest I felt inadequate, unable to do my job properly.

Distancing teachers from the knowledge which would enable them to give 'adequate advice' to their students about TVEI, prevents their constructing an 'enabler' relationships with their students for this option at subject choice time. From having a role which necessitates a variety of knowledge to enable form teachers to play an effective part in advising students about their choices, they are deprived of the 'tools' with which to do this (i.e. adequate information about TVEI):

> I knew very little about TVEI, certainly not enough to even begin to advise students about it or answer their questions as I'd have liked. (Mr Brown)

From perceiving their role to be concerned with generally advising students about new subjects on offer (see pp.121–3), these form teachers were distanced from the role of academic advisor. They were placed in the role of an intermediary with regard to TVEI, becoming agents of referral to those who *have* the necessary knowledge. Again, this indirect effect of TVEI can be seen as accentuating the process of deskilling identified by Apple, Ozga and others. Instead of being able to inform and advise about the whole process of option choices, the referral of students interested in TVEI to others brings the 'breakdown' of that advisory role with 'tasks' effectively 'assigned to different individuals' (Ozga 1981; 40). This situation was expressed by form teachers through the following such comments:

> In the end I had to tell anybody who was interested to go and see (the school TVEI co-ordinator). (Mr Simpson)

> Well, I knew something of TVEI through a colleague who is involved in it, but I also told them to go and see (the co-ordinator). I didn't know anywhere near as much as I'd have needed to answer most of the questions I was asked. (Ms Jennings)

If this position were to continue, the role of form teachers as academic and vocational guides might be substantially reduced. Form teachers could be left with a greater part of their role concerned with pastoral matters. Their ability to offer adequate advice and construct an 'enabler' relationship with students would be removed for TVEI.

Now, such a situation might be seen as overcoming the problems faced by those responsible for achieving a 'balanced intake':

> The dilemma of those occupying central position (in front line organizations) is that they are responsible for policy and maintaining standards of performance for the organization as a whole, while occupying positions from which this responsibility can least effectively be exercised as authority. (Smith 1965; 395)

Bypassing form teachers may place those in charge of TVEI in a better position to 'exercise effective authority' over the recruitment of students. However, a feature of front-line units is the difficulty of controlling the activities of those working in them. Form teachers may have their role reduced, but the ensuing distance they may feel from TVEI is not necessarily neutral in the effects it may have on student subject choice. As illustrated by three of the Borough form teachers who felt distanced from advising about the course, such teachers may not encourage any of their students to opt for TVEI:

> I didn't push or promote the course to anyone in my form. (Ms Blackwell)

> I wasn't going to advise any of them to take TVEI. It was just another option choice as far as I was concerned. (Ms Jennings)

> I didn't say anything about it. As I said, I didn't really know anything much about it. (Mr Brown)

Furthermore, even if such form teachers assume the role of an agent of referral to the school TVEI co-ordinator, this does not ensure a satisfactory meeting. Blackburn, in discussing careers teachers, points to one possible problem:

> The careers teacher...may be friendly...but many pupils will need an initial introduction before they will feel free to approach them. (1975;105)

The lack of a close source of information embodied in the familiar figure of the form teacher, may prevent TVEI from being considered by some students.

At Borough, three of the five form teachers who felt distanced from TVEI did not promote it to any in their group. The other two promoted the course, but to 'low-ability' students who they thought would benefit from it (Mr Osgood and Mr Simpson). Indeed, *not in one case* did any of Borough's third-year form teachers promote the Initiative to both sexes across the ability range. The erratic dissemination of knowledge about TVEI and the 'enabler' view Borough's form teachers had of their role appeared to contribute to this situation. However, a number of other sources of influence can also be seen as impinging upon form teachers and producing this situation.

2 *The potential divisiveness of TVEI*

The potential divisions generated by TVEI can be seen as a source of influence posing an even greater threat to the recruitment of a 'balanced intake' than the poor 'dissemination of TVEI'. Nationally, TVEI has injected millions of pounds into selected areas of the educational system. At the level of the school, favoured subject areas have received thousands of pounds extra to their usual capitation allowance. In common with other schools, science and technology areas at Borough were benefitting at the same time that certain other subjects were struggling with falling resources.

I will mention two, interrelated factors which can lead to division within TVEI schools; the distribution of resources, and what will be represented as the MSC's 'paradigm of relevance'.

(a) The distribution of resources

The concentration of resources at Borough had equipped certain subjects with new 'up-to-the-minute' hardware. Classrooms had been filled with new computers, typewriters and other electronic equipment. Furthermore, it was not simply 'core' TVEI subjects such as Information Technology and Business Studies which benefitted. The Maths department argued for, and won, extra money and extra teacher time for participating in the Initiative. As one form teacher who taught maths put it:

> We went to the Head and said, 'If we're going to be teaching TVEI groups of fifteen, it's going to create more strain on other classes. We need more resources, including staff, to cope.

Similar problems were created for the P.E. department through having to teach TVEI students in a separate group. As the third-year form teacher who taught P.E. noted:

> It has meant that on Mondays we have the TVEI group of sixty, followed by the rest of the year group which consists of well over a hundred...that causes problems!

The differential allocation of resources within and outside TVEI areas is clearly another source of influence which may impinge upon form teachers' views. Furthermore, the resources factor is unlikely to stop at differences between subjects. TVEI has provided for some activities to be funded while their pre-existing counterparts within the school remain unfunded and often 'voluntary' activities.(9) For example, residential experience forms a central part of TVEI and is heavily resourced. This is in contrast to the usual school trips which are funded from school finance, contributions from students, and require teachers to volunteer time and take the responsibility for looking after students. As the recent deaths of children from Bucks, and the subsequent resignation of teachers involved in the outing, illustrate, this entails a substantial unpaid risk for teachers (*TES* 15.11.85).

The differential allocation of resources extends to reports and their TVEI equivalent, student profiling. Profiling requires that teachers (including form teachers) and students spend a number of periods over the year together as individuals, negotiating formative and summative profiles. At Borough, this amounted to finding the time to enable students to write in close consultation with teachers, up to fifty per cent of their profile report. The MSC has provided resources to enable this to take place. Such financial support contrasts with the long-standing practice of teachers having to complete hundreds of reports in their *own time*. It would not be surprising if this left a 'bitter taste' with those teachers who did not benefit from MSC resources.

(b) The MSC's paradigm of relevance

In establishing TVEI, the MSC has created what can be seen as a paradigm of relevance. This consists of those subject areas considered as meeting the 'rules and standards' which prepare students for working life (Kuhn 1962).

Despite the flexibility of the MSC's national guidelines for TVEI programmes, there is an emphasis on 'technical and vocational education' (MSC 1984). This alone may not, perhaps, create status differences between 'applied' subjects and others. Indeed, much evidence attests to the great difficulty applied technical and vocational subjects have had in attempting to achieve equal standing with 'traditional sciences' (McCulloch *et al.* 1985). However, the existence of financially privileged areas of the curriculum (which may include traditional and applied science) considered 'relevant' to students' needs, creates areas of 'exclusion'. Subjects left outside have, by definition, something about them which is irrelevant to the objective of enriching and widening 'the curriculum in a way that will help young people to prepare for the world of work, and to develop skills and interests, including creative abilities' (MSC 1984).

This area of relevance applies also to teachers. It is those *within* TVEI subjects who are implicitly defined as having the skills to help young people in these ways. Moreover, their skills are often rewarded by finance which enables their departments to be lavishly equipped with new resources. What then of the teachers excluded from involvement with TVEI? The implication is that the MSC does not view them as having the necessary skills to contribute to the above objective. It may well be the case that such teachers see themselves demoted to 'second-class' status.

To experience such 'exclusion' may lead to antagonism towards the structure which created it (i.e. the establishment of TVEI) and those subjects which effectively define others as 'irrelevant'. The following comment illustrates how one form teacher I spoke to experienced her location within this situation:

> I'm against it (TVEI). It creates a hierarchy between subjects making them into 'first' and 'second' rate parts of the curriculum. It's elitist and divisive. The MSC are telling teachers in subjects like mine (humanities) that we're irrelevant to the education of children. (Ms Blackwell)

As mentioned earlier, form teachers are not just people who 'look after' groups of students. They are also subject specialists who have to work within the confines and demands of their departments. If the interaction of sources of influence, which are seen to revolve around and stem from TVEI, are experienced by form teachers as a burden, this may well affect their opinion of TVEI and their advice to students. Such a tendency may be reinforced by the possibility that it could be rational for form teachers of subjects outside the Initiative *not* to promote it. Heavy student demand for TVEI would serve to 'confirm' the second-class status of other areas of the curriculum implied by the MSC, and the lack of relevant teaching skills held by those within these areas. This was articulated most strongly at Borough by Ms Blackwell (see above). An undersubscribed Initiative, however, releases students for recruitment to other subjects. This would create a situation whereby the consumers of options contradict, by their choices, the MSC's paradigm of relevance, and, for non-TVEI teachers, reaffirm the importance of other subjects. It would be surprising if this was not a factor which entered into the minds of form teachers who did not promote TVEI. For example, neither Ms Jennings nor Ms Lawson promoted the course to their form despite viewing TVEI as a 'good course' from what they had heard.

Up to this point, I have examined certain sources of influence which may work against the promotion of TVEI. However, elements of the politics of the Borough school curriculum constituted a source of influence which acted as a mitigating force for some form teachers. Senior teachers viewed TVEI as a curriculum development which coincided with the direction in which they wanted the school to develop. The existing curriculum was viewed as one which 'did not meet the needs or interests of a large proportion of our students' (deputy head). It was not only senior teachers who were concerned that Borough should move toward a more 'practically based curriculum'. A concrete rationale existed in the minds of many teachers which supported such a view. This stemmed from the day-to-day problems they and their colleagues often faced in the classroom.

Borough's catchment area covered a population which included many with serious social and economic problems. Years of Conservative financial stringency had exacerbated this situation and had not helped the many young people entering Borough who brought social and emotional problems with them. Teachers often had an exhausting job just coping with these, as they manifested themselves in the eruption of discipline problems in the classroom. Many teachers I spoke to were grateful for any course which was 'more practical' and 'got the kids out of school' and, in the cases of two form teachers, it overrode the reservations they had about TVEI:

> Though I don't know much at all about TVEI I've heard it's a practical scheme which keeps them occupied in and outside of school. Those in my group weren't the brightest of kids — far from it — but I directed them toward it. I thought they'd benefit from such a course. (Mr Osgood)

> Anything with a practical bias which sometimes gets the kids out of school such as TVEI has got to be a good thing with the intake we have got at Borough. While I wasn't consulted about the course, or told anything about it, I've got to say that it might help reduce the appalling truancy and discipline problems we've got. (Mr Simpson)

3 *Ideology — a countervailing tendency*

Before tabulating some of the information relevant to the recruitment of a 'balanced intake' to TVEI, which I gained from the eight form teachers I spoke to, it is important to mention a further countervailing source of influence.

The rationale with which the Government and MSC have promoted vocational/training schemes gives great significance to equipping young people with 'relevant' skills (e.g. MSC 1978). This has been built into a political and ideological discourse which views a lack of training as a major reason for youth unemployment, and posits school as having a responsibility for this inadequacy. TVEI has been promoted as a major response to this.

To the extent that form teachers believe that TVEI may help students gain employment, or even a sought-after YTS course at sixteen, they may encourage their group to opt for the course irrespective of their subjective experience of the Initiative. This was the case for Mr Osgood who, despite having to teach larger English groups as a result of his departments involvement in TVEI, still encouraged many in his group to opt for the Initiative:

> I've heard from someone it helps equip them with skills which should improve substantially their job chances. That's got to be a good thing.

Ms Jay was involved in teaching TVEI, and viewed it in terms of the ideology attached to the course by the MSC:

> TVEI has a lot to offer in terms of training opportunities and increasing job and college chances.

Over the last few pages I have mentioned a number of factors, or sources of influence, which could impinge upon form teachers' views of TVEI. At times I have suggested certain factors which could affect the type of students for whom they see the course as suitable. Others have been viewed as having the potential to alter form teachers' perceptions of the Initiative. I have attempted to suggest that these factors do not exist separately but are often interrelated within the school and may intersect at different points depending on individual form teachers. I have also noted the importance of schools as front-line organizations, which make it difficult for those in charge of the Initiative to reduce the autonomy form teachers enjoy even if they manage to reduce the advisory role of such teachers. A centralized recruitment process may attempt to bypass form teachers through removing them from the information necessary to give 'considered advice' about the scheme, but their influence is likely to remain while the school is organized into form groups. In the front-line units of the classroom, form teachers are free to translate their views and experiences of TVEI into concrete advice to students.

In itself, this is obviously not enough to identify individual form teachers' positions on TVEI. Teachers may interpret their experience of a number of sources of influence in a variety of ways. It should not be thought that merely identifying all the relevant sources of influence would allow the action of a particular subject specialist form teacher to be specified in advance. It would be a positivist flaw for sociologists of education to treat schools as 'closed systems' (Bhaskar 1979; 58), or teachers as mere dupes of those systems.

I have attempted to develop a picture of a number of interrelated 'reasons' whose relative significance remains open — a matter for empirical investigation. At Borough, though I have identified 'countervailing' factors, not in one case did those sources of influence experienced by form teachers lead them to promote the Initiative to both sexes across the ability range.(10) Table 2 summarizes some of the views of Borough's form teachers in a more systematic manner than would have been appropriate in the main body of this paper.

Conclusion

In outlining form teachers' views of TVEI, I hope to have demonstrated the relevance and importance of building an overview of a number of interrelating sources of influence, stemming from the school organization of TVEI, which impinge on form teachers in a variety of ways. At Borough, for example, the dissemination of knowledge about TVEI had failed for Mr Simpson. His experience of distance from the course combined with that of a deskilling in his role. He had to refer students to others who had the information not available to him. Despite this, he still viewed TVEI as a 'practical course' which might help some of the needs of Borough's students and this was the dominant factor in his judgement of the Initiative.

The interaction of various sources of influence produced a somewhat different outcome with Ms Blackwell, who taught a subject which was excluded from the MSC's paradigm of relevance at Borough. Ms Blackwell viewed TVEI as elitist and divisive and did not encourage any in her form to take it. She experienced the implied irrelevance of her subject and teaching skills in a direct manner, and this reinforced the view she held of TVEI as 'creating first- and second-rate subjects and marking the reintroduction of the tripartite system'. Despite this, Ms Blackwell still saw her role as a form teacher as an impartial 'enabler', and was 'neutral in what advice I could give when asked about TVEI by a couple in my form'. Such a role, in common with the other form teachers who adopted it, may well be useful for students, but does little to promote the recruitment of a 'balanced intake'.

It has been seen how form teachers did not promote TVEI to both sexes across the ability range. The end result of the option choice process at Borough was that only forty-five students, out of a year group of around 230, opted for TVEI. In an effort to get numbers up to the sixty required for the course, a central recruiting drive was established by senior teachers. Third-year girls were seen as a group and certain students from 'alpha' sets were seen individually in an attempt to persuade them to reconsider their choices. Eventually only two places remained unfilled although there was what the school TVEI co-ordinator described as a 'male, low-ability' bias to the intake.

Table 2

Teacher and subject specialism	*'Model Role'* Viewed their activities as a form teacher as including pastoral, academic, and career matters.	Perceived their role in terms of an 'enabler' at option choice time?	Satisfied with their knowledge about TVEI within the school?	*'Deskilling'* Expressed the experience of a distancing from any role concerned with advising students about TVEI?	Did the form teachers subject department benefit from TVEI resources?	Aware of aim to recruit a 'balanced intake' to TVEI?	Promoted TVEI to a 'balanced intake'?
Mr Peebles (Maths)	Yes	Yes	Yes	No	Yes	Yes	No
Mr Brown (Craft)	Yes	Yes	No	Yes	No	No	No
Mr Osgood (English)	Yes	Yes	No	No	No	No	No (Encouraged 'low ability')
Mr Simpson (Physical Education)	Yes	Yes	No	Yes	No	Yes	No (Encouraged 'low ability')
Ms Blackwell (Humanities)	Yes	Yes	No	Yes	No	Yes	No
Ms Jennings (Home Economics)	Yes	Yes	No	Yes	Yes	Yes	No
Ms Jay (Maths)	Yes	Yes	Yes	No	Yes	No	No (Encouraged 'high ability')
Ms Lawson (Languages)	Yes	Yes	Yes	No	No	Yes	No

From the limited information I had gained about the TVEI course at Borough, it was impossible to discover exactly why it had been undersubscribed. However, it would be surprising if the interaction between students and form teachers was not of some significance in this. As has been seen, the autonomy within front line units allowed form teachers to translate their views of TVEI into concrete action — whether this was in treating TVEI as 'just another option choice', by encouraging only a specific ability range of students to take it, or by not 'saying anything to anyone about it'. The varieties that exist in the position of form teachers between schools makes it difficult to draw general conclusions from the findings of this paper. The following remarks may well be limited in their applicability to those schools where form teachers occupy a position similar to that in Borough (see pp. 120–2).

Form teachers are just one possible influence on students' option choices. However, that they may occasionally be *the* causal factor means that they should be significant for senior teachers and policy makers aiming for a 'balanced intake' to a new curriculum development. A recognition of this by those responsible for TVEI would seem to lead to two possible policy conclusions, both of which are relevant to the 'model' role of form teachers, and their position within front-line organizations.

Firstly, central policy makers within the school could introduce further 'mechanisms of control adapted to regulating autonomy' (Smith 1965, 397). It has been seen how form teachers at Borough felt removed from the course and sometimes unable to give informed advice about TVEI. An intensification of the centralized aspects of recruitment to the course, as occured at Borough in an attempt to 'fill the course up', could help bypass form teachers. However, this would exacerbate what has been seen as the deskilling of form teachers. Their ability to give general academic and 'first level' career advice would be severely limited and the 'model' role I have seen Borough's form teachers approximating to, would need to be replaced with one which recognized their 'function' as agents of referral. Furthermore, this would not alter the fact that teachers antagonistic to the Initiative (whose numbers may well increase if they perceive the organization of TVEI as reducing their ability to advise students) have the autonomy within the front-line units of the classroom to *influence* students. To change this would require a complete reorganization of the school away from the 'form group' or its equivalent. An alternative to such reorganization would be for senior teachers to take on the role of 'charismatic leaders'. This would supplement the bypassing of form teachers with their extensive supervision. As Smith notes:

> Control of front-line agents is maintained by intensive ideological conversations, which expose front-line performances to the corrections and advice of the leader. (p.398)

How form teachers would react to such 'conversations', however, is a variable which might not work in favour of senior teachers seeking a 'balanced intake' to TVEI. Moreover, other sources of influence may impinge upon form teachers which may override the effect of any 'ideological conversations'.

The second possible conclusion, which could be relevant for policy concerning TVEI, would be for senior teachers to recognize the sources of influence which are likely to impinge upon form teachers of different subject specialisms, and act to change the school organization of TVEI in a way which would alter these factors in a 'favourable' direction. For example, a more egalitarian structure and distribution of resources might remove the 'creation of first- and second-rate subjects'. For this to be effective, all teachers would have to be 'drawn into' the aims and objectives of a course they actively supported. However, this would seem to contradict the very rationale of a course seemingly designed to create an asymmetry between 'relevant' and 'irrelevant' areas of the curriculum.

If, as appears likely, the introduction of technical and vocational courses within schools is increased, the roles of many form teachers may well undergo a significant change.

Acknowledgements

I would like to thank Roger Dale for his useful comments and suggestions on various drafts of paper. I am also grateful to Colin Lacey and Barry Cooper for their comments.

Notes

1. At a minimum, form teachers have a responsibility for the pastoral care of their students, and have a legal obligation to maintain a register of attendence for those in their group.
2. TVEI is a 14–18 years course but students who opt for it may leave half way through it at the end of their fifth year.
3. The potential influence of form teachers would depend on the organization of particular schools.
4. This took place just before the 1985/86 teachers' dispute with the Government, at which point teachers withdrew from such activities as parents' evenings.
5. Both Ball (1981) and Wood (1979) stress the importance of teachers' perceptions of the academic ability of students in relation to their placement in certain subjects (and groups within that subject).
6. I asked the teachers what activities they were involved with in their capacity as form teachers.
7. 'Alpha' groups consisted of those students expected to follow examination syllabuses in at least four to five subjects. The school TVEI co-ordinator and others I spoke to regarded these students as of relatively 'high academic ability', a definition I adopt throughout this paper. To achieve a 'balanced

intake', the co-ordinator was hoping to recruit around fourteen 'alpha' students to the Initiative.

8. Borough's TVEI co-ordinator doubted this explanation and argued that the form teachers probably did not check their pigeonholes. However, those I talked to said they regularly cleared their pigeonholes.
9. Whether such activities are voluntary was an issue at the centre of the recent dispute and is likely to remain a point of contestation for some time to come.
10. While I have stressed the difficulty of generalizing the points made in this paper, there is some evidence to suggest their relevance to other TVEI schools. Borough's LEA recognizes the promotion of TVEI to be a difficulty and I have been told that those concerned have had at least one meeting concerned with this. Furthermore, when I presented this paper to the Open University's TVEI Evaluation Group, several of its members mentioned that schools they were involved with had encountered similar 'problems'.

References

Apple, M. (1985) *Education and Power*. London, Ark Publishing.

Ball, S. (1981) *Beachside Comprehensive*. Cambridge, Cambridge University Press.

Bhaskar, B. (1979) *The Possibility of Naturalism*. Brighton, Harvester Press.

Blackburn, B. (1975) *The Tutor*. London, Heinemann.

Dale, R. (1985) The background and inception of the Technical and Vocational Education Initiative. In Dale, R. (ed.), *Education, Training and Employment: Towards a 'New Vocationalism'?* Oxford, Pergamon.

Dale, R. (1986) Examining the gift horse's teeth: a tentative analysis of TVEI. In Walker, S. and Barton, L. *Youth, Unemployment and Schooling*. Milton Keynes, Open University Press.

Hamblin, D. (1974) *The Teacher and Counselling*. Oxford, Basil Blackwell.

Hamblin, D. (1981) *Problems and Practice of Pastoral Care*, Oxford, Blackwell.

Kuhn, T. (1970) *The Structure of Scientific Revolutions*, 2nd ed. University of Chicago Press.

Lawn, M. and Ozga, J. (1981) The educational worker? A reassessment of teachers. In Barton, L. and Walker, S. *Schools, Teachers and Teaching*. Barcombe, Falmer Press.

MSC (1978) *Young People and Work*. London, HMSO.

MSC (1984) *TVEI Review*. Manpower Services Commission.

Marland, M. (1974) *Pastoral Care*. London, Heinemann.

McCulloch, G. et al. (1985) *Technological Revolution? The Politics of School Science and Technology in England and Wales Since 1945*. London, Falmer Press.

McCulloch, G. (1986) Policy, Politics and Education: The Technical and Vocational Education Initiative, in *J. Education Policy* **1**,(1).

Ozga, J. (1981) *The Politics of the Teaching Profession*. The Open University E353, Unit 14. Milton Keynes, Open University Press.

Pyart, B. (1985) An overview of TVEI. In *School Organisation* **5**,(4).

Rees, B. (1985) Developments in Pastoral Care and Counselling. In *The Counsellor* **5**,(2).

Smith, D. (1965) Front line organisation of the state mental hospital. In *Administrative Science Quarterly* **10**.

Times Educational Supplement, 15.11.85.

Woods, P. (1979) *The Divided School*. London, Routledge & Kegan Paul.

This paper first appeared as 'Implementing the contract: the Technical and Vocational Education and Initiative', in *Brit. J. Sociology of Education* **7**,(4), (397–414) (1986).

Douglas Barnes

8

A First Impression: TVEI in Six Schools

When in Autumn 1986 my colleagues and I began our study of TVEI curricula* many of the programmes which we saw had already been in progress for more than two years. We had undertaken to carry out case studies of twenty-six schools. For our first visits a team of two investigators spent two weeks in each school, talking to teachers and students, observing lessons, and endeavouring to understand not only how the school was putting TVEI into action, but why they were doing so in that manner and no other. What follows is a shortened version of a working paper which I wrote at an early stage of these visits; it was based on casework dossiers in which were recorded our data from the first six schools visited.

The paper begins by discussing how the content of courses is related to activities in the world outside school, and goes on to refer to teaching styles, problem solving, what teachers said about the idea of negotiating the curriculum, and aspects of the integration of TVEI courses. (The original paper dealt with other issues too.) In choosing to write about these issues I was guided partly by MSC's aims for TVEI, partly by the concerns which were implicit in the schools' activities or expressed to us by the teachers we talked with, and partly by my own priorities and values.

* The National Evaluation of TVEI Curriculum is based in the University of Leeds School of Education, and is funded by the Manpower Services Commission, I am indebted to my co-director David Layton and my colleagues Peter Medway, George Johnson, Steven Jordan, and David Yeomans for agreeing to my use of the material in this paper.

Learning in a context

Schooling, while itself a part of the normal social world of our time, projects images of the world that are edited in various ways that can be described. TVEI schools have undertaken to make their courses practical and relevant to the world which students are likely to experience, so it is appropriate to ask what progress they have made in this direction. Few teachers see their task as training their students for a particular occupation. They do not see themselves as engaged in narrow vocationalism but in helping students to master skills, knowledge and understanding that will be widely useful to them in their lives, and not only in employment. The phrase 'transferable skills' is commonly used. One crucial distinction between narrow and broad learning lies in the context in which the practice of the skills is embedded. There are occasions when skills are taught for their own sake because the teacher judges that they will be necessary at a later stage of the student's learning, or directly relevant to some aspect of a particular employment, but this is different in kind from learning which places the skills in a context which will lead to a wider understanding of that field of activity.

There seem to be three aspects of the creation of a successful context for the learning of a skill. First, the skill needs to be learnt in a context which attributes a purpose and a set of criteria to it; for example in one Business Studies course the teacher had embedded the study of maps in a context of trying to understand the criteria which influences a firm in the siting of a factory. When in another school some students wished to write a letter to a firm that manufactured electronic components, their teacher made this an opportunity to persuade them to consider alternative forms of expression and the tone that each of them would be likely to convey.

The second requirement is that the question, even if it originates with the teacher and not with the students, should be adopted by them as if it were their own. Students are unlikely to learn unless they either recognize the task in hand as potentially relevant, or can be persuaded by a teacher that it will indeed be so one day. The teachers observed were not always very successful in this. One teacher of a course on Land Based Industries, who was very concerned to involve his students actively in the choice and conduct of their work together, said that they seemed unable to suggest concerns that could be investigated within the framework of the course. (One wonders how he set about encouraging them to think about it.) Some of the tasks that he had previously set had caught their interest; for example, he had invited a farmer to set a task to the class, and the farmer had responded by giving them the task of designing new dairy facilities for his farm. When we were observing his teaching he had chosen as topic the impact on farming of the recent bad weather, a focus that on the face of it seems practical and likely to appeal. After the visit to the farm the students had been set the task of making a tape-recorded programme on the subject of the effects of the weather. Our observer reports, however, that the question had remained the teacher's, and had not been taken on by the students. The results were that their approach to it was perfunctory; they showed more interest in manipulating the tape-recorder than in the set topic.

The third aspect relates to the complexity of the task. On the one hand, tasks may be simple, pre-analysed, routine sequences of skills, or they may be pre-digested uncontroversial accounts, of the kind common in traditional school textbooks. Such tasks are based on what are sometimes called 'well-formed' problems: all the necessary data are given, there is no irrelevant or distracting information, the criteria of success are clear, and there is a single right answer. But in the real world few problems are like this. In solving real-world problems one finds oneself at one and the same time seeking to define the goals, to decide what information about both context and means are relevant, and at the same time generating an array of possible methods. Real-world problems are 'noisy', complex, and seldom lead to an unambiguously 'best solution'. The real world is full of uncertainty, ambiguity, and controversy, and an education which is to prepare for that world needs at some times to reflect this and prepare for it. However, we are not making the assumption that the curriculum should always reflect this complexity and uncertainty; there are clearly arguments for stages of induction when young people are introduced to specially simplified versions of the world in order to develop skills and understanding that will stand them in good stead later.

Teaching styles

It was never our intention to categorize the teaching that we were permitted to witness in TVEI courses in order to pass judgment upon the work of individual teachers. Nevertheless TVEI aims directed our attention to the way in which different styles of teaching enabled students to participate in learning in different ways. The aims imply that young people are to engage in active problem-solving of a kind that will strengthen their initiative and their ability to monitor their own learning and therefore take some responsibility for it. Observing lessons in the light of this has led us to outline three styles of teaching: Controlled, Framed and Negotiated. Since these styles are 'ideal types' some teachers' work may display elements of more than one style.

The controlled style

In the 'controlled' style, the teacher sets out to hand over to pupils a set of skills or a body of knowledge, often simplifying what is to be learnt into sequential sub-tasks. The pupils are to master the skills and knowledge rather than to understand why these are to be mastered and not others.

The teacher judges on the basis of his or her expertise that there is a body of competences that can be defined in advance and taught directly. As one member of our teams said, 'How would you teach students to plant bulbs except by showing them how and then giving them some to plant?' An alternative might be to teach the skills in the context of flower-growing for market, which would make it possible to discuss the advantages of different methods. Skills such as typing may be taught either in a Controlled fashion or in a context which considers current changes in office practice and their implications for employers and employees.

In one school a teacher of Communications told us that it was the subject to which the least able children in the TVEI group were directed. This seems to have persuaded her to adopt a policy of containing the pupils by occupying them with activities that would make minimal demands on them. The work was controlled by worksheets; there was much 'filling-in' of missing words, or looking for errors in diagrams. During one lesson which we observed, the class was required to find a single word that would appropriately describe the expression on a pictured face provided in the worksheet. Such a use of worksheets is unlikely to contribute to the TVEI aims of involving students actively in their work, and of relating it closely to the concerns of the real world. However, teachers are not only responsible to curricular aims but also have to manage groups of young people who may at times prove uncooperative.

The framed style

In the 'framed' style, the teacher's central concern is to offer to students an induction into the 'framework' of an established discipline or a set of techniques. The students' task is to take over the framework and learn to use it in their own thinking and action. Within the frame, however, the students may be given considerable freedom to make choices of subject matter, task and methods, and may be invited to express opinions, so that they do not have to take their learning 'on trust' from the teacher.

To illustrate the Framed style, we begin with a course in Technology, which carried a Mode III CSE qualification. The criteria to be used in assessing the students' achievement included problem-solving, researching, manipulative and analytical skills, as well as knowledge and understanding. The teacher made it clear that he preferred to introduce students to practical inquiry rather than to present them with authoritative statements. We observed a sequence of lessons about stresses in bridge-like structures. At one point he placed a weight on the centre of a model of a bridge but a student objected:

S: But you put that weight in the middle where it's strongest.
T: That's an assumption; we can't do that (i.e. make assumptions). We've got to investigate that assumption.

As the students began practical work he advised them:

> Do a sketch. Estimate what you think. Analyse it. Do your investigation and see.

This is described here as an example of a typical 'Framed' pedagogy. The teacher is maintaining a tight control of progress through the subject-matter but the students, far from being inactive, have ample opportunity to get access to the underlying principles involved, and to join in the teacher's thinking in a manner typical of good traditional teaching.

The next example is drawn from a lesson taught to a group of boys and girls as part of a course called 'Community Studies'. The lesson began with a film about Caesarian section during childbirth. The teacher next led class discussion, first eliciting some central concepts and terms used in the film and then endeavouring to encourage discussion of their feelings about the topic. The students next worked in small groups discussing issues defined for them by the teacher, and completing worksheets that required them to rehearse the information given in the film. They were next asked to discuss questions such as:

> Doctors may treat pregnant women as if they were ill. Why do you think this is?
>
> Why do you think some mothers may feel cheated when they have had a baby delivered by Caesarian section?

Thus while the teacher was in tight control of the more 'technical' elements of the topic she expected the pupils to consider the socio-ethical issues for themselves. This worksheet, unlike many we have seen, led into discussion rather than shutting it off. Finally, the teacher required each group to report their findings orally, and she commented on what they said by way of placing the whole discussion in a framework. Within the Framed style, a teacher may from time to time give a good deal of autonomy to pupils to choose content or activities, yet all the time the implicit message will be that these are to be chosen so as to exercise the framework of skills and knowledge.

The negotiated style

The teacher who adopts the 'negotiated' style places a major emphasis on involving his or her students in the decisions and choices which shape the work that they are doing. Through continual discussion teacher and class together make joint decisions about the area of content being dealt with, the approaches to be tried, and the methods to be used. Upon occasion the teacher may give his or her support to ideas and methods that seem immature or inappropriate so that students have an opportunity to learn from their misconceptions. From one point of view, this can be seen as a way of putting a high priority on personal and social goals, since the effect is likely to be to strengthen students' sense of responsibility for their work. Its prime purpose however is to see to it that they are fully involved in the thinking.

In the six schools being described here we found only two undeniable examples of the Negotiated pedagogy. In one case a teacher of Technology told us that he saw it as his responsibility to make available to his students an experience of the decision-making process without himself making decisions for them. For example, he used deliberate techniques for helping them to generate ideas, as on one occasion when a group of students was about to choose problems for a project:

> I'm not sure what will help you best forward, how we'll settle on something. Tell you what, Mrs B—'s room is free; we'll go through and get stuff, see what's there, get catalogues. *You* need brainstorming — jot down remotely possible ideas, up to twenty, quite separately of each other. Play with equipment, make something work. In the last fifteen minutes we'll talk.

In our view his approach not only invited his students to participate but went far towards enabling them to do so.

The second clear example of a Negotiated pedagogy occurred in a TVEI option in Performing Arts which was taught by a drama specialist. When asked what 'negotiating the curriculum' meant to her she said:

> It is about the group making decisions, constantly. As I said, by fifth year, hopefully, with a good group, they should be totally in control of the style, content and organization of their work. There are times obviously when I say, 'Right, I think that this is the right section of the piece to look at now. What do you feel about that?' If they say, 'No,' and totally disagree, I say, 'O.K., fine. What are we going to do then?' Obviously sometimes I set a topic...as an introduction to the course, just to get everybody working together.

In an interview she made her purposes explicit:

> They have to work as individuals within [the] group, they have to learn the group pressure, they have to cope with it, they have to be prepared to teach each other, they have to be prepared to be taught by each other, they have to learn to give and to accept criticism positively rather than negatively, they have to learn the most immense amount of self-control, they have to learn communication skills, they have to learn the relationship between the thinking of an idea, deciding you want to communicate, putting that into a form that is accessible to an audience, seeing that through and then looking back and saying, 'Did we succeed in that...?'

In both of these cases a need had to be identified and its parameters explored, possible responses considered, a choice made and put into effect, and the results evaluated. Both teachers avoided making the decisions and teaching the course as a set of pre-specified skills and competences.

Problem-solving

Three of the six schools provided an introduction to problem-solving at the beginning of their TVEI courses. One school made problem-solving a central element in the residential experience provided for all TVEI students at an early stage of the course. Another school began its TVEI provision with a six-week course which included a range of problem-solving from interpersonal communication and relationships to designing a poster and making a burglar alarm. A third school provided a TVEI core which included problem-solving as the first element in a rather miscellaneous programme.

Commendable as such introductory courses no doubt are, they seem no substitute for the use of problem-solving as a normal part of everyday teaching. There are problems and problems, however. We conventionally apply the word 'problem' to tasks which require students to apply a routine they have been taught to a situation that the routine is obviously relevant to; we are all familiar with these from conventional mathematics textbooks. Within a 'controlled' teaching style, teachers set tasks to pupils which ask for the application of routines to standard tasks, for example the lay-out of a business letter. It is a very different kind of 'problem' which requires the student to analyse the requirements of the situation and search his or her repertoire for models that might aid understanding and action. At what point can a distinction be made between standard exercises and problems? The criteria must include (a) the distance of the problem task from any previous task dealt with during the course, and therefore the degree of generalization required, and (b) the degree of autonomy given to the student to analyse the requirements of the task and to generate and evaluate alternative solutions. TVEI goals give some prominence to problem-solving that reflects something of the complexity of the real world, and links it with the development of self-reliance and initiative.

An example of the second kind of problem-solving though within a relatively tight frame occurred in one lesson that was observed from a course in Information Technology. The teacher spent a substantial proportion of the time in teaching pupils a standard format for presenting written documentation to accompany the computer programs that they were writing. As soon as this ended, the students went back to individual work on their programs, which might be concerned with calculating percentages or constructing an English/French dictionary. Such tasks gave students the opportunity to exercise skills, judgement and analytical abilities within a predetermined framework. A less tightly framed example occurred when we observed some lessons from an Electronics course; one group of students was working under the teacher's direct supervision, another was working on separate sections of a joint project; one student for example had drawn in his 'Project Book' a series of six possible circuit diagrams which he thought might be suitable for the part of the task that had fallen to his share. A third group was setting up circuits that they had previously drawn. The emphasis fell upon the testing of hypotheses. Here is a typical exchange between the teacher and a member of the second group of pupils:

P: Sir, will that work?
T: Well, you say, 'Will that work?' What's the straight answer to that now? Am I going to tell you if it works or not? So what are you going to do? What you are going to do in about five minutes' time, you're going to come to me and say, 'Can I switch this on now so I can see if it works?' won't you?
P: Yeah.
T: Go on then.

We were told that the coursework that was being done would be assessed against the following criteria: originality, flexibility, resourcefulness, understanding of physical principles, practical skill, quality of product, and presentation of written report. The work of this class threw considerable responsibility upon individual pupils and also required collaborative effort. It would certainly encourage self-reliance. Since we were observing at a relatively late point in the process, we were not able to be sure how far the students had grasped underlying principles or had worked by rule of thumb. Moreover, the more freedom the students have to choose the problem they will address, the less certain that it will allow them to practise any particular skills, including those they have been taught in preparation for the problem-solving exercise. Such is the paradox of realistic problem-solving.

We found very few occasions when teachers picked up real-life problems as they arose, though in my view many of them would do well to consider what value there might be in helping students to engage in what has been called 'problem-finding'. Most students need help in finding problems; it is not enough merely to tell them that the time has come for them to choose the focus for a practical project. Some teachers provide a list for their students to choose from; this has the advantage of ensuring that no one chooses something entirely impracticable, yet deprives the students of a valuable opportunity for learning, since many real-world problems do not come to us ready formulated. Unfortunately, some students develop ways of persuading teachers to do the thinking for them. One teacher of Motor Vehicle Technology, however, was determined that he was not to be manipulated in that way. The class was working on another matter when a student pointed out that a particular car engine was overheating. The teacher accepted this new focus, elicited a range of suggestions for the possible cause, asked the group to evaluate them, and then shared among the group of students the responsibility for testing the more likely suggestions. He was clearly determined that the students would have to go through the thought processes for themselves. This was a good deal closer to the disorganized way in which problems arise in real life than the well-defined tasks which were commonly set in many of the courses observed, and it can be surmised that the two call upon different personal resources.

The same teacher explained the rationale of his concentration upon problem-solving in this way:

> I might present the problems or if they have problems of their own they can present them.

He saw his students as people who had a voice that ought to be heard.

> It doesn't really matter what the problem is so long as it's a problem...Dangle ideas around...Try to coax them through.

He did not believe that many of his colleagues shared his views.

> I think some people might cringe at the thought of pupils having an input into any lesson. There's quite a few teachers who, rightly or wrongly, have been brought up with the system of didactic teaching and that will stay.

We might permit ourselves to hope that he was mistaken.

We found worksheets to be widely in use, and the investigators' comments on the effects of these upon teaching frequently implies a negative judgment. This is because some teachers, mainly from the Controlled category, use them as a means of withdrawing from direct interaction with students. On the other hand worksheets need not necessarily perform this function, but can fill a valuable role by structuring parts of the work in order to free the teacher to work with individuals, and by setting up occasions when students are required to collaborate and discuss their work. It seems that the proper use of worksheets in a pedagogy committed to encouraging problem-solving, initiative, and collaboration might be a suitable subject for further investigation and for INSET. Indeed, a number of TVEI teachers have suggested that the most valuable in-service education teachers new to TVEI could receive would be to engage in experiential learning for themselves.

Conceptions of 'negotiating the curriculum'

I am giving some prominence to the concept of 'negotiation' since it would seem an essential component in any teaching strategy that is designed to encourage young people to take a more active part in learning, to develop qualities of initiative and self-reliance, and to take more responsibility for their own activities and achievements. We must however ask how far it is reasonable to expect teachers to be successful in negotiating aspects of their courses with their students.

When we have discussed this matter with teachers involved in TVEI courses they have mentioned many of the pressures that discourage such a change in teacher–student relationships. Among, these are the size of some of the groups taught (in spite of the special advantages of TVEI funding), the amount of time available for teaching the course, the requirements of certain examinations which do not allow the necessary freedom of manoeuvre, and even the administrative requirements of some schools (for example those which do not allow students to undertake tasks outside the building). Moreover, teachers of subjects such as technology are more likely than teachers of some other subjects (personal and social education is an example of the latter) to take the view that the subject they are teaching has a core of knowledge and skills that is not negotiable. It was plain in the case of the Communications course mentioned above that if a group of students is unmotivated or demoralized it becomes much harder even to begin to discuss with them the purposes and procedures of the work in hand.

School TVEI co-ordinators were more ready than other teachers to talk to us of negotiating the curriculum, and displayed, as one would expect, a good grasp of what it would entail. However, even they were not always sanguine about the likelihood of its implementation by their colleagues. One said that negotiation occurred only in 'those subjects suited to it' and by that he meant subjects other than two-year courses leading to an examination. He saw the examination system as the major obstacle to the changes in teaching methods which are invited in the TVEI aims.

Some of the teachers whom we saw with their classes had a clear conception of negotiation and expressed approval of it. I have already quoted from an interview with a teacher of Performing Arts about how she negotiated with her students. One of her colleagues, an English teacher who expressed enthusiasm about TVEI (and especially about the value of word-processing in English), defined negotiation in this way:

> What I think it means is to avoid an authoritarian approach to telling kids what they must do and why, and arriving at some agreed or half-way point where they are working more independently at their own levels in ways that they see as more practical, or having more application.

A number of teachers, asked directly about negotiating the curriculum with their students, said quite frankly, 'I haven't tried it to any large extent.' In spite of undeniable difficulties, it is my view that teachers whose normal teaching methods could be called Controlled should ask themselves whether they should be reaching towards a Framed pedagogy, and that those who are already comfortable in using Framed methods might well consider whether there are not occasions when they can aid their students in taking more responsibility, and even attempt the joint planning of part of a course with them.

The head teacher of one of the schools when asked about negotiation first equated it with pupils having a choice of subject options, and then went on to associate it with his own version of profiling and counselling.

> What it should primarily mean is that you discuss a piece of work with a pupil and you say, 'I think this particular piece of work, you have done well with this aspect of it, but here...[omission] you should have done such and such, and here quite frankly you have been very lazy, because you've not done it at all. And then you should say, 'Do you agree?' or, 'Do you think I'm being fair?' and then you should let the pupil say what he feels about what you've said...

This head teacher's conception of negotiation, far from increasing the student's initiative, seems to use a version of profiling as a way of strengthening the teacher's control over the student. His view of profiling was far from typical: in several schools we have been told that profiling has been essential to the changes in teacher–student relationships which many teachers saw as central to TVEI.

Integration

In the context of the impact of TVEI on schools, 'integration' may have either of two meanings: it may either refer to previously discrete areas of study which had been amalgamated in order to construct one of the TVEI options, or it may refer to special arrangements intended to pull together the whole of the students' experience of the courses. It is the latter we are concerned with, since it is of more central importance to TVEI.

Secondary schools have seldom taken it to be their task to help their pupils to interrelate the various kinds of learning that they have experienced in different subjects, so it was no surprise to find that two of the six schools made no attempt to find a means of integrating the students' experience of TVEI. In one of the other schools the course began for all TVEI students with a six-weeks introduction to problem-solving. All students then devoted six periods each week to 'Breadth Studies', two periods being given to Social and Life Skills and four to other activities, such as Careers, Health Education, and Information Technology. A particularly interesting aspect of the compulsory Information Technology course was that it was based on a body of classroom materials prepared by a specialist teacher but taught by a large number of non-specialist volunteers, thus involving a wider group of teachers in TVEI work than would otherwise have been the case. In none of these schools did it seem that the structures set up to integrate the students' experience of TVEI were achieving that end; the core modules ensured that students had a *common* experience but did nothing to aid each of them to interrelate the various options they had chosen.

It is not easy to see how an integrated experience can be achieved by solely administrative means. The school mentioned above had gone far in this direction by setting up occasions when skills and knowledge learnt in specialist areas can be applied to tasks and issues that transcend subject boundaries. However, the perceptions of the teachers are at least as important as formal arrangements. (On one occasion when a group of students returned empty-handed from an attempt to obtain copies of their work from an adult who operated the school's photocopying machine, the teacher made of it an occasion to point out the part played by human relationships in the effective solution even of what seem to be technical tasks.)

One school's experience of a system set up to encourage integration of the individual student's work deserves to be reported in more detail. The TVEI project in question had been centrally planned in the first instance, and one of the central decisions had been to timetable time for students to work under non-specialist supervision on what were called 'Personal Assignments'. The central planners had envisaged that teachers would set students to work on tasks or larger projects during the more specialized lessons and that the students would thereafter be able to work on these tasks and projects during the Personal Assignments time. In the event, the time was not being used for that purpose, but for remedial and other teaching. (As one teacher said: 'The original idea behind Personal Assignments was that students would bring work to catch up or extend from their TVEI course, but these were run on traditional lines that did not make this possible. So the teacher in these periods has to devise work specially to occupy the students so that he can do the central profiling process with individuals.') It was not clear whether the teachers did not understand how the time was intended to be used, or whether they were unsympathetic towards the arrangement. The teacher referred to above blamed his colleagues' pedagogical conservatism, and this was probably part of the explanation. It is frequently suggested in the literature on curriculum development that to make central decisions about pedagogy without involving affected teachers in the necessary rethinking is not likely to be a successful strategy.

It will have been clear to the reader that this paper is a collection of rather diverse concerns that happened to be at the forefront of one person's attention in the very early stages of the project. During the case studies, information on a far wider range of issues has been collected, and is being analysed. Our original impressions drawn from only six schools have inevitably been modified as the study took us to other schools where the approaches to TVEI were quite different. This paper is offered as a first impression and no more.

Murray Saunders

9

At Work in TVEI

Students Perceptions of Their Work Experience

Introduction

As in the case of many practices emerging or re-emerging under the auspices of TVEI, 'work experience' is far too slippery to define with any confidence. As a curricular practice its form has developed through 'custom' and can signify quite different types of activity (see Eggleston 1982, Watts 1983). While this is certainly the case, there is also little consensus on the purpose of work experience and a lack of clarity concerning the less obvious or unintended effects.

Derek Black, writing in 1976, notes that work experience has been defined as disparately as a half-day visit to a place of work (a talk and tour) or one week or more actually participating in some working practices. He defines work experience, on behalf of the Trident Trust, as an activity in which a school pupil spends a significant and continuous period of time performing a realistic job of work on the premises of an employer (Black 1976, p. 89).

It is interesting to note that the Trident Trust follows closely the guidelines suggested by the British Government Circular 7/74 on Work Experience. In the circular, it is the general *educational* value of work experience which is stressed rather than specifically vocational training or the production of articles for sale which would not satisfy the requirements of the 1973 Education Act concerned with Work Experience (DES 1974). Since this Circular, the governmental preoccupation with work experience has grown considerably with the relationship between the 'school curriculum' and work the object of official scrutiny. The Green Paper 'Education in Schools' (Cmnd 6869) in which authorities were asked to review their curricular arrangements signalled a specific interest in this area. Questions were set out subsequently in Circular 14/77 for authorities to answer. The most extensive section was that called 'Preparation for Working Life', in which authorities were asked, for example, 'What steps has the authority taken to promote the development of work experience and work observation where appropriate in relation to school courses and needs of an industrial society?' (DES 1977).

We have in these earlier pronouncements, the seeds of the uneasy relationship between the different stated purposes of 'work experience', i.e. an emphasis on possible educational needs of pupils on the one hand and the needs and requirements of the 'work place' on the other. Although the DES was explicit about the intended group of pupils who should engage in work experience — 'Work experience should have value for pupils of varying ability and aptitudes and neither be designed as vocational training nor aimed at a limited range of ability' (DES 1974) — in practice it is likely that work experience has involved those students who were not successful in the 'academic' curricula. For example, the Head of the Barrymoor Unit at Banbury School in England noted that the course which had developed at the Unit, committed to work-experience orientation, is really open only to pupils who were of below-average academic ability. Those who initially showed an interest in the fourth year, in particular of average or above-average academic ability, met strong counselling against the Barrymoor courses (Farlam 1977, p. 366).

While this conflict of definition of 'vocational' (academic routes for high ability, experience of work for lower ability) acts as a legacy for current moves toward work experience and creates a continued tension for those planning curricula in schools, current orthodoxy has moved some way from this blunt division between students of different ability and has reasserted the 'across-the-board' theme in Circular 14/77.

What we may have embedded in TVEI culture, particularly in the stress on work experience, is an interesting shift in the interpretations of what compulsory schooling is all about emanating from Government via the MSC. Hudson, in a paper given to the BERA conference of 1980 experimented by using the economic categories of exchange value and use value to analyse teachers' professional ideologies. To use these categories here to reinterpret shifts in government focus represented by TVEI and work experience in particular might be useful. If a course of study has predominantly exchange value for those students experiencing it, then its use to students lies primarily in what it can be exchanged for (jobs, higher education entrance), irrespective of the skills and capacities the courses were intended to develop. Thus, in this case the use value of a course, lies in its exchange value. If a course of study has primarily use value rather than exchange value, the skills and capacities the course was intended to develop in students would *actually* be intended for use in, for example, a job. The use value of a course could lie, not in its exchange, but in the extent to which it actually prepared students for work or the next stage of their education.

These categories are not, of course, mutually exclusive, but are intended to indicate a shift of emphasis which underlies the current drift away from literary, symbolic modes of learning and teaching (the modes usually associated with liberal notions of education that emphasize the liberating qualities attributed to universalistic meanings or knowledge forms) toward the inclusion of (to use Bruner's 1978 categories) enactive (gaining knowledge from direct action) and iconic (gaining knowledge from the imitation and observation of models) modes of learning of which work experience is a part.

From the government's perspective, the concern with the lack of 'use value' of courses or its preoccupation with 'relevance' (another way of putting it) has been gaining momentum in recent years, certainly since Callaghan's 'Ruskin College' speech of 1976. 'Use value' appears to refer to the extent to which school students have skills and capacities on leaving school which are of direct benefit to the productivity of British Industry. In other words, a series of connections were made between what went on at school and what was failing to go on at work. The argument that schooling (in particular) has not been 'relevant' either to society's or individual pupils' needs is a hardy perennial.

The central position of the two issues of industrial decline and unemployment in public debate has sharpened the re-emerging discussion concerning the connection between education and other areas of social life, in particular 'work'. At the same time the function of technology and technological change has featured strongly in the analysis. This has provided a fertile seed bed for the growth of arguments concerning the need for national governments to adopt a more interventionist stance on the curriculum and teacher effectiveness. In a nutshell, the issue of educational effectiveness has become important enough in the public and political mind for an attempt, by government, to readjust the traditional 'autonomy' of schooling characterizing British education and to move toward more direct forms of influence. It is clear that part of the 'problem' of industrial decline/competitiveness and unemployment is identified by government as a 'deficiency' in the school system in terms of what and how students learn.

Notwithstanding the shaky logic of these 'connections', the analysis has gained sufficient currency for it to be tacitly accepted by the schools. Not least because acceptance also brought with it the opportunity, by way of MSC funding, to innovate in a period of unprecedented contraction and trauma in the teaching profession.

While the governmental view can be characterized as a form of functional analysis of the connection between school and work, which, although questioned, has become part of the broad vocabulary of 'relevance' now embracing discussions on curricula, curricula which display 'use value' also have a progressive and educationally persuasive pedigree going back for many years. John Dewey in Democracy and Education for example asserted that useful learning could occur only through 'experience', and reflection upon it, various Schools Council Projects, the Plowden report, all these have emphasized 'enactive' modes of learning; the list is a long one. The paradox is that many of those who may harbour suspicions about the government analysis and governmental motives, are as equally committed, on educational or socio/political grounds, to precisely those areas of practice the government appears to be promoting. Stephen Castles and Wiebke Wustenburg (1979), from a deeply critical marxist analysis of schooling within capitalism argue that the breakdown of the barrier between learning and work is a step in the right direction. However, John Clarke and Paul Willis (1984) from a similarly critical stance, stress that the 'social control' elements of such curricula, as youth unemployment bites still harder, are paramount.

Thus, as the viability of the exchange value of courses of study is reduced to a smaller and smaller group of students, the use value imperative grows. This tendency is to be found in the TVEI aims and criteria in which the desired connection between work and school is made quite clear. Although, as Clark and Willis suggest, 'work' has always been present in the classroom, it was never made this explicit. Perhaps the most obvious expression of this affirmation of the 'use' value of schooling is in number (vi) of the *TVEI Aims and Criteria*:

> The construction of the bridge from education to work is begun earlier by giving these young people the opportunity to have direct contact and training/planned work experience with a number of local employers in the relevant specialisms (p.34)

The 'bridging' between eduation and work that the MSC stressed so clearly as an aim is manifest in the compulsory inclusion in each TVEI submission of a work-experience component. It is not my intention here to analyse these submissions, but all submissions include at least one week of work experience for all TVEI students from the age of 15+ at a 'place of work'. The following section explores the broad perception of fifth-year TVEI students of their work experience.

Students' perceptions of work experience

Irrespective of the competing perspectives on work experience (functional preparation or social control), its growing inclusion in the school curriculum suggests that 'practical action' or 'experience' are becoming legitimate forms of knowledge. As such, work experience constitutes an attack on the assumption that 'education' and the 'literary prose tradition' are the same thing.

The following analysis draws on survey data collected in the Spring of 1986 from TVEI students from twelve authorities, as part of the Lancaster

TVEI Evaluation Programme, open-ended written comments derived from the same survey and discussions and written comments from students in three student forums established to encourage students to evaluate their experience of TVEI. Of the 2143 TVEI students who answered the work experience item on the questionnaire, 54.3% (1163) said they had participated in work experience. This compares with 29.7% of a non-TVEI comparison group.

Feeling good about work experience

Of these students 90.2% said they had enjoyed work experience, with 60.5% *strongly* agreeing it was enjoyable, while 89% of students thought it helped them to understand what work was like and 87.5% considered the experience helped them to get on with adults. This is a strong message. However, these positive responses did not entirely coincide with work experience perceived as a 'rehearsal' for the kind of work students wished to do after leaving school. While this was the case for just over half (54%), 46% were not sure or had not done the kind of work they wished to do when leaving. For many students then, enjoyment of work experience was not conditional on it being a 'taste' of a particular job, more generalized or intrinsic value may have been perceived. Although we can characterize work experience as an enjoyable practice, according to this data, is this the same as saying it was 'worthwhile' or 'valuable' or 'educational'?

A constant criticism of curricula which appear to have a more direct 'use' value is that they encourage specific, non generalizable experiences thus having little broader *educational* value. Notwithstanding the way in which these criticisms suffer from what Olsen (1977) has described as a 'naïve psychology of learning', the charge is important. If work experience is 'worthwhile' in what sense is it? Very few students (15%) found work experience difficult; however, 73.9% of students considered that work experience had taught them new skills. At the same time, the use of skills learned at school, during students' work experience, was either unclear or did not happen for 50.4% of students. These data suggest that for many students, work experience was enjoyable precisely because it was different from school (interacting with adults, learning *new* skills) and may not be justified in conventional liberal educational terms. On the other hand, the data shows that half of the students did perceive a connection between work experience and what they had learned at school, although we cannot tell from the survey what kind of skills they are.

A clue to some of these issues may be in the open-ended statements we invited students to make. We analysed 1163 separate statements, however, because students could say whatever they chose, the categories we established are illustrative of what students considered to be an appropriate statement rather than the distribution of actual perceptions. The gamble we take in giving validity to these data is based on the assumption that given a completely 'open' opportunity, students considered these comments to be significant enough to choose to make in particular to others. Each statement contained several separate references to aspects of their experience. The distinction between a *statement* and a *reference* is important in this analysis. Many statements were not qualified, i.e. they were simply statements like: 'It was more interesting and the people were much nicer than I thought. Betty was a lovely woman.' In such a case, we could not know what the work was or why it was interesting, but we did know that the student had been treated well by working colleagues. In such an instance, the statement was categorized as having two references, one to the work being 'interesting' and one to working colleagues being 'kind, nice, helpful or friendly'. In this way, Table 1 categorizes the 'positive' references the students made within the total of 1163 statements.

Table 1

Reference category	*Number of references*	*Percentage of total of routine references*
Work experience was enjoyable, good, exciting	295	27.5
The work was varied	154	14.3
Work experience was interesting	131	12.2
People were kind, nice, helpful or friendly	94	8.7
Work experience taught new 'job related' skills	90	8.4
Work experience increased confidence, helped to know how to get on with people	70	6.5
Work experience was not what was expected	49	4.5
Work experience confirmed a liking for this kind of work	45	4.2
Work experience was what was expected	42	3.9
Treated the same as everyone else/like an adult	36	3.3
There was more to the job than thought, found did more than they thought they would	29	2.7
Work experience was a change from or better than school	19	1.7
Work experience was enjoyable, but not intended career	16	1.4
Total number of respondents	1070	

Although many of the positive statements contained unqualified references to work experience as good or enjoyable, there were sufficient qualified references to 'enjoyment' or 'interest' to make some tentative suggestions on what constituted a 'good' work experience for students. In general there were relatively few direct comparisons with or references to school (1.7%) and a relatively small percentage of references made positive connections between students' work experience and intentions about future work (4.2%). Important student definitions of a 'good' work experience may contain the followng characteristics:

1 Friendly, helpful colleagues who accept the student as 'one of them'.
2 Work which is varied, containing many different aspects.
3 Opportunities to 'cope' with other people, particularly adults, in a working environment.
4 Opportunities to learn new 'skills' related to the work the student was required to do.

The kind of learning these characteristics suggest is non-specific (in terms of conventional 'knowledge areas') and enactively derived. The 'use value' of such experiences may be considered high. The assessment systems which can do justice to these experiences (and with reference to the so-called 'negative' experiences see below) are difficult to devise and standardize and thus the exchange value may be low. At the same time, the enactive rather than symbolic learning characterizing work experience suggests an undervaluation of such experiences at a wider cultural level. Proponents of work experience are therefore faced with a double bind in legitimizing work experience for all students, i.e. giving work experience exchange value. There may be competing definitions of the use value of work experience emanating from students with different ability/achievement on the one hand and government on the other.

Added to this tendency we may suggest that the underlying imperatives of selection still impel students toward conventional, symbolically expressed evidence of their capacities (written exams). As students progress past the 16+ compulsory education divide, this imperative may become stronger. Tensions in the organization of work experience for 'A' level TVEI students suggest this clearly. The use value of 'A' level courses is very much in their 'exchange' value in applications for courses in Higher Education. The exchange value of work experience in this scenario is unclear, if non-existant, for such students.

Critical perspectives on work experience

While the survey data presented above give an overwhelmingly positive view of work experience from the students' point of view, the open-ended written statements allow a more problematic picture to emerge within this overall message. Table 2 categorizes references within each statement which suggested a more critical view of the work experience for the student. It is of note that these 329 critical references constitute just under a third of the 1070 which we categorized as 'positive'.

Table 2

Reference category	*Number of references*	*Percentage of total of critical references*
The work was boring, monotonous, or too easy	129	39.2
The work was hard or tiring	114	34.6
The tasks given were trivial	35	10.6
The work experience was not enjoyed	25	7.5
The work experience put the students off this kind of work	19	5.7
The people were unhelpful	7	2.1
Total	329	

Part of the explanation for the discrepancy between the survey data and the open-ended comments may be that students' critical references were compounded or several were included in the statement. At the same time, that the work was hard or tiring may not necessarily constitute a 'critical' view, but we included it in this category. A problem with this analysis is in understanding the way in which the student interpreted the experience as, for example, 'boring'. Was this in relation to the expectations the student had of work, or in comparison with school, or a reference to the intrinsic qualities of the experience? In the latter case it seemed that the references could give an indication of some important distinctions. The first instance is where the student was given work to do, which was representative of the nature of the work situation in which the student was placed, and the student found the work unrewarding, boring or monotonous. We could still say the experience had high 'use value' for the student in providing a critical insight into the nature of many semi- or unskilled occupations. Some references were explicit in this respect:

> Work experience was good because it made me realize work is as tedious as school.

Most, however, did not make these comparisons, but simply described the nature of the work:

> It was very boring. Day in day out we would come in and open parcels, letters, and, very rarely, filing.

> I didn't like the work as I was stacking shelves and generally standing around.

When I went on work experience I worked in an office, it was not bad but I found filing very boring.

I went to Asda on work experience, it was my third choice. I found the job monotonous.

It was hairdressing, my second choice. But now I am not that interested. I was quite bored.

Second, the critique could be, not so much in the nature of the work itself, but in the *management* of the students' work experience by those charged with its provision 'on site' or by the school (in searching out placements and in 'preparing' students for their experience). In this case students were critical of the way in which they were 'surplus to requirements'. The work experience had not been considered by those responsible at the work face and students had not been absorbed into routine working practices.

I worked in the Red Lion and they didn't really know what I could do down in the cellars.

It was boring — there wasn't anything to do. I would not like a job like this.

On my works experience I sat behind a desk all day — doing nothing.

No one gave me work, the hours were too long. I had to make up my own work, I never want to work in an office again.

Sitting down reading a newspaper and coffee all day.

A variant of this problem is where the student did not really have a task to perform or had not been exposed deliberately to a variety of tasks but, instead, had been used as a general dogsbody and had been asked to perform a series of trivial jobs, often for particular individuals.

All I did was clean the place up and helped a bit.

All I did was sweep up and clear wood out of the workshop and move wood around.

I hated this experience ... They used me just to get their dirty jobs done.

I thought work experience was to help the kids and work with them, not get the toys out and tidy the cupboard and paints away. I only played with kids a little.

I was supposed to be a panel-beater but I just did all the grubby jobs to save the workers doing it.

I just ran a few errands for the boss and brewed up.

In these cases the use value of the work experience for students may be unclear. In one sense they may have gained a distorted picture of the tasks associated with these jobs because they were really non-essential or formal. On the other hand, the students were still able to talk with working colleagues, observe and come to conclusions about the overall nature of the working situations in which they were placed. It is interesting to note that, in this usage of the concept of 'use value', those work experiences which allowed the student to try out or be exposed to a variety of tasks, may not have high 'use value' because it is an unrealistic experience of 'work', i.e. 'artificially' interesting or varied. If the aims of the experience offered by the school is to introduce the student to the realities of work, then a positive experience for the student may in fact have less use value than the negative experiences described in the first case above.

In general we are able to suggest student definitions of a 'poor' work experience. For those students who may have already begun to 'penetrate', to use Willis' (1977) vocabulary, the nature of aspects of routine or unskilled work, being exposed to boring or monotonous jobs may still be interpreted as a good experience even though there was little 'enjoyment'. However, the single most important characteristic of a poor 'work experience' was where the student was not involved in the routine work practice and was left to either make his/her own work or simply sit around doing nothing. This was perceived not only as a waste of time but also humiliating for the student. Interestingly, there were several references to the work not being what the student wanted to do or intended to do in the future, but they were nevertheless positively surprised and classified the experience as a good one.

Summary

The data analysed here suggest, overall, a positive yet complex picture. Clearly, most students perceived their work experience as a good thing. While many references to the work experience were unqualified statements of enjoyment, references were made to the importance of the interactions students had with those they were working with as of key significance. Learning 'new' task-related skills and being exposed to a variety of jobs were also aspects of work experience students chose to single out for particular mention. A 'poor' experience was characterized as one in which the student was outside normal working practices, treated, as one student said 'like a lemon', and left with no real job to do.

The distinction was made between the exchange and use value of particular types of curricula. This distinction is not on the basis of abstract logical categories but represents differences in interpretation and practice. It is quite clear that the categories are not necessarily mutually exclusive, they just tend to be. The dichotomy points to quite fundamental conceptions of what learning and legitimate educational practice is, and is expressed, for example, in the distinctions made in the new orthodoxy represented in TVEI, between 'student and teacher centredness'. The preoccupation of government with 'relevance' (interpreted here as an explicit connection between what is learned within educational institutions and what are the perceived needs of the labour market) has been interpreted as a shift, at least in the rhetoric, toward curricula which have an emphasis on use value rather than, or as well as, exchange value. The kind of curricula associated with these two categories are those involving enactive modes of learning in the case of the former and symbolic modes in the latter. In that work experience is predominantly 'enactive' and is perceived as having an explicit connection with the labour market, it falls into the 'use' value category. However, the nature of the use value of experiences of work were complex.

For the students, they tended to be in the development of generalized interactional competencies and the learning of different and varied 'action' skills; it also included the development of a critical perspective on aspects of work. Whether these characteristics coincide with those of the government conception of 'preparation' is unclear. Also, whether these competencies lend themselves to assessment procedures may determine the extent to which they gain exchange value.

There are other areas of practice in TVEI which 'suffer' the same problem. Work experience can be grouped with residential, leisure and PSD education in this respect. The current practice is for such experiences to 'stand alone' and to have only a tenuous connection with other, more 'exchange' oriented courses. At present our evidence suggests (see Saunders 1986, Fuller 1986a) that work experience is predominantly 'placement' rather than 'curriculum' led. By this we mean that because of the organizational difficulties associated with placing large numbers of students in work experience (usually carried out over and above teachers' normal working time), such organizational demands greatly determine how placements are made. Although most projects attempted to match students demands with placements, how the experience connected with other curriculum experience was rarely considered.

At a recent conference on schools/industry links (see Fuller 1986b), it emerged that preparation for work experience usually took the form of behavioural instructions. Although students were often asked to diarize their experience, follow-up work was patchy and uneven. In order for integration with the broader curriculum to occur, it was considered that work experience may have to be radically rethought and reorganized.

However, the likelihood is that in order for this to occur, the competencies thus developed will have to be expressed symbolically (files, reports, integration into conventional curricula, etc.) which will yet again retreat to an assessment of competence in symbolic modes rather than the iconic or enactive modes that work experience was actually all about. How to generalize from experiences of work and to explore intellectually the learning undertaken by students in such a way that we don't fall into the trap of 'naïve psychology' Olsen (1976) alerts us to, remains perhaps the most important challenge in work experience programmes.

References

Black, D. (1976) Work experience: a systematic approach. *Brit. J. Guidance and Counselling*, pp. 88–97.

Bruner, J.S., Olsen, D.R. (1977/78) Symbols and texts as tools of intellect. *Interchange* **8**, (4).

Castles, S. and Wustenburg, W. (1979) *The Education of the Future*. London, Pluto Press.

Clarke, J. and Willis, P. (1984) in *Introduction to Schooling for the Dole*, by Bates, I., Clarke, J., Cohen, P., Finn, D., Moore, R. and Willis, P. London, Macmillan.

DES (1974) Work Experience, Circulars and Administrative Memoranda, *Circular 7/74*. London, HMSO.

DES (1977) Local Education Authority Arrangements for the School Curriculum Circulars and Administrative Memoranda, *Circular 140/77*. London, HMSO.

Egglestone, J. (1982) (ed.) *Work Experience in Secondary Schools*. London, Routledge & Kegan Paul.

Farlam (1977) On the Barrymoor Unit — Banbury School, Coombe Lodge Reports, Study Conference 77/19. *The Vocational Preparation of Young People* **10**, (8).

Fuller, A. (1986) *Beyond TVEI: A Study of 16+ TVEI Leavers From Six First Round TVEI Projects*. Manpower Services Commission.

Fuller, A. (1986) *TVEI: Education and Industry Links — Constraints and Strategies*. Manpower Services Commission.

Hudson, G. (1980) Use and exchange values and teachers' professional ideology. Paper to the BERA Conference, Cardiff.

MSC (1986) *TVEI Review '85*, p. 34. Manpower Services Commission.

Olson, D.R. (1976) The language of instruction. *The Literate Bias of Schooling*. OISE mimeo.

Saunders, M. (1986) Three reports on *Students' Evaluation of Their Experience of TVEI* (Unpublished).

Watts, A.G. (eds) (1983) *Work Experience and Schools*. London, Heinemann Educational Books.

Willis, P. (1977) *Learning to Labour*. London, Saxon House.

Val Millman and Gaby Weiner

10

Engendering Equal Opportunities

The Case of TVEI

In this chapter we explore the progress of TVEI in its brief to promote equal opportunities between the sexes, and compare the work being undertaken by TVEI with earlier gender initiatives in education. First we shall consider the reasons for the inclusion of equal opportunities as a TVEI criterion and the ways in which TVEI co-ordinators and teachers have come to grips with equality issues. We shall then ask questions about the kinds of initiatives which have been developed within TVEI to promote sex equality. Have they developed along the same lines as other educational initiatives on gender or has TVEI developed innovative strategies of its own?

Since the Sex Discrimination Act and the Equal Pay Act came into force in 1975, considerable efforts have been made by some teachers and educationists to develop ideas about how to challenge sex inequalities in education. Several national projects (e.g. Girls into Science and Technology (GIST), Schools Council Sex Differentiation Project) have developed strategies for combatting sex-stereotyping in option choice and teacher perceptions. A number of LEAs have made substantial progress in recognizing gender (and race) as mainstream educational issues, and individuals or groups of teachers have tried to promote change in their schools.

Until the 1960s concern for redressing gender inequalities in education was directed mainly towards gaining *access* to education courses, qualifications and benefits for middle-class girls. More recently there has been more emphasis on *content* and *outcomes* for *all* girls in terms of curriculum content, option choice, examination results and career destination.

It has been argued elsewhere (Weiner 1986) that two different approaches to gender issues in education are evident post World War II. The 'egalitarian' approach which draws on ideas of equality of opportunity, first formally acknowledged in the 1944 Education Act; and the 'radical' approach which has its origins in the civil rights and women's movements of the late 1960s and 1970s, and has a more girl/woman-centred orientation.

The concept of equality of opportunity expanded from an emphasis originally on levels of ability in the 1940s and 1950s, to class in the 1970s, and race and gender in the 1970s and 1980s. Since the Fish Report (1985) it has been further widened to include disability and children with special needs. The concern of this approach has been with extending educational opportunities to hitherto under-represented and disadvantaged groups. So, in the case of gender, its main campaigning issues have included persuading more girls to take up science and technology, ensuring a higher proportion of women in senior educational management, and encouraging girls (and boys) to make non sex-stereotyped career choices which will lead to better-paid and higher-status jobs. There have, however, been few examples of boys being encouraged to develop, for instance, their aesthetic, caring or inter-personal qualities and skills.

The 'radical' approach, on the other hand, has emphasized the unequal power relationships between men and women, girls and boys in education and in other social institutions such as the family and the workplace, and has argued for major changes in the structure of schooling. For instance, it has been critical of existing staff hierarchies, focused on the importance of sexuality in school life by drawing attention to the incidence of sexual harassment and verbal abuse, and challenged existing forms of school knowledge on the ground of male bias.

In the early 1970s, at the height of women's entry in greater numbers into the labour market and at a time of expansion and optimism for the future, ideas about sex equality flourished. Support came from central government in the form of proposed anti-discriminatory legislation which was to include education (the Sex Discrimination Act was passed in 1975), and cautious encouragement was provided by the DES in an important HMI survey conducted in 1973 (DES 1975).

Both the approaches mentioned above, drew on *feminist* ideas; that is ideas concerned with changing the position of women in society. Many of the 1980s *strategies* developed by teachers to promote equal opportunities between the sexes in education were thus premised on feminist ideas. For instance, value was placed on the importance of individual experience, working in non-hierarchical and collaborative ways, and coming to grips with the main characteristics and explanations for girls'/women's underachievement or subordination. As a consequence many of the in-service courses, teacher group meetings and 'action research' projects on gender drew on these ideas, for example, by initiating discussion-led or experiental workshops, establishing support networks, and sharing information through newsletters. There was also some support from central government, mainly through HMI discussion papers (for example, DES 1980) and individual HMI commitment.

In contrast to these approaches to gender divisions in education, the TVEI initiative on equal opportunities appears to draw on neither concepts of equality or justice, nor feminist ideas. It constitutes the biggest national initiative on gender so far proposed, backed by a powerful government agency which has the authority to withold funding if TVEI criteria are not met (Arnot 1986), yet the general philosophy of TVEI appears to be at odds with the gender initiatives mentioned earlier.

TVEI was created by the Department of Industry, not the DES, and its agenda was therefore 'set outside the education apparatus — even outside the DES; its most immediate stimulus was probably the National Economic Development Council's deliberations on education and training' (Dale 1986, p.61). It was also premised on the belief that education and schools were partly responsible for the fact that many young people were failing to find employment.

> The problem was conceptualized as one that was rooted in the individual who had failed to acquire rudimentary skills during schooling, and therefore... a special effort (was needed) to deal with inadequacies in... indivduals with whom the schools failed to cope.
>
> (Wickham 1986, pp.53–4)

David Young, the chairman of the Manpower Services Commission (MSC), said at the outset that TVEI was aimed at producing 'more skilled youngsters' adding, 'I hope that the schemes we set up will act as a catalyst to increase the pace of change.' Beyond that, it was noted, Young seemed to offer little indication of expected outcome or long-term objectives (Millman 1985).

So, why has TVEI become involved with equal opportunities given that:

> the current Conservative government embraces a political ideology which, however muted in practice, is certainly against the kind of governmental intervention that using the tools of contracts and finance to open up the labour market and training to women could ensure. (Wickham 1986, p.120)

One of the reasons, perhaps, centres on the notion of a flexible workforce. The production of a non sex-differentiated workforce could make adaptation to future (unknown) changes in the manufacturing and service industries much more practicable. Despite a massive rise in youth unemployment a MSC document in 1981 promised a brighter future which required a 'better educated, better trained and more adaptable workforce to take advantage of the new opportunities presented by new technology (*A New Training Initiative*, 1981).

Support was also forthcoming from committed individuals within the senior echelons of the MSC who were themselves pushing for a policy on gender, as well as from the European Economic Community (from which the MSC receives a proportion of its funds) and from the Trade Unions (Arnot 1986).

Tentative steps towards providing new opportunities for women had already been made by the MSC through the Training Opportunities Scheme (TOPS) and Wider Opportunities for Women (WOW). However, the MSC had found it particularly difficult to redirect young women in the new youth training programmes (YOP and, later, YTS) towards 'non-traditional' crafts and courses because many young women lacked school experience in the science and technical crafts. It seemed logical, therefore, to try to influence the secondary school curriculum; TVEI provided a useful vehicle and it therefore included in its criteria one which stated that 'equal opportunities should be available to people of both sexes and they should normally be educated together on courses within each project. Care should be taken to avoid sex-stereotyping' (MSC 1984). LEA interpretations of this statement have undergone rapid evolution since 1983 when the fourteen selected pilot authorities first made a contractual commitment to offer equal opportunities in their schemes. It remains to be seen whether TVEI's growth from a 'new' initiative to an LEA-wide approach to the education of 14–18 year olds will be paralleled by an extended capacity to promote sex-equality among this age group.

TVEI, equal opportunities and the LEAs

When TVEI was first launched, only a handful of the pilot LEAs had previous experience of equal opportunities work relating to gender. Initial interpretations of the equal opportunities criterion therefore tended to focus on ensuring that equal numbers of girls and boys participated in the project. The structure of most pilot programmes remained, however, strongly sex-stereotyped. Other government organizations with a specific 'equal opportunities' brief, namely the Equal Opportunities Commission (EOC) and the Women's National Commission (WNC) pressed the MSC to provide more 'detailed central guidance' to LEAs. The MSC was adamant that it must avoid being prescriptive; but it was also apparent that despite expecting 'firm evidence that authorities are developing strategies to overcome sex-stereotyping' (Wilce 1984), the MSC itself was unclear as to what form such strategies might take. As one local TVEI evaluator put it, 'tension exists between the rhetoric being dictated from outside whilst the reality was to be performed by practitioners' (Herbert 1985).

An immediate outcome, therefore, was that if LEAs were to be told what to do, they expected guidance as to how to do it. The contractual requirement of the MSC and the LEAs consequent commitment to provide equal opportunities for both sexes suddenly propelled both parties into the formulation of working definitions. For many LEAs this was the first time that they had considered issues of gender and the problem proved more complex than anticipated. It also led to a plethora of 'hit-and-miss' initiatives based on confused and ill-informed understanding of the issues under consideration:

> The teachers' confusion seemed not only a personal confusion, but also a confusion inherent in the TVEI brief...The staff have been handed a brief which is, for many, fudged and hazy. To date they have reasonably taught within those personal parameters which offer control, success and survival. Tackling sex stereotypes and equality are part of a package which includes handling new content, new equipment and new teaching methodologies. In an environment ill equipped to provide the training, support and information necessary for such a massive initiative it is small wonder that little regarding equal opportunities is visible in schools. (Herbert 1985)

In attempting to interpret the MSC equal opportunities brief,

> the teachers, co-ordinators, supervisors and heads were handed ambiguity to unravel and they accurately intuited the deeply hidden societal confusion of conflicting pressures and issues. In part, it could be argued that it is an amalgam composed of the particular experiences that the teachers brought with them. Their own conditioning, private agendas, assumptions and habits all have bearing on how they tackle the problem. Together with this personal baggage there was also the political environment in which they lived and worked. Their private experiences of marriage or relationships and their own children's upbringing and education, plus the larger pressures beyond the school and the home, are more likely in tune with the school's traditional policy and hierarchy. Society provides a framework of tradition and stereotyping which is difficult to thwart. (ibid.)

It is to the credit of the LEAs therefore, that their teachers had the courage to undertake practical work on gender while remaining uncertain about its ultimate objectives. This is particularly problematic in an area where success and failure are so difficult to measure. But equally it is worrying that in one of the first national education schemes to prioritize equal opportunities, the 'delivery' of so many initiatives has been uneven, threatening to present pupils with confused sets of messages. Where TVEI pupils have been in a significant majority in a school, positive action by TVEI teachers, for example observation of each other's classroom management styles, sometimes successfully stimulated debate across the school. But in other cases, wider exploration of gender issues has been limited. There have been few attempts to raise awareness of whole-school staff, a necessary prerequisite to ensuring that the TVEI experiences of pupils are premised on a coherent working definition of equal opportunities throughout the school.

In response to the confusion voiced by TVEI teachers, particularly the majority of male teachers charged with managing local schemes (Millman 1985), the MSC ran a series of regional workshops (1984, 1985) aimed at defining the issues more clearly and encouraging the exchange of practical ideas among participating authorities. For the majority of TVEI teachers and personnel who were new to the issues, these workshops provided an important source of professional support. They helped participants to explore their own definitions of equal opportunities within TVEI, and to consider the messages they were conveying, implicitly or explicitly, to girl and boy pupils. Which of the following messages, for instance, were they giving?

The unlocked door — 'We're not blocking your path'
The open door — 'Welcome aboard'
The special escalator — 'All aboard'
Equal outcomes — 'We'll see you there'

(MSC Regional Workshop papers, 1984, 1985)

The workshops also helped participants to define their own needs in relation to their capacity to promote equal opportunities among their pupils, and to meet some of the more tangible requirements by the provision of resource lists, etc. But for the minority of teachers, mainly women, who had been attempting to address issues of gender in their own schools over a number of years, there was frustration at the 'repetition of old circular arguments' and some concern that in the desire for immediate, highly visible solutions, strategies for ensuring more than cosmetic change seemed to have little attraction. While TVEI has rapidly succeeded in putting equal opportunities on to the educational agenda, how long would it remain there once the 'immediate solutions' were found to be flawed?

'Hit-and-miss' strategies

In the first instance, most TVEI schemes identified 'positive counselling' as the immediate solution to differences of pupil choice and career aspiration. When this appeared to fail, or not yield the results expected, they looked to other strategies such as removal of choice, modular curricula and 'raising awareness' among teachers and pupils.

The goal of positive counselling for some teachers meant making sure that there were equal numbers of girls and boys on courses; for others it meant persuading more girls to go into traditionally male subject areas. For most, the sheer difficulty of achieving either of these, despite extensive attempts at persuasion, began to raise questions about the relationship between 'sex stereo-typing' and 'freedom of choice'. TVEI projects, on the whole, showed a tendency to move towards less choice. In Clwyd and Coventry, where there was an emphasis on a modular approach, it was evident, however, that a strong compulsive element was not the only solution. Sensitive one-to-one counselling *could* encourage students to risk choosing a non-traditional module for a period of only ten weeks, provided other measures were also taken to ensure that this was a positive experience. Other LEAs such as Leicestershire, offered a compulsory core to students:

> Physics, computer studies and technology made up part of the compulsory core of study (at Beauchamp College)......fifty per cent of the places on the TVEI course are reserved for female students. (*TVEI Insight*, September 1986)

One female student from Beauchamp commented:

> I had reservations about computer studies as I'd no previous experience, whereas some students had been programming, etc. for the previous two or three years. However, there were several students in the same predicament so I wasn't alone in my anxieties. (ibid.)

Hertfordshire TVEI project favoured compulsion as a positive action strategy, having concluded that:

> extensive guidance and counselling, staff working parties, statements on equal opportunities, programmes of persuasion using videos, role models, 'Opening Windows on Engineering', and so on, seem doomed to marginal success or downright failure. A considerable waste of energy, ingenuity and time is involved. (Luxton 1985)

In Hertfordshire, girls entering TVEI had to study at least one of the following: manufacturing technology, modular technology, electric instrumentation. The TVEI co-ordinator recognized the risks of compulsion:

> It is an easy step to take. But one may simply be postponing the standard stereotyped decisions on areas of interest, on jobs and careers and life-style for two years. Equally, one may be creating, at least in the short term, a large number of highly dissatisfied girls who feel they have been forced into quite unwanted, unnecessary territory — a reservoir of disaffection and indiscipline. (ibid.)

Tideway school in East Sussex, also chose a measure of compulsion, but recognized the importance for boys, as well as girls, of gaining non-traditional skills. At the end of the first year of the Vocational Studies course,

> all pupils spend a week at the college where they follow a series of 'taster' courses; each student takes the same options which include bricklaying, vehicle maintenance and hair and beauty care. In the second year all pupils will follow a week of work experience.... both girls and boys are linked to a firm for the industrial study section of the vocational studies course. This ensures that each firm has a boy and girl associated with it and overcomes any notion that any firm or job within it, is only open to one of the sexes. (*TVEI Insight*, July 1986)

Some TVEI projects tried to circumvent the change process and took 'easy steps' in the hope of producing immediately visible results with little attention to the consequences of such strategies for pupils and teachers. The following comments, from a Beauchamp pupil, indicate the need for carefully planned change at *all* levels of school life if the girls themselves are not to be left to bear the burden of institutional contradictions and inconsistences:

> Girls should not be forced to take sciences such as physics but only be encouraged to do so. I personally think that girls are put off physics by their

> high schools and teachers.....I, for one, need to enjoy a subject to want to take it. From previous experience, physics has always been boring. Nothing has been done to make the lesson enjoyable or even pleasant. The work seems to be done in such a way that you don't understand it and it doesn't seem relevant to your everyday life....
>
> Girls and boys are obviously different, but should be, and in some cases are, treated more equally. Boys should be made or encouraged to be more considerate and caring, etc. as well as not treating girls as people not so clever as themselves. (*TVEI Insight*, ibid.)

Bedford TVEI sponsored a small study of pupils (girls and boys) who had already opted for non-traditional options and careers, in an attempt to identify 'key factors' in producing change. A number of interesting features were identified by the study: the close relationship between option choice and career aspiration for pupils; the importance of parental support; the influence of friends.

> Well, they (my friends) couldn't believe I was taking physics because I act stupid, so when they found out I was really brainy they couldn't believe it.
>
> Well, a lot of my friends think I'm a 'pouff' for choosing a girls' option, but it doesn't bother me. (Weiner 1985, p.18)

Most importantly, the influence of teachers, whether negative or positive, was consistently reported by pupils. Girls frequently mentioned that the intervention of a particular teacher had caused them to consider opting for what they believed to be an 'unusual' subject though others were rather more critical of the teachers' behaviour towards pupils. The following examples from the Bedford report illustrate these two views.

> Because he (the woodwork teacher) does not treat girls as the weaker persons, even though many people think so. He treats us all the same.
>
> Some teachers, you'll ask them, say Technology or Computer Studies, you'll ask them something and ask how to do it but they won't just tell you how to do it, they'll do it for you and I dislike that. (ibid, p.17)

LEAs found that the vocational focus of TVEI pilot projects has been as responsible as its technical elements for eliciting sex-stereotyped responses from pupils. Girls and boys, for example, may aspire to different (traditional) skills and careers even when their work experience placements are in the same firm. Attempts to challenge the traditional attitudes of employers have often been tempered by pragmatic needs — to aim for harmonious relationships with local firms in order to maintain a 'bank' of placements. In this context teachers have been obliged to devise alternative means of challenging pupils' traditional expectations. Some teachers have asked pupils to observe gender differences in the work place by logging their daily experiences in diary form. This material has been used back in school in debriefing sessions; and issues such as sexual harassment or the sexual division of labour have been followed up in counselling sessions or in English or General Education modules.

Simulated work experience and residential periods have offered teachers greater opportunities to challenge, in practical ways, traditional sex roles. Careers advisers have also tried to achieve this by putting pupils in contact with adult men and women working in non-traditional areas. For instance the careers officer for Newcastle TVEI organized a careers convention for pupils, and invited representatives from sixty different careers. He reported:

> We feel that the only way for young people to see that it is possible for girls to move into traditionally male preserves and boys to move into traditionally female preserves is for the pupils to get the chance to meet and talk to people who have done it.
> (*TVEI Insight*, July 1986)

A rather more ambitious approach was adopted by some teachers of courses with a strong vocational emphasis whereby they created new teaching materials and adopted new approaches within their classrooms. In Coventry, teachers of the 'product development' module addressed some of the following questions:

- Will the range of products/services 'on offer' appeal as strongly to girls as to boys?
- Will both sexes see the activities as having relevance to their present and future experiences?
- What aspects of the enterprise are run hierarchically?
- How can girls be helped to gain confidence e.g. in management positions?
- Are there theoretical concepts and practical skills in which members of one sex show less confidence? If so, could intensive work in single-sex groups overcome this?
- Are there ways of demonstrating that girls' interests, experiences and learning styles are as highly valued as boys?
- Are positive interventions made when sexist attitudes are expressed in the working area?

(Coventry LEA, 1985)

Summary and discussion

TVEI strategies on equal opportunities moved from attempting to change pupils' voluntary choices at option stage through career counselling and advice on the benefits of non-traditional courses, to providing substantial compulsory elements in the TVEI curriculum. More sophisticated attempts to achieve equal opportunities included the revision of materials and teaching styles to make the TVEI curriculum more accessible to girls, and 'raising the consciousness' of pupils and teachers through discussion and experiential workshops.

Some LEAs now have a deeper understanding of the MSC 'equal opportunities' criterion. In certain cases, the deeper understanding resulted from a negative evaluation of strategies which were hurriedly and inappropriately implemented. This has, in turn, provided a stimulus to the formulation of more appropriate questions and objectives. In others, teachers have retreated from the complexities of the problem. This was acknowledged by the Buckinghamshire TVEI co-ordinator as follows:

> Equality of opportunity is a very sensitive issue. Almost by definition it implies a criticism of current practice and has to be handled with care if it is not to provide a defensive reaction. Yet the evidence strongly suggests that the status quo has to be challenged. (Vincent 1986)

At the point where TVEI moved from its pilot to its extension phase, the success of its equal-opportunities policy was open to a variety of interpretations. TVEI's equal-opportunities criterion had obliged many LEAs who had not previously addressed gender issues to at least look as if they were doing so, though the almost exclusively male dominance of the TVEI hierarchy meant that there was little knowledge of earlier equal-opportunities initiatives. Whilst most TVEI personnel were initially ill-prepared, persistent requests from the MSC for 'hard evidence' of progress on equal opportunities prevented LEAs from backing away from the undeniably complex issues. Some projects maintained a superficial concern but others, the Buckinghamshire project for example, moved towards a deeper personal and professional understanding of the underlying issues, accompanied by a stronger commitment to tackle them. These are likely to continue asking questions beyond the lifetime of TVEI, reflect on earlier feminist initiatives, and dismiss Luxton's assertion, quoted in this paper, that awareness-raising measures are a 'considerable waste of energy, ingenuity, and time'. They will have realized, as did Pratt et al. (1984) in their study of option choice patterns, that changes in the aspirations of pupils will occur only if preceded by similar changes in teachers.

Conclusions

The TVEI approach towards gender inequality in education has been, for us, somewhat contradictory. On the one hand, its equality stance has provided possibilities for change in the relations between the sexes in school, on a scale, hitherto, unexpected and unknown. The greater the integration of TVEI within existing LEA structures, the greater the likelihood that gender issues arising from TVEI initiatives will have become embedded in LEA practice and firmly fixed on LEA agendas. The collection of data required by the MSC and the availability of resources which could be diverted towards equal opportunities, has already assisted this process.

On the other hand, the promotion of equal opportunities within TVEI by a government whose 'own political and economic ideology wishes to limit state intervention in all areas of life and give free reign to the market'

(Wickham 1986, p.34), is confusing, unless we accept the 'flexible workforce' explanation, mentioned earlier. Further, why, even when the government, LEAs, employers and unions all make verbal and public commitments to equal opportunities, is it so difficult to make changes? Wickham suggests:

> One element of the answer must be, of course, the general social attitudes shared by mostly male members of these institutions. They have been educated, and grown to manhood, in a society which still clings to the belief that women only have a secondary role in paid employment and that their primary role is within the home....Women's secondary role in the labour market keeps the primary one for men: the better jobs, the positions of authority and power, the better levels of pay all go to men who would not willingly lose such privileges. (Wickham 1986, p.34)

Consequently it is not surprising that the debates about equality and change stimulated by TVEI, which involved members of the MSC and LEA personnel, did not explore more deeply the contradictions underlying the different strategies adopted, say, by the Hertfordshire and Buckinghamshire projects, reported in this article. Neither is it strange that the MSC TVEI unit and the individual projects disregarded the importance of aiming for equal representation of women and men at the senior and management levels of TVEI.

If TVEI is serious about addressing gender issues, it seems to us that a rigorous evaluation of current TVEI policy is needed, informed by the evidence from earlier gender initiatives in education. If this had been considered earlier, LEAs might have been encouraged to ask more appropriate questions prior to entering the new (extension) phase of TVEI's development. For instance, what are the chances of successfully encouraging girls to broaden and raise their career aspirations if most TVEI staff, particularly in management, are male? Much of the emphasis within TVEI has been on 'process' rather than 'product'; nowhere is this more important than in the changes of attitude clearly needed if the perceptions and behaviour of girls and boys in school are to change.

Achieving equal opportunities in education is conceptually and qualitatively different from, say, acquiring computing skills or developing pupil profiles. If equality is a serious consideration of TVEI, it needs to address the psychological, social and *political* perceptions of teachers, the MSC and employers before it can tackle the pedagogical problems of how to provide equal opportunities for pupils. The odd workshop or conference on equal opportunities is clearly inadequate.

A carefully developed equal-opportunities programme which includes long-term commitment as well as immediate changes, and which builds on the experiences and acquired knowledge of ten years of equal-opportunities work in education is the least that can be expected. It is important that the MSC, TVEI, LEAs, etc. come to realize this, and tackle gender issues in education with due understanding, resource and responsibility. Then progress will be less patchy, and pupils in schools (particularly girls) will be helped to use their talents and energies in more challenging, economically rewarding and personally satisfying ways.

References

Arnot, M. (1986) *Race, gender and policy-making*. Open University course E333, module 4. Milton Keynes, Open University Press.

Coventry LEA (1986) *TVEI product development: teachers' guide*. Coventry Education Authority.

Dale, R. (1986) *Industry, vocationalism and employers' needs*, Part 2, Open University course E333, module 3. Milton Keynes, Open University Press.

Department of Education and Science (1975) *Curricular differences for boys and girls; Education Survey 21*. HMSO.

(1980) *Girls and science: HMI Matters for Discussion 13*. HMSO.

East Sussex LEA (1986) *TVEI Insight*, July. Sheffield, Manpower Services Commission.

Herbert, C. (1985) *TVEI: Equal opportunities*. Centre for Applied Research in Education, UEA.

Inner London Education Authority (1985) *Educational opportunities for all?* (The Fish Report). Inner London Education Authority.

Kennerley, G. (1986) *TVEI Insight*, September, Sheffield, Manpower Services Commission.

Luxton, R. (1985) The participation and performance of the girls on the Hertfordshire TVEI Project: an interim statement. Hertfordshire Education Authority.

Manpower Services Commission (1981) *A New Training Initiative*. HMSO.

(1984a) *TVEI Annual Review*. Sheffield, MSC.

(1984b) *Regional Workshop Papers*. Sheffield, MSC.

(1985) *Regional Workship Papers*. Sheffield, MSC.

Millman, V. (1985) The new vocationalism in secondary schools: its influence on girls. In Whyte J. *et al.* (eds). *Girl-friendly Schooling*. London, Methuen, pp. 45–70.

Newcastle LEA (1986) *TVEI Insight*, July. Sheffield, Manpower Services Commission.

Pratt, J., Bloomfield, J. and Seale, C. (1984) *Option choice; a question of equal opportunity*. London NFER/Nelson.

Vincent, G. (1986) *TVEI Insight*, September. Sheffield, Manpower Services Commission.

Weiner, G. (1986) Feminist education and equal opportunities: unity or discord?. *Brit. J. Sociology of Education* **7**, (3), 265–74.

Weiner, G. (1985) What the customers have to say; interviews with pupils who have made non-traditional choices. Unpublished report to the Bedfordshire TVEI steering committee, February.

Wickham, A. (1986) *Women and Training*. Milton Keynes, Open University Press.

Wilce, H. (1984) 'Professor speaks out for sex equality'. *Times Educ. Suppl.*, 30 March.

Denis Gleeson and Gordon Smith

11

16–18 The Neglected Territory of TVEI Provision

Introduction

When TVEI was announced by the Prime Minister in the House of Commons, on 12 November 1982, it signalled the demise of a long tradition of democratic consultation on educational matters. The speed with which TVEI was introduced was unprecedented and only ten months after the announcement, the scheme was operational. The result of these circumstances and requirements appears to be a tendency, as identified in most projects, towards a degree of retrospective policy formation or making policy 'on the hoof'. This, in turn, has led to a massive concentration on the *immediate* front-loading of resources in the 14–16 age range of TVEI. One consequence of this has been a serious neglect of 16–18 provision in the hurried events of early planning and development — a factor which causes innumerable problems as the project has caught up with itself.

An important feature of TVEI is that it represents a four-year package, beginning at fourteen and progressing beyond the compulsory leaving age to eighteen. Within this programme, curricular coherence and progression towards nationally recognized qualifications constitutes a major objective. Inherent in the initiative is co-operation between schools and colleges in the form of linked courses backed by coherent programmes and inter-institutional provision. Yet, in practice, this co-operation remains patchy and uneven rendering TVEI a 14–16 school-based phenomenon. What this paper seeks to do is to examine the reasons behind this neglect of the 16–18 phase and to outline some of the policy issues which need to be overcome if progression is to take place.

In announcing the extension of TVEI (DES/DEP 1986) the government has effectively removed the 'pilot' status of the initiative and firmly replaced it with TVEI as the 'recommended' framework for mainstream national schooling 14–16. However, the 16–18 phase is still left to compete with MSC's financially attractive 16–18 initiative, YTS (an issue taken up later). With a £900 m budget over ten years, TVEI is clearly being promoted as a 'success' despite there being few evaluation results. This is especially true of the 16–18 phase and could be interpreted as further evidence of neglect.

It is worth noting here that inherent in the extension proposals is the same hurried timescale as experienced in the pilot projects. Despite the announcement of further large-scale funding for TVEI replication (in a year approaching a General Election) LEAs were still experiencing government cuts in expenditure — school buildings were in urgent need of repair, books and other essentials were in short supply and there were teacher shortages in vital curricular areas. This, coupled with the after effects of teacher action and the general low morale of the profession, will no doubt have an effect on the reception of TVEI extension in schools and colleges.

The apparent 'success' of the pilot projects and the instruction given to LEAs in the extension documentation to base their submissions on 'the lessons emerging from the pilot TVEI projects', raises the question: What are the lessons of the pilot projects? In particular, what are the lessons for the least evaluated and reported phase of TVEI, the neglected post-sixteen element?

Background issues

The rapid nature of TVEI implementation and the 'front-loaded' highly selective resourcing, affecting a small number of pupils in a small number of schools and colleges, led to fears of TVEI being divisive at all levels of the educational system. Other initial fears concerning the new initiative were centred on arguments of tripartism and the vocationalization of the school curriculum. Some critics, for example, argued that TVEI would lead to a return to tripartism and signal the destruction of the comprehensive system (Chitty 1986, Golby 1986). Others maintain that it was the potential narrowing and instrumentalization of the curriculum that caused the greatest concern. Dale (1985), for example, views TVEI as a political intervention 'unlike any other curriculum innovation we have seen before in this country'. Finn (1985) criticized the 'New Vocationalism' movement and particularly recent MSC initiatives such as TVEI and YTS, citing their centralism as being non-democratic, ideologically-based and 'signalling the abandonment of equal opportunity as the central reference point of educational policy'. At the local level, contractual obligations entered into between LEAs and MSC and the 'bidding' system encouraged by MSC for specific funding has been criticized as divisive (Chitty 1986). Moreover, the effects of centralized control, categorical funding and binding five-year contracts has radically altered LEA and institutional autonomy.

The generous funding of the pilot projects led many staff concerned to ask the question: 'What happens when the money runs out?' This appears to have been answered by the national extension of TVEI. However, the level of the new funding arrangements is far less generous than for the pilot projects. If one of the anomalies about funding the pilot project is that it focused on a relatively small pupil cohort, another is that it created discrepancies in staffing and resources within and between schools. The likelihood that government policy designed to extend TVEI post 1987/88 will rectify such anomalies is unlikely to succeed, not least because the level of funding is inadequate to meet the needs of the majority of institutions to be involved. With reference to 16–18 provision, for example, the signs of neglect are already there. Within TVEI projects there has been wastage of resources, particularly early on in the project, due mainly to the rapid 'front-loaded' nature of the funding, which has resulted in a failure to even consider planning and resourcing 16–18 provision in many areas.

The lack of planning, difficulties in achieving a coherent curricular provision and 'structural' problems within projects and individual institutions are just some of the factors that have been combined to make many of the first attempts at post-sixteen TVEI somewhat difficult. Others revolve around what is emerging as the key issue in 16–18 TVEI pilot projects, *numbers*. Low numbers combined with a lack of curricular coherence has led to a situation in many schools and colleges where TVEI post-sixteen is almost non-existent. Competition from traditional courses and the attraction of YTS are blamed by many for this situation although other factors, including historical and cultural aspects, have also been influential.

From pilot to system

The main implication of TVEI extension is that TVEI and its philosophy will become part of British mainstream education. As a consequence, MSC will have a major stake in the compulsory sector of education to complement their already large stake in post-sixteen education and training via Work Related Non-Advanced Further Education (WRNAFE), the Youth Training Scheme (YTS) and the Adult Training Strategy (ATS). Although there is little evidence to date of MSC using its 'muscle' in these areas it is obvious to many involved that a certain degree of muscle flexing is taking place. Further, when areas of MSC activity such as the Training Standards Advisory Service (TSAS), and the National Council for Vocational Qualifications (NCVQ) are considered, the enormity of their involvement becomes apparent and the fears of centralized control seem to be very real. These moves are highlighted when one reads that the job details for the TSAS clearly state that MSC's new YTS 'inspectorate' may be operational in other areas of MSC involvement. The possibility of the new service moving into schools (via TVEI) and colleges (via WRNAFE and TVEI) must enhance further the arguments of central control of education from an 'outside' body.

Before discussing TVEI further, it must be appreciated that TVEI is itself neither a universal nor, particularly as a process of innovation, a static thing. It varies widely across the country and each LEA Project differs in its institutional arrangements and model of delivery depending upon the local perception and interpretation of the Initiative (Gleeson and Maunders 1985). This variability of TVEI nationally derives from the original and apparently 'bottom-up' design in which (while broad national criteria and guidelines were established) the detailed curriculum design, planning and implementation was left in local hands. As MSC itself concluded (in the 1984 TVEI Review), without criticism, the resulting projects were ... 'diverse' and ... 'responsive to local circumstances'. Such diversity and responsiveness within broad guidelines affected the content of TVEI in that ... 'activities vary considerably between projects, and to an extent, between colleges and schools within them'. Indeed, within each LEA Project, individual institutions often differ *greatly* in their approach to TVEI, depending on their traditions, aspirations and their perceptions of the initiative both at a national and local level.

Indeed, the majority of TVEI pilot projects have evolved to accommodate numerous internal and external changes in a variety of ways. Since 1984, emphasis on enrichment of the curriculum, teaching methods and assessment based upon learning by doing, problem solving and practical experience, has become more noticeable. However, this is perhaps not so surprising as most major curriculum development projects have a tendency to take on a momentum of their own over and beyond their original conception and in this respect TVEI is no exception. Hence, the question — What is TVEI? — must be answered in terms of place, time and circumstance (Gleeson and Maunders 1985).

Within many LEAs and individual institutions there was an early assumption that TVEI constituted a technical and vocational thrust into the school curriculum, a thrust that aimed to alter traditional subject hierarchies ('the technicians' revenge'). This initial assumption has however, proved to be unfounded as the 'bottom-up' nature of TVEI has ensured that rather than being 'New Vocationalism', TVEI is becoming more and more 'New Educationalism'. Initially, in keeping with the original perceptions of TVEI, many Projects had an explicitly Technical and Vocational bias, many seeing the initiative as a 'Hi-Tech' venture and directing their resources accordingly. Once again the emphasis was on the *immediate* and funding tended to be towards schools and the 14–16 area to the neglect of the 16–18 sector, the assumption being that post-sixteen, especially FE, already possessed the perceived 'Technical and Vocational' requirements of TVEI. However, in the national scheme as a whole, the operational focus has now moved more and more towards aspects of learning and teaching styles, curriculum and staff development and away from the early 'Technical and Vocational' perceptions.

To say that the operational focus has *moved onto* staff development when a project is in its third year would seem to be a nonsense. Surely, staff development should precede and be part of the planning and development of any new initiative? Yet, awareness of TVEI aims and philosophy are sadly lacking in many schools and colleges engaged in piloting the initiative. Moreover, TVEI Related In Service Training (TRIST) with its financial input specifically for this 14–18 area was implemented only in the third year of TVEI. The neglect of staff development 16–18 in many projects appears to be the result of a variety of circumstances concerning numbers of students, priority afforded to TVEI 16–18, initial planning and status within the post-sixteen sector — issues taken up later.

Curriculum and control

Central control was one of the early criticisms of TVEI and from the evidence of TVEI research and evaluation the following comment provides an appropriate summary:

> Whatever the view of the proper relationship between government and education, we can recognize TVEI as a massive attempt by Central Government to effect, in a direct way, changes in the curricula priorities of secondary schools and FE. (Saunders 1986)

The arguments of central control lead to other early criticisms of the initiative and, in particular, that of a return to tripartism being inherent within TVEI. Within schools there is no evidence to suggest that this is the case and, indeed, in many schools TVEI has been used to reinforce comprehensive ideas. However, it is at the post-sixteen phase of TVEI, it may be argued, that there is a real danger of the re-emergence of tripartite education. Ranson, Taylor and Brighouse (1986), for example, argue that:

> What has almost been eliminated from secondary education is now re-appearing at tertiary level with Advanced levels forming a more entrenched grammar stream, TVEI..... indicating a technical track, with YTS comprising the new tertiary modern sector.

Could this be the reason that TVEI and YTS are being kept apart by MSC knowing that traditionalists within education will fight to preserve the third route, the 'A'-level route, outside TVEI?

The subject of tripartism is also central to the emerging debate concerning the proposed City Technology Colleges (CTCs). It is apparent from the CTC paper (Annexe A, 1986) that there is a clear link with the TVEI concept in curriculum content but any other links must be viewed as tenuous. Indeed, the future of the CTCs must be seriously in doubt when practical problems such as management and the 'promoters' of the CTCs are considered. When other factors such as falling rolls and local politics (particularly in the inner-city areas suggested for the colleges) are thought through, it becomes apparent that a new school/college of 1000 students in these areas would seriously affect the viability of existing establishments and lead, inevitably to lengthy political wrangles. Finally, what of the specialist teachers of shortage subjects required to staff such institutions and the implications for the staffing of other schools in the locality?

The neglected territory 16–18

When the first cohort of TVEI students reached the post-sixteen phase in Autumn 1985 most projects were operating a 'set' and individually specific model of TVEI delivery. For some, this delivery meant a continuation in the same establishment, for others a change of institution was required and for the rest provision was a combination of both. It is true to say that the institutional provision has varied as much as the 'up-take' of post-sixteen TVEI.

One of the fundamental concepts of TVEI is that it is a 14–18 initiative. The implications of this are that those embarking on a TVEI scheme at fourteen are 'expected' to remain within that scheme until eighteen and, as a planned and well-resourced 14–18 initiative, TVEI reasonably may have been expected to increase 'staying-on rates' post-sixteen. However, national figures (MSC 1986) show that 'staying-on rates' in full-time education, for the first TVEI cohort to reach this stage, were, to say the least, varied. 'Win some, lose some,' reported the *TES* at the time. Some schools and some LEAs managed to increase their staying-on rates significantly, others experienced disappointingly low rates and many found no significant change at all. From early information, a similar situation appears to have occured in the 'second round' LEAs and the second cohort in first-round authorities who began their post-sixteen phase in Autumn 1986. To many, this apparent failure of TVEI is seen as a damning criticism. However, it must be said that in many projects early cohorts of TVEI students experienced little to suggest that these rates should change, mainly due to the bottom-up, front-loaded nature of pilot projects and the rapid implementation of TVEI. Moreover, the statistics are dealing with a comparatively small sample of 'selected' pupils and, as such, are particularly vulnerable to distortion.

The significance of the number of TVEI 'arrivals' post-sixteen is one that cannot be over-emphasized at a time of falling rolls, school reorganization and increased competition. Post-sixteen, schools and colleges are geared to 'numbers' and when insufficient students arrive to form specific groups/courses, all but the most imaginative of institutions experience difficult decisions and institutional problems. This has been the experience of many schools and colleges involved in TVEI over the past year and must be seen as problematic in a planned 14–18 initiative.

In seeking to establish the influencing factors behind staying-on rates and, indeed, pupil destinations generally, three main 'areas of influence' may be explored and related to practice — the school, the college and the 'ecological'....environmental, historical and economic influences, social and cultural background....and so forth (Eggleston 1977).

In terms of the ecological it is suggested that the immediate and specific influences of a pilot curriculum project like TVEI may be considered as marginal to the long-term economic and sociological trends of 'ecology' in an area. None the less, possible short-term attitudinal and organizational influences which might be effective in changing the pattern are a neglected area of evaluation. With the extension of TVEI developments into mainstream schooling the need for such further evaluation would seem pressing.

In terms of the school the initial perceptions and reactions concerning TVEI entry and the way in which they have influenced the management, planning, allocation of resources, staff attitudes and actions, are discussed in detail by Saunders (1985) and are reported on by HMI (1985), NFER (1986) and others. These reports confirm that the influences of the school are complex, varied and inter-related. They have, as their background, the political, the 'ecological', the 'culture' of pupils (Willis 1979), the traditions and 'ethos' of the school (Rutter 1979) and the attitudes and experiences of staff. It is against this background that the factors affecting destinations of pupils post-sixteen must be viewed.

When considering the school influence on pupil destinations the focus often falls on the amount of liaison between schools and colleges, their relationships and traditions, staff attitudes and personal experiences. These may be expressed through the 'hidden curriculum' and in guidance given throughout the school. There is ample evidence from evaluation reports that these factors are prevalent and influential in schools within TVEI Projects. However, this appears to have been an area neglected by the planning process in many projects. A further area related to attitudes, perceptions and aspirations within Projects and individual institutions is that of the curriculum *content* provided and its coherence with post-sixteen provision. This will affect the 'bias' of the project, largely dictate the ability and gender spread and influence institutional liaison, providing a further area of influence for pupils post-sixteen. Relating directly to this is the issue of the selection of pupils for TVEI participation within institutions which may prove to be a significant influence on destinations statistics. The selection of pupils is discussed further by Evans and Davies in Chapter 5 of this book. However, in terms of national replication, this may not be as contentious an area *providing* that all pupils share the TVEI experience.

The curriculum content of individual schools and its coherence with post-sixteen provision provides evidence of further neglect in many cases and yet is a vital area of influence for pupils deciding on post-sixteen destinations. In many schools the initial model of TVEI provision was one of 'containment' (Saunders 1985); curriculum change was minimal, the introduction of 'vocational' qualifications (CGLI, B/TEC, etc.) was often rejected and coherence with much of the FE provision therefore minimized. However, in maintaining traditional school structures in this way, a continued coherence with Sixth Form provision was often maintained. In other schools the reliance on 'low-level' provision for TVEI ensured that none of the vocational 'goats' were mixed with the academic 'sheep' (Golby 1985) and hence there was little coherence of provision at Sixth Form level. The solution to this problem of 'Fixing the Mix' (Evans and Davies 1986) can only be if there is no mix to fix and that TVEI extension has a 'whole-school' approach with corresponding coherence of provision for all ability levels post-sixteen. If it is to succeed, TVEI must not be used as a device to placate and control the average to less able while allowing the high flyer to pursue the traditional academic and prestigious route.

An often-expressed reason for low numbers in TVEI 16–18 is the attraction of YTS with its employment potential and financial incentive. It is ironic that in a planned 14–18 initiative now being extended throughout the country and promoted as being a 'success' by MSC, that the same government 'QUANGO' should be promoting its other 16–18 'success' YTS and positively discriminating in its favour by offering payment to participants. For many TVEI youngsters there is no option of staying in full-time education and completing their TVEI programme when faced with the financial attraction of YTS, or the fact that some industries recruit only through YTS. The MSC (*TVEI Review* 1985) partially touched on this issue by suggesting that a progression into YTS is acceptable 'in cases where YTS is the only route to a particular industry'. In any other case YTS is seen as 'not normally the route of progression which TVEI intends'. Paradoxically, this same body claims to be pursuing a policy of rationalization of education and training 14–18. There are now links between YTS and CPVE (via the 'alternative route') and moves to introduce more nationally recognized qualifications into YTS via NVQ. The question to be asked is: Will there be a YTS/TVEI link (an area some TVEI pilot projects are investigating) or is this to remain an element of the new post-sixteen tripartism?

In looking at the question of numbers and TVEI 16–18, as with schools, 'ethos', staff attitudes, experiences and perceptions and the 'ecology' of the area are all background influences within which actions must be viewed. Add to this the 'special' nature of FE, in terms of legal status, entrepreneurial spirit and establishment structure, based on the 'points' system and course gradings, it is within this context that the entry of TVEI into the post-sixteen sector must be considered.

TVEI 16–18 experiences

The post-sixteen TVEI experience is as varied as TVEI 14–16 and has been delivered in a variety of ways. School Sixth Forms, Sixth Form Colleges, Tertiary Colleges, Colleges of Further Education, Agriculture and Horticulture have all been involved, as have other specialist provision such as TVEI centres and establishments of Higher Education. In most projects, local colleges have formed part or all of the provision post-sixteen and have often had an involvement pre-sixteen within a variety of linked provision. However, many difficulties have been experienced in the area of linking institutions where there are differences of funding, administrative structures, payment and conditions of service and qualifications of staff. Some further examples of organizational considerations which have affected colleges are outlined by McCabe (1986) and discussed in more detail later:

> Within a college, there is eagerness to be involved in the project but some concern as to how TVEI's specialist requirements could be met without distorting the complex programmes of a large interlocked organization. If TVEI students, individually, could be 'slotted into' already existing programmes it would be simple enough ...
>
> TVEI requirements add the complications of more intensive tutorial guidance and record keeping plus an 'enhanced' programme — one principal has estimated that to accept about 70 students, who would have come to college in any case, on TVEI terms would represent an extra work load equivalent to three or four lecturers plus some timetable reorganization.

This is perhaps the main stumbling block for colleges as they may feel that their commitment would have to be estimated and underwritten in advance before the implementation of TVEI. A further problem to college departments is that ... 'there is, it is said, no slack in college staffing — in new technology areas, for example, there may already be many students and not enough staff while other courses depend on a considerable proportion of part-time staff' ... (McCabe 1986). This could be a serious problem for in the very areas that TVEI is promoting (new technology, business studies, food and related services ... etc.) many colleges are already operating at capacity.

In many post-sixteen college situations there is a vision of the project being planned by 'school-oriented people' and an apparent assumption of minimal change on the basis that 'We already provide technical and vocational education'. In some cases this has led to a lack of interest in the preparation of courses to accommodate the prospective TVEI clientele. This attitude is reinforced by the views of many post-sixteen staff who feel that they provide appropriate courses anyway and that if TVEI students enter courses of their choice, leading to nationally recognized qualifications, then all is well and no change is needed. A further assumption is that TVEI only provides colleges with the students that they would have had anyway.

In striving to achieve a coherent programme 14–18 the 'drop-out' rate at sixteen has been, and is, an important factor for post-sixteen institutions involved in pilot projects. However, these same institutions must also look to their own responses to the initiative when questioning the coherence, progression and numbers staying in the project. The situation is now changed somewhat and for institutions preparing for involvement in TVEI replication (where it could be that all their feeder schools are providing a TVEI experience for their students), the importance of creating a planned, coherent progression and maximizing staying-on rates at a time of falling rolls and increased competition, is one that cannot afford to be missed.

The point at issue is that TVEI is a 14–18 initiative and, as such, should be planned by *all* institutions involved, from the beginning. It has been suggested that in certain Projects this joint planning has been minimal and that the Projects were planned with little input from the post-sixteen sector, especially FE. Any such lack of integrated planning may result in a fragmented project, lacking coherence and hence not providing a 'natural progression' for students involved. This, in turn, is likely to have an effect on staying-on rates and involvement in TVEI post-sixteen. By not involving FE at an early stage in the planning process, as an equal partner, not only is the chance of coherence minimized but considerable expertise is also lost. This has particular significance for the planning of TVEI replication.

According to FEU (1985):

> Colleges will wish to ensure the status both of their contribution to the planning process and of the new development within the college by allocating staff of the appropriate seniority and experience to the planning groups. They must also be concerned to stress the cross-departmental nature of such developments.

One of the implications of this statement is that the *co-ordinator* of any TVEI project within an establishment must have the necessary status, time and experience to plan, co-ordinate and develop a cross-curricular initiative involving changes in curriculum content, learning strategies and teaching styles. This co-ordination will, of course, not only involve one institution but often a whole consortium. The need for status and the 'institutional clout' associated with it is one issue that has been identified in pilot projects (NFER 1985). Indeed the status afforded to the co-ordinator within an institution is often seen as a reflection of the priority placed on the project by the management of that institution. It has been suggested above that the issue of priority and status afforded to TVEI by the post-sixteen sector and by others in the initial planning of TVEI is an important factor in the 16–18 debate. It is here and in the area of planning a coherent progression 14–18 that the future of the 16–18 neglected area lies.

Progression

One area of school and college contact where coherent planning could begin is the link course. It is suggested (FEU 1985) that FE will have to rethink the rationale of link courses and review the relationship between existing provision and TVEI requirements in seeking to plan a coherent progression 14–18. Much existing link course provision is seen as in direct contrast to this and the views of 'consumers' of link courses often reflect a negative influence in terms of progression and coherence. Indeed a view expressed by some FE staff is that link courses actively discourage participation in post-sixteen education.

In some projects link courses are seen to fall into this category, with few being specially designed for TVEI. Many of these courses use part-time FE staff and are based in schools or annexes and by the nature of their certification ensure an 'average' ability clientele. Further, there is often no recognized progression to many link courses. This has been confirmed by students in post-sixteen TVEI, who were link-course 'graduates', the same students often reporting repetition and duplication of work in their first year at college. This must be viewed as a major area of concern, for if TVEI students can see no apparent and obvious progression to their 14–18 programme then it is hardly surprising if they leave that programme at sixteen or seventeen. However, this is not the case in all colleges and it is suggested that successful link course provision and school/college consortia arrangements may form a sound basis for initial TVEI programme planning. Many colleges have established a successful and impressive array of link-course provision, utilizing resources to the full thereby avoiding costly duplication. It is suggested that it is upon this type of relationship that TVEI links should be established and a planned 14–18 progression developed.

Much of the debate in and around link courses is concerned essentially with the status and priority given to them and of who attends the courses and why. School teachers tend to feel that FE staff have an 'instrumental' approach and are critical of the priority that link courses are afforded. FE staff, on the other hand, are critical of schools and often feel that link courses are used by schools to accommodate the less able and 'problem' students. However, most of these criticisms tend to be founded on misunderstandings of the problems, difficulties and conditions of the criticized. This, of course, is an all too common problem within education but is especially ominous in a 'planned' 14–18 initiative linking schools and colleges in what should be a coherent four-year progression. In terms of the school-to-college transition and staying-on rates these attitudes must be influential.

Clearly, what is needed is a planned, coherent system of link-course provision within TVEI, offering pupils a clear progression post-sixteen. Status and priority of provision must be ensured within the project and institutions and their programmes must accommodate the whole ability range. Since TVEI is essentially an integrated scheme, liaison between institutions and the development of understanding between schools and FE should be afforded priority in any project. Better inter-institutional co-operation will develop only through contact, involvement and communication at all levels in the initial overall planning of TVEI, in curriculum and staff development and in assessment and evaluation of TVEI.

In many of the pilot projects the development of sound inter-institutional relations are being fostered through the meeting of staff from collaborating institutions. These meetings are varied and numerous, involving senior management and classroom teachers in planning, developing, administering and evaluating their project. All the indications are that such meetings are beneficial, and it is suggested that time devoted to such liaison must be considered a worthwhile investment of TVEI funds. One project, for example, reports 'some encouraging signs of an emerging new relationship between schools and the FE college, a relationship which simply did not exist prior to TVEI' (McCabe 1985).

Bridging the compulsory to post-sixteen education 'time-gap' has proved a further area of concern within some projects, as has the enrolment of TVEI pupils by individual colleges where a school-to-college transition has occurred. In certain pilot projects, following initial correspondence and interviews, there has often followed a period of up to three months where no contact between the Project and the student has been made. It is felt by staff involved that this period has contributed to numbers of 'intending' students never arriving at the post-sixteen phase. Clearly, in a 14–18 continuum this gap must be bridged in order to minimize these transitional difficulties. This experience highlights the administrative difficulties that may be faced post-sixteen and points to the need for a planned policy to bridge school and college, thereby maximizing staying-on rates in post-sixteen TVEI.

At the commencement of the post-sixteen phase, further complications have been experienced. One central issue revolves around numbers and the use of 'infill' to make viable TVEI groups. This poses the question; Who is a TVEI student? Is it a person who has followed a TVEI course for two years 14–16 and then transferred to the 16–18 phase to attend an appropriate course which is *not* designated as being TVEI-related? Or, is it someone attending a designated TVEI course who has not previously followed a TVEI course at 14–16? Either way, this situation poses problems in an initiative designed on the basis of a coherent progression 14–18. Often the majority of students on 'TVEI courses' post-sixteen are 'infill' students who have not followed a TVEI programme previously. This situation makes a nonsense of curricular links 14–18 and the continuity and progression implicit within TVEI. To further compound the problem, students' experiences of TVEI pre-sixteen often vary so greatly as to make any notion of coherence and progression 14–18 impractical with this first cohort. MSC (*TVEI Review* 1985) acknowledges these difficulties by suggesting 'induction' courses for this type of 'infill' student, 'to enable new entrants to gain maximum benefit from the last two years of the four-year programme'.

This situation could, of course, change with the general replication of TVEI within LEA areas. Dependent upon local arrangements, large numbers of students entering post-sixteen education will have experienced TVEI provision. The challenge is then for the post-sixteen sector to provide the appropriate experiences leading to nationally recognized qualifications and further progression across the whole ability range and across their total 14–18 provision.

For post-sixteen TVEI based in school Sixth Forms some of the problems concerning continuity of provision mentioned above are lessened. On the other hand, problems of appropriate course provision in a comparatively limited curriculum are increased unless local institutions of FE are used in a consortia of provision. This, however, raises a number of issues in and around student numbers, tertiary reorganization and academic entrenchment, which affect perceptions, decisions and, ultimately, the kind of TVEI provision that such institutions can offer to the whole ability range. The issue of 'ownership' of students is one such issue, especially when institutions are operating within a consortium of post-sixteen provision. Indeed, this is a prime consideration for many institutions faced with reorganization and falling rolls.

One universal panacea for many of the problems associated with appropriate course provision has been the use of the Certificate of Pre-Vocational Education (CPVE). Although this may be seen as highly appropriate by some, it must be acknowledged that CPVE is only a one-year course and has, in many cases, reduced TVEI to a three-year initiative. For students who entered the 16–18 phase and TVEI/CPVE, many are moving out of TVEI after three years; in some cases after their institutions had not accepted them on to courses of their choice at 17+. This raises the issue of selection for courses within the post-sixteen sector and the perceived 'value' of TVEI and CPVE to those who are selecting students for such courses. What price progression in these circumstances?

The challenges post-sixteen

TVEI is nudging for reform post-sixteen but it is doubtful whether it alone will be enough to succeed. However, TVEI is only one of the major challenges facing the post-sixteen sector in the immediate future. The requirements of WRNAFE are already making an impact on FE colleges as are new YTS demands. GCSE, A/S levels and CPVE are beginning to initiate qualification-led change in both schools and colleges and corresponding curriculum change will be required by TVEI. The forthcoming National Vocational Qualifications (NVQ) framework will be fully operational by 1991 and, by introducing competency-based assessment into a restructured national system, will demand radical changes in curriculum content, methods of delivery and assessment procedures. It is the combination of these challenges that will undoubtedly change the post-sixteen sector. These changes will require an appropriate staff development programme which, in turn, entails institutional development.

In terms of the changes required to provide an appropriate TVEI experience within a framework of nationally recognized qualifications, an inter-institutional curriculum will need to be examined. Any such change will also need to be set against the background of TVEI aims and criteria. In practice these challenges have been met in a variety of ways through the development of new courses, the 'enhancement' of existing provision, the 'bolting-on' of TVEI elements to conventional courses and the use of 'similar' courses such as CPVE — in some cases all within one institution! One model that appears to be particularly appropriate to post-sixteen provision is that of a TVEI 'core' within existing nationally recognized and prescribed qualifications which have been suitably enhanced. To co-operate fully with TVEI a college would need not only to provide all of these 'enhancements' but would also need to build into its programmes special tutorial arrangements and profiling/record of achievement continuity from school. A certain degree of control as to who does what in terms of course provision would also be necessary.

Further, curricula change is required at the post-sixteen phase to accommodate innovation and developments taking place 14–16. Developments such as modular provision will need to be responded to by colleges in terms of linked courses/modules and generally by the post-sixteen sector in terms of progression. The move towards more active approaches to learning now taking place in schools as a result of TVEI, and in response to GCSE, will need careful consideration in terms of progression and the provision of a coherent 14–18 continuum. Already there are signs that within TVEI, students in their first year post-sixteen are reporting duplication of provision and a more didactic approach in teaching method than they experienced within TVEI at school. This, in some cases, has led to their leaving the post-sixteen TVEI programme and opting for the more practical work-based YTS.

Explicit within TVEI is that work experience is a compulsory element of every programme: 'the construction of a bridge from education to work is begun earlier by giving young people the opportunity to have direct contact and *planned* work experience with local employers in the relevant specialisms.' According to MSC, work experience should be *planned and appropriate* and be an integral part of TVEI programmes (MSC 1986). Although many post-sixteen courses of study contain some element of work experience, leading to comments of 'we already do this', it is suggested that many such courses do not see this experience as part of an *integrated* course element as demanded by TVEI and that contrary to the belief of many, especially in FE, this constitutes a neglected area within the post-sixteen provision of TVEI.

A further 'challenge' embodied in TVEI is that — 'care should be taken to avoid sex-stereotyping' (MSC 1985). So far, despite efforts in certain areas, this appears to be of secondary concern to many when faced with the task of planning and implementing a TVEI programme. Little has changed in the numbers of students undertaking non-traditional curriculum areas and post-sixteen courses, although to expect significant change in a project barely into its fourth year (second year post-sixteen) and so hastily implemented, is perhaps to expect too much. However, TVEI is only reinforcing what has been advocated since the passing of the Sex Discrimination Act in 1975 and schools and colleges have since been urged by various DES, HMI and Equal Opportunities Commission reports to review their curriculum content and organizational structures and to evolve strategies to avoid sex-stereotyping. Despite these exhortations, progress towards equality of opportunity has been made with a varying degree of success and commitment.

Summary

Experiences of TVEI within the post-sixteen sector indicate that without the appropriate joint planning and delivery, together with sufficient curriculum and staff development, it is difficult to provide a coherent TVEI programme and ensure that the MSC's 'aims', 'criteria' and 'content of programme' are implemented. Many of the problems experienced in the first year of TVEI post-sixteen are felt to be due to lack of initial planning, curriculum and staff development and 'institutional difficulties'. Others may arise from the management structure, size, status and traditions of institutions and consequent perceptions of, and status afforded to, TVEI. The organizational form of an institution has a major influence on determining the actions and attitudes within that establishment. Schools and colleges may, for example, experience difficulties implementing an initiative such as TVEI, which is cross-curricular, within a rigid departmental structure.

From what is known of TVEI post-sixteen, it has proved to be different in many respects from TVEI pre-sixteen. Much of this appears to be connected with the nature, scale and priorities of the post-sixteen sector. There are numerous areas of concern for those looking for the initiative to have a major impact on post-sixteen education. Many of the implications that can be drawn from comments above reinforce much of what is said in the recommendations made by FEU (*Supporting TVEI* 1985). The need for a planned, coherent progression within TVEI is of paramount importance for any scheme. Adequate curriculum, staff and institutional development must be embarked upon and the breaking down of school/FE barriers and the strengthening of links and liaison should be a priority. The unique nature of FE in the educational system and the inherent differences between school and college must be appreciated, planned for at all levels and afforded status, in order to achieve the desired smooth transition and coherence of provision expected within TVEI. Unless these things are implemented in the neglected territory of 16–18 TVEI the four-year programme is in grave danger of becoming a two-plus-two divided initiative, with this second phase offering little coherence and progression.

Conclusion

TVEI is not simply a number of interesting pilot schemes. It represents a major initiative to change the education and training of 14–18 year-olds and a move towards a more vocationally relevant system. At policy level, TVEI represents an impetus in restructuring the education and training experiences of 14–18 year-olds and reorganizing the environment in which they learn. It is claimed to be a catalyst for change by some and divisive by others. Within it, however, there is certainly potential for curriculum change, changes in teaching styles and for a better deal for many young people in schools and colleges.

Most of the fears expressed about TVEI have not, as yet, materialized. What has emerged from the pilot schemes is an enthusiastic response from many teachers and students leading to a broadening of the curriculum and involving more student-centred, activity-based learning — often with new methods of assessment. In the words of the Secretary of State for Education: 'Our plan is to put within the reach of all 14–18 year-olds in schools and colleges the lessons of the TVEI pilot projects.' (*TES* 4.7.86). This may well be the case for the much evaluated 14–16 phase of TVEI but it is not the case for post-sixteen TVEI. For this group the targeting of resources to specific curricular areas and age groups remains questionable. Moreover, the announced extension of TVEI will not have the same resourcing as did the pilot projects. This again raises the question of allocation and priorities within LEAs in the post-pilot phase. Will there continue to be the emphasis on TVEI 14–16; will this reduced resourcing lead to further neglect of the post-sixteen phase of TVEI, or will the initiative develop into a coherent 14–18 programme? Only time will tell.

References

Chitty, C. (1986). TVEI: The MSC's Trojan Horse, in Benn and Fairly (eds). *Challenging The MSC: On Jobs, Education and Training*. London, Pluto Press.

Dale, R. (1985). *Education, Training and Employment: Towards a New Vocationalism?* Oxford, Pergamon Press.

Department of Education and Science/Department of Employment (1984). Joint White Paper: *Training for Jobs*. HMSO.

Department of Education and Science (1985a). White Paper: *Education and Training for Young People* (Cmnd 9482). HMSO.

Department of Education and Science (1985c). HMI Report: *The Technical and Vocational Education Initiative: Early Developments*. Stanmore, Department of Education and Science.

Department of Education and Science/Department of Employment (1986). Joint White Paper: *Working Together — Education and Training* (Cmnd 9823). HMSO.

Department of Education and Science (1986). *A New Choice of School*. Stanmore, Department of Education and Science.

Eggleston, J. (1977). *The Ecology of the School*. London, Methuen.

Evans, J. and Davies, B. (1986). Fixing the mix in TVEI. Paper presented to the International Sociology of Education Conference, Westhill, Birmingham, January 1986.

Farley, M. (1985). Trends and structural changes in English vocational education, in Dale, R. *Education, Training and Employment: Towards a New Vocationalism?* Oxford, Pergamon Press.

FEU (1985). Supporting TVEI. Stanmore, Further Education Unit.

Finn, D. (1985). The Manpower Services Commission and the Youth Training Scheme; a permanent bridge to work?, in Dale, R. (ed.), *Education, Training and Employment: Towards a New Vocationalism?* Oxford, Pergamon Press.

Gleeson, D. (1985). Privatisation of industry and the nationalisation of youth, in Dale, R. (ed.), *Education, Training and Employment; Towards a New Vocationalism?* Oxford, Pergamon Press.

Gleeson, D. and Maunders, A. (1985). *Curricular Issues in TVEI Evaluation: A Discussion Document*. University of Keele TVEI Evaluation Unit.

Golby, G. (1985). The coming crisis at 14+. *Forum* **27**, (3).

McCabe, C. (1986). The management of sixteen plus choice, in McCabe, C. (ed.), *The Organisation of the Early Years of the Technical and Vocational Education Initiative*. Avon, Multilingual Matters.

MSC (1985). *TVEI Review 1984*. London, Manpower Services Commission.

MSC (1986). *TVEI Review 1985*. London, Manpower Services Commission.

MSC (1985). *TVEI National Pupil Teacher Database Figures*, London, Manpower Services Commission.

MSC (1986) *TVEI: Progress Report on the 16–18 Phase* (NSG/86/11). London, Manpower Services Commission.

NFER (1985). The Management of TVEI. Sheffield, Manpower Services Commission.

Ranson, Taylor and Brighouse (1986). *The Revolution in Education and Training*. Harlow, Longman.

Rutter, M. *et al.* (1979). *Fifteen Thousand Hours; Secondary Schools and their Effect on Children*. Shepton Mallet, Open Books.

Saunders, M. (1985). *Emerging Issues in TVEI Implementation*. Document of the University of Lancaster TVEI Evaluation Programme.

Saunders, M. (1986). TVEI — a tiger by the tail? *Business Education*, November.

Smith, G.D. (1986). *TVEI — The School to College Transition — A Case Study*. University of Keele.

Smith, G.D. (1986). TVEI replication and FE. *NATFHE Journal*, December.

TES (1986). Drop-out rates underline patchy effect of TVEI. *Times Educ. Suppl.*, 31 January.

TES (1986). Fewer stay on as YTS recruiting takes off. *Times Educ. Suppl.*, 6 June.

TES (1986). Carry on, TVEI; Young takes over vocational exams; Ten year programme to extend TVEI. *Times Educ. Suppl.*, 4 July.

Willis, P.E. (1977). *Learning to Labour*. London, Saxon House.

Wragg, T. (1984). Evaluating TVEI programmes, in *TVEI Perspectives 14*. University of Exeter.

Wringe, C. (1981). Education, schooling and the world of work. *Brit. J. Educational Studies* **29**, (2).

Glossary of Terms

ATS	Adult Training Strategy.
BERA	British Educational Research Association.
B/TEC	Business and Technician Education Council.
CARE	Centre for Applied Research in Education.
CCCS	Consultative Committee on the Curriculum (Scotland).
CD	Curriculum Development.
CDT	Craft, Design and Technology.
CEO	Chief Education Officer.
CGLI	City and Guilds of London Institute.
CPVE	Certificate of Pre-Vocational Education.
CSE	Certificate of Secondary Education.
CTC	City Technology College.
DE	Department of Employment.
DES	Department of Education and Science.
DOE	Department of Employment.
DTI	Department of Trade and Industry.
EC	European Community.
EITB	Engineering Industry Training Board.
EOC	Equal Opportunities Commission.
ESG	Education Support Grant.
FE	Further Education.
FEU	Further Education Unit.
GCE	General Certificate of Education.
GCSE	General Certificate of Secondary Education.
GIST	Girls into Science and Technology.
GRIST	Grant Related In-Service Training.
HCP	Humanities Curriculum Project.
HE	Higher Education.
HMI	Her Majesty's Inspector (or Inspectorate).
IMS	Institute of Manpower Studies.
INSET	In-Service Education for Teachers.
IS	Integrated Science.

IT	Information Technology.
LEA	Local Education Authority.
MDDMER	Manage, Devolve, Develop, Monitor, Evaluate, Replicate.
MSC	Manpower Services Commission.
NAFE	Non-Advanced Further Education.
NATFHE	National Association of Teachers in Further and Higher Education.
NCVQ	National Council for Vocational Qualifications.
NEDC	National Economic Development Council.
NFER	National Foundation for Educational Research.
NSG	National Steering Group.
NTVEI	New Technical and Vocational Education Initiative.
NUS	National Union of Students.
NVQ	National Vocational Qualifications.
PICKUP	Professional, Industrial and Commercial Updating.
PS	Problem Solving.
PSD	Personal and Social Development.
PTRs	Pupil/Teacher Ratios.
PVE	Pre-Vocational Education.
RAC	Regional Advisory Council.
RCB	Regional Curriculum Base.
REPLAN	A DES programme to promote the development of educational opportunities for the adult unemployed.
RSA	Royal Society of Arts.
RVQ	Review of Vocational Qualifications.
SCDC	Schools Curriculum Development Committee.
SI	Sociology Interaction.
SIP	Schools Industry Project.
SMA	Science Masters' Association.
TOPS	Training Opportunities Scheme.
TUC	Trades Union Congress.
TRIST	TVEI Related In-Service Training.
TSAS	Training Standards and Advisory Service.
TVEI	Technical and Vocational Education Initiative.
UEA	University of East Anglia.
UVP	Unified Vocational Preparation.
WEP	Work Experience Programme.
WNC	Womens' National Commission.
WOW	Wider Opportunities for Women.
WRNAFE	Work-Related Non-Advanced Further Education.
YOP	Youth Opportunities Scheme.
YTS	Youth Training Scheme.

Name Index

Subject Index